# POCKET SIZE 5

## BORNSTONE'S ELIXIR

*The Akiko Series,*
*Issues 26~31*

**SIRIUS ENTERTAINMENT**
**UNADILLA, NEW YORK**

*This book is dedicated to my good friends*
*Dennis & Mary Moylan,*
*and to their children: Tyler, Alec, & Lydia*

AKIKO POCKET SIZE 5 FEBRUARY, 2006.
FIRST PRINTING. PUBLISHED BY SIRIUS ENTERTAINMENT, INC.
LAWRENCE SALAMONE, PRESIDENT. ROBB HORAN, PUBLISHER.
KEITH DAVIDSEN, EDITOR. CORRESPONDENCE: P.O. BOX X, UNADILLA, NY 13849.
AKIKO AND ALL RELATED CHARACTERS ARE TM & © 2004 MARK CRILLEY. SIRIUS AND
THE DOGSTAR LOGO ARE ® SIRIUS ENTERTAINMENT, INC. ALL RIGHTS RESERVED. ANY
SIMILARITY TO PERSONS LIVING OR DEAD IS PURELY COINCIDENTAL.
PRINTED IN THE USA.

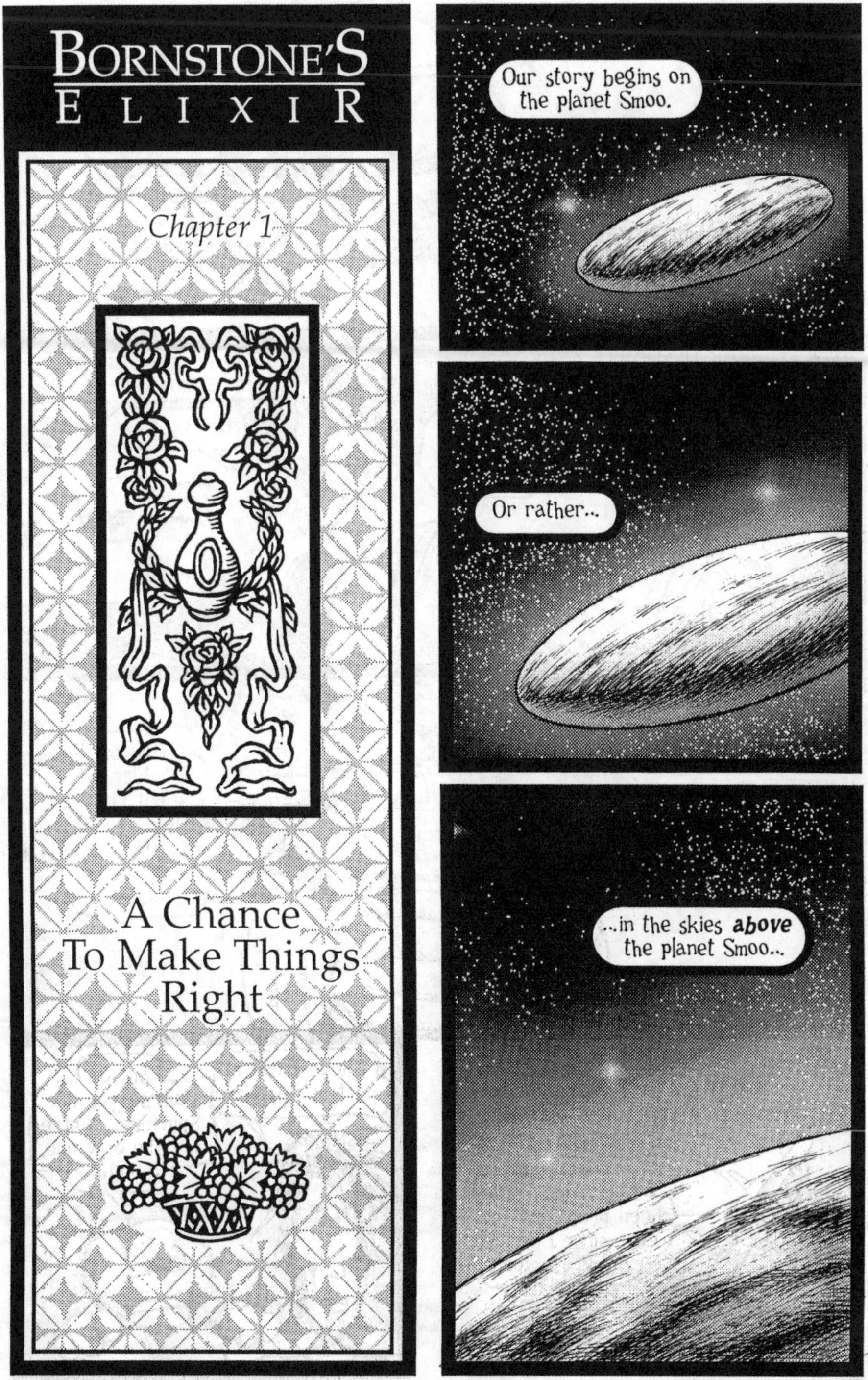
BORNSTONE'S ELIXIR
Chapter 1
A Chance To Make Things Right
Our story begins on the planet Smoo.
Or rather...
...in the skies **above** the planet Smoo...

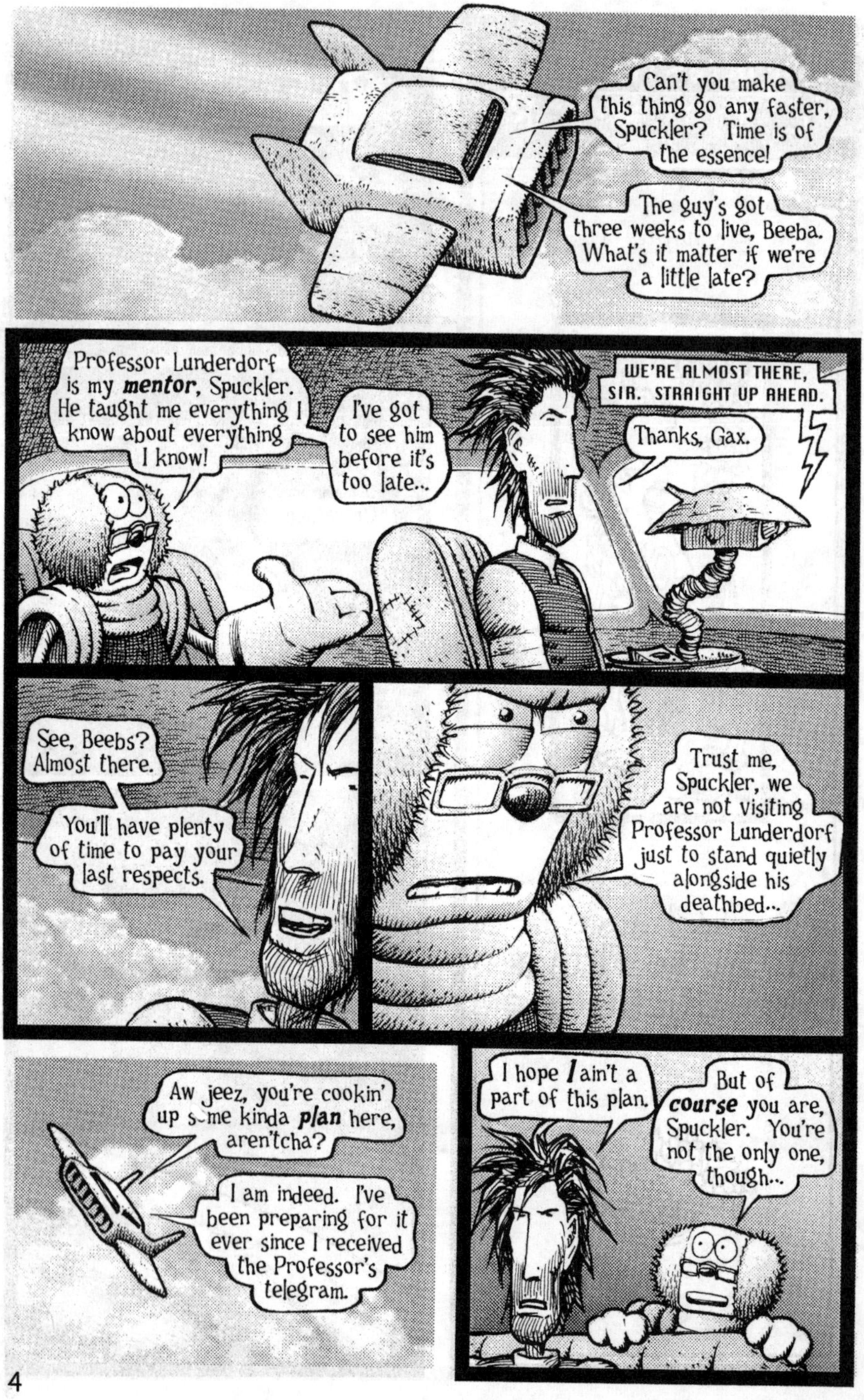
Can't you make this thing go any faster, Spuckler? Time is of the essence!
The guy's got three weeks to live, Beeba. What's it matter if we're a little late?
Professor Lunderdorf is my **mentor**, Spuckler. He taught me everything I know about everything I know!
I've got to see him before it's too late...
WE'RE ALMOST THERE, SIR. STRAIGHT UP AHEAD.
Thanks, Gax.
See, Beebs? Almost there.
You'll have plenty of time to pay your last respects.
Trust me, Spuckler, we are not visiting Professor Lunderdorf just to stand quietly alongside his deathbed...
Aw jeez, you're cookin' up some kinda **plan** here, aren'tcha?
I am indeed. I've been preparing for it ever since I received the Professor's telegram.
I hope **I** ain't a part of this plan.
But of **course** you are, Spuckler. You're not the only one, though...

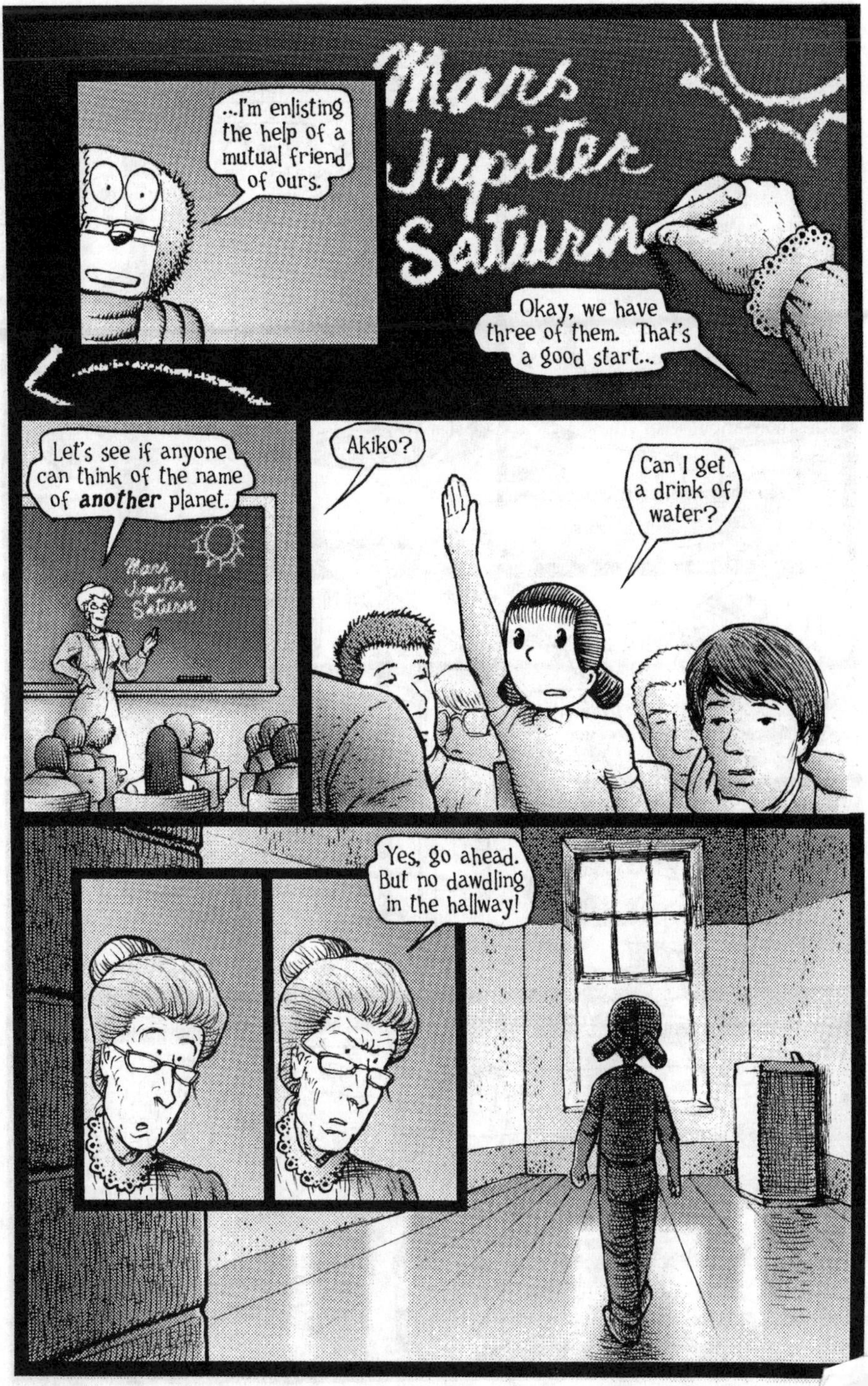
...I'm enlisting the help of a mutual friend of ours.
Mars
Jupiter
Saturn
Okay, we have three of them. That's a good start...
Let's see if anyone can think of the name of **another** planet.
Akiko?
Can I get a drink of water?
Yes, go ahead. But no dawdling in the hallway!

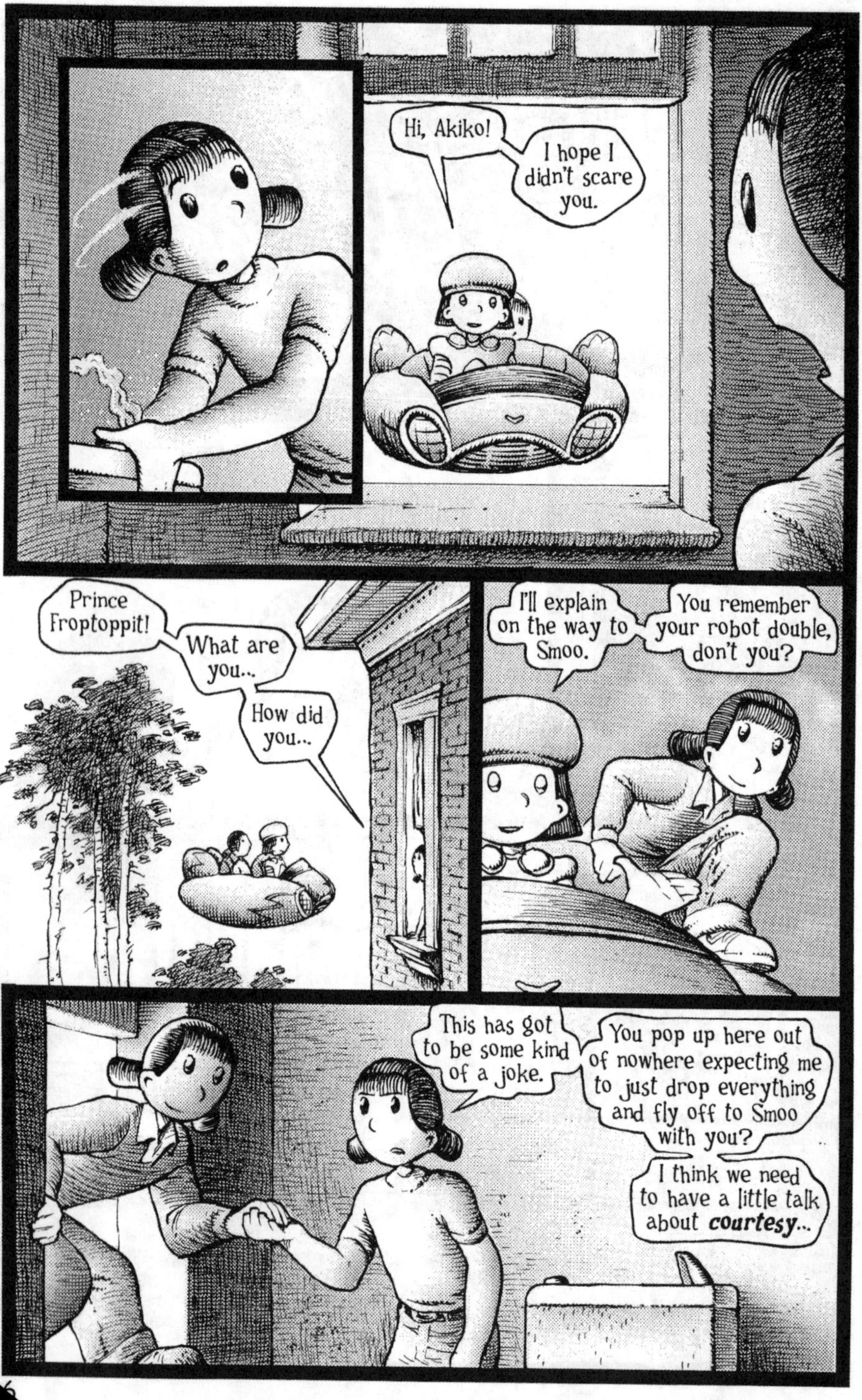

Hi, Akiko!
I hope I didn't scare you.
Prince Froptoppit!
What are you...
How did you...
I'll explain on the way to Smoo.
You remember your robot double, don't you?
This has got to be some kind of a joke.
You pop up here out of nowhere expecting me to just drop everything and fly off to Smoo with you?
I think we need to have a little talk about ***courtesy***...

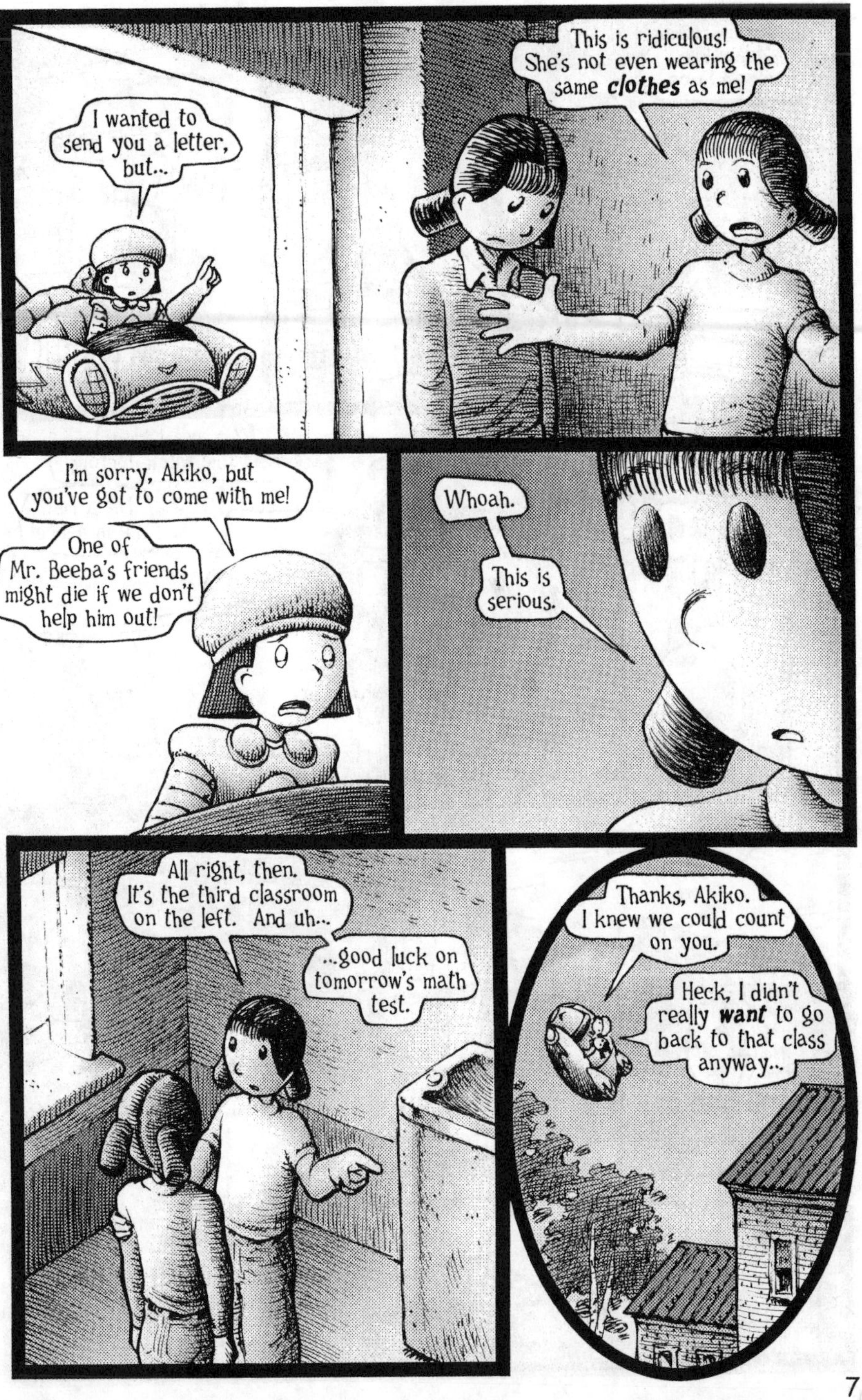
I wanted to send you a letter, but...
This is ridiculous! She's not even wearing the same ***clothes*** as me!
I'm sorry, Akiko, but you've got to come with me!
One of Mr. Beeba's friends might die if we don't help him out!
Whoah.
This is serious.
All right, then. It's the third classroom on the left. And uh...
...good luck on tomorrow's math test.
Thanks, Akiko. I knew we could count on you.
Heck, I didn't really ***want*** to go back to that class anyway...

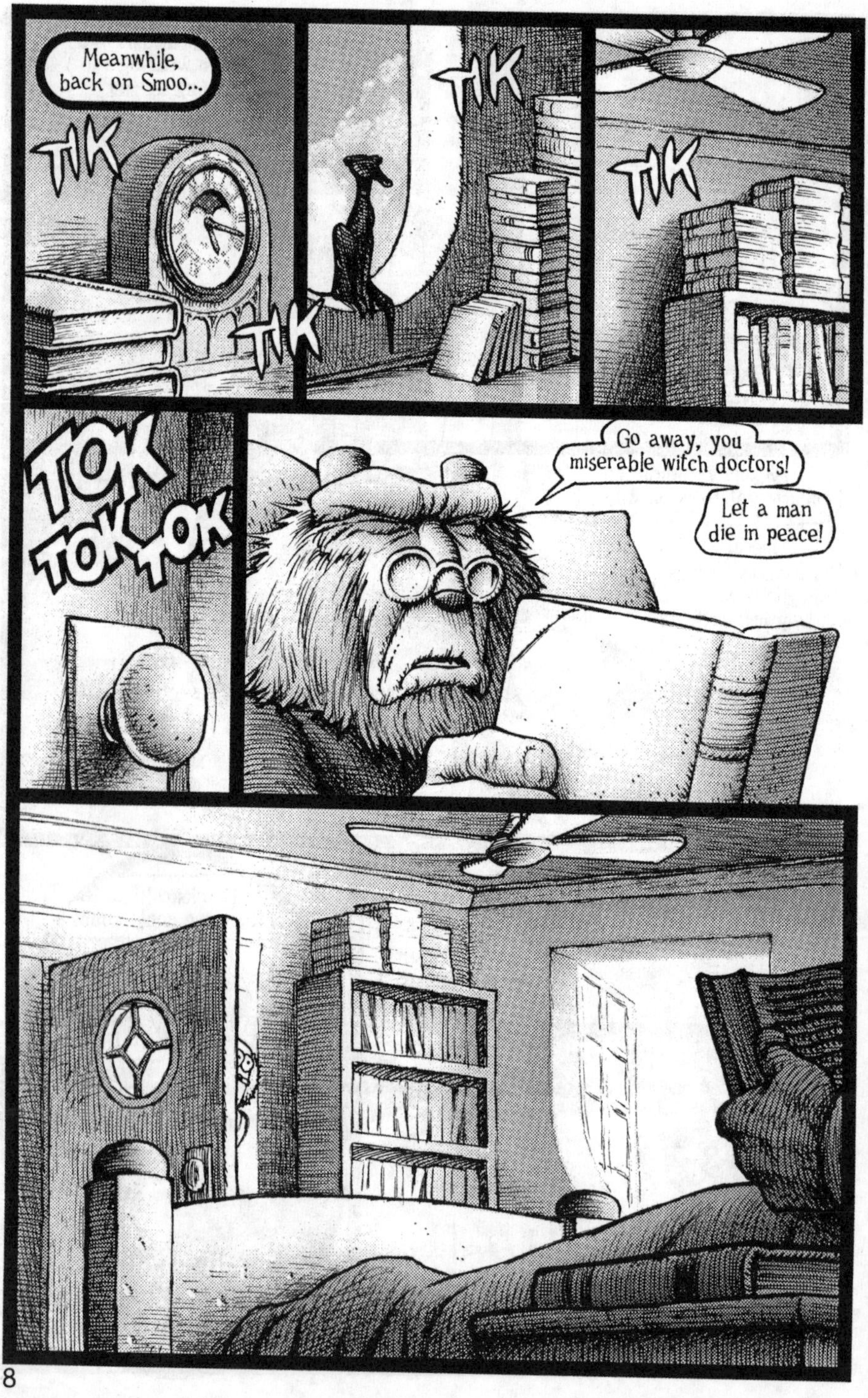
Meanwhile, back on Smoo...
TIK
TIK
TIK
TIK
TOK TOK TOK TOK
Go away, you miserable witch doctors!
Let a man die in peace!

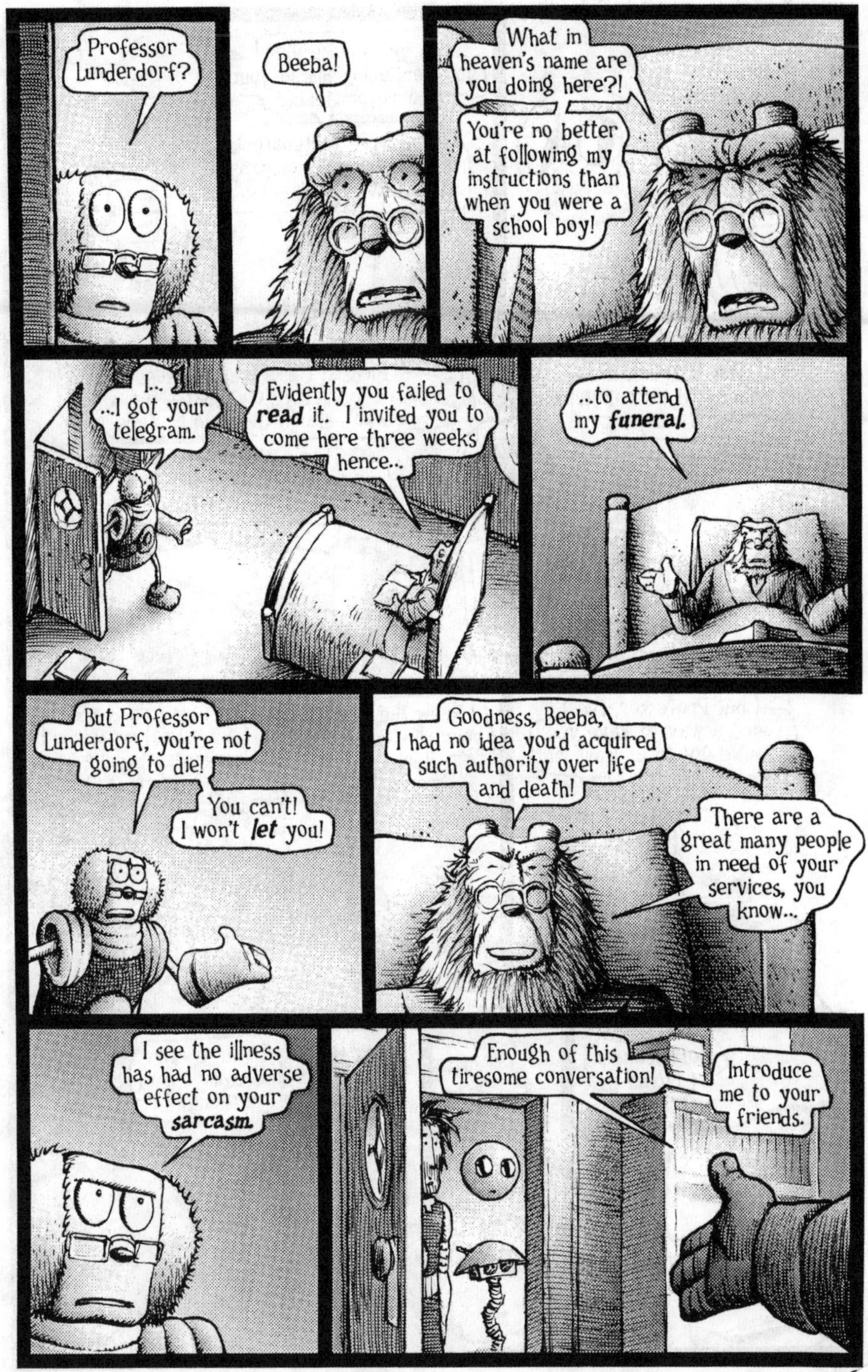
Professor Lunderdorf?
Beeba!
What in heaven's name are you doing here?!
You're no better at following my instructions than when you were a school boy!
I... ...I got your telegram.
Evidently you failed to **read** it. I invited you to come here three weeks hence...
...to attend my **funeral**.
But Professor Lunderdorf, you're not going to die!
You can't! I won't **let** you!
Goodness, Beeba, I had no idea you'd acquired such authority over life and death!
There are a great many people in need of your services, you know...
I see the illness has had no adverse effect on your **sarcasm**.
Enough of this tiresome conversation!
Introduce me to your friends.

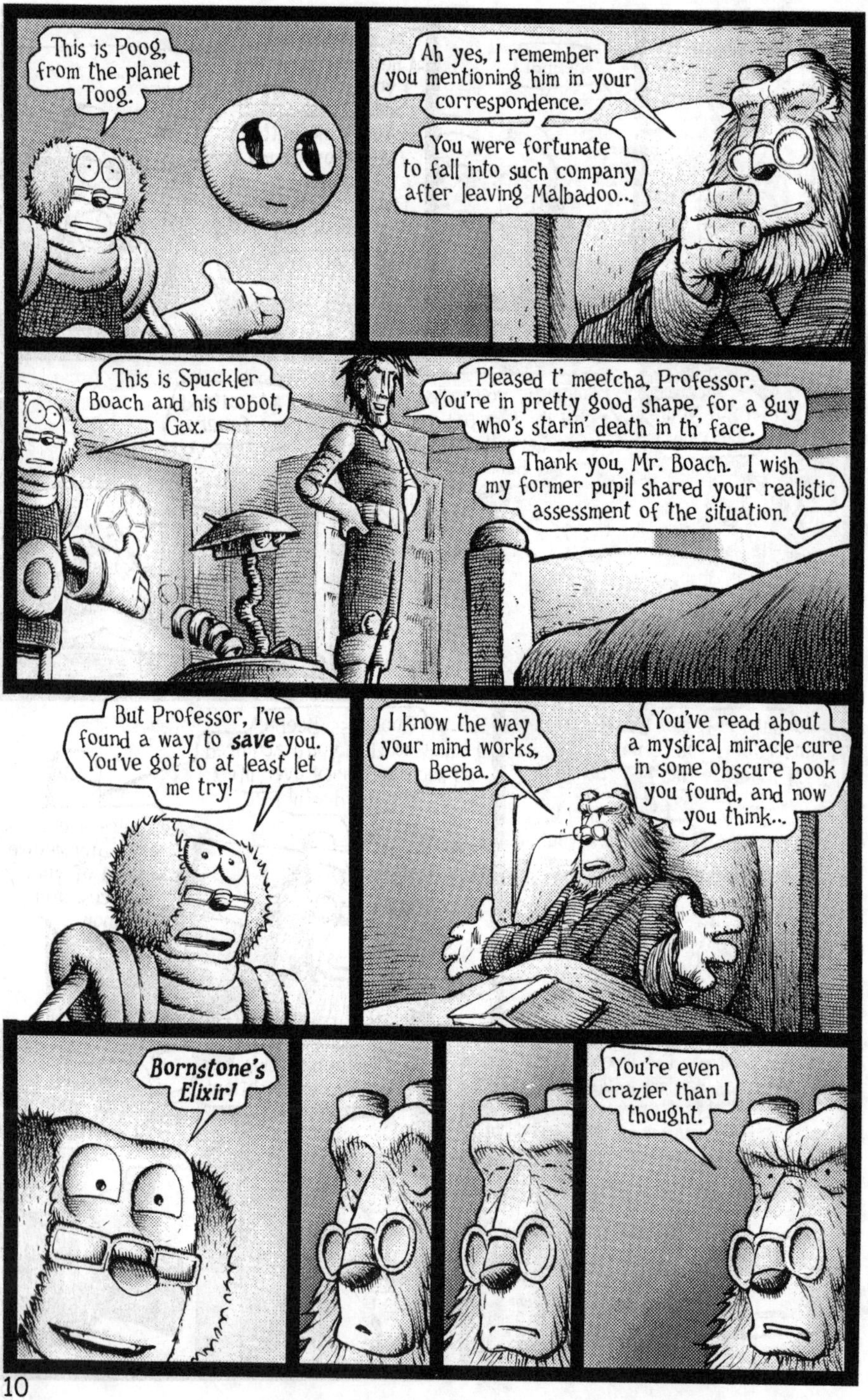
This is Poog, from the planet Toog.
Ah yes, I remember you mentioning him in your correspondence.
You were fortunate to fall into such company after leaving Malbadoo...
This is Spuckler Boach and his robot, Gax.
Pleased t' meetcha, Professor. You're in pretty good shape, for a guy who's starin' death in th' face.
Thank you, Mr. Boach. I wish my former pupil shared your realistic assessment of the situation.
But Professor, I've found a way to ***save*** you. You've got to at least let me try!
I know the way your mind works, Beeba.
You've read about a mystical miracle cure in some obscure book you found, and now you think...
***Bornstone's Elixir!***
You're even crazier than I thought.

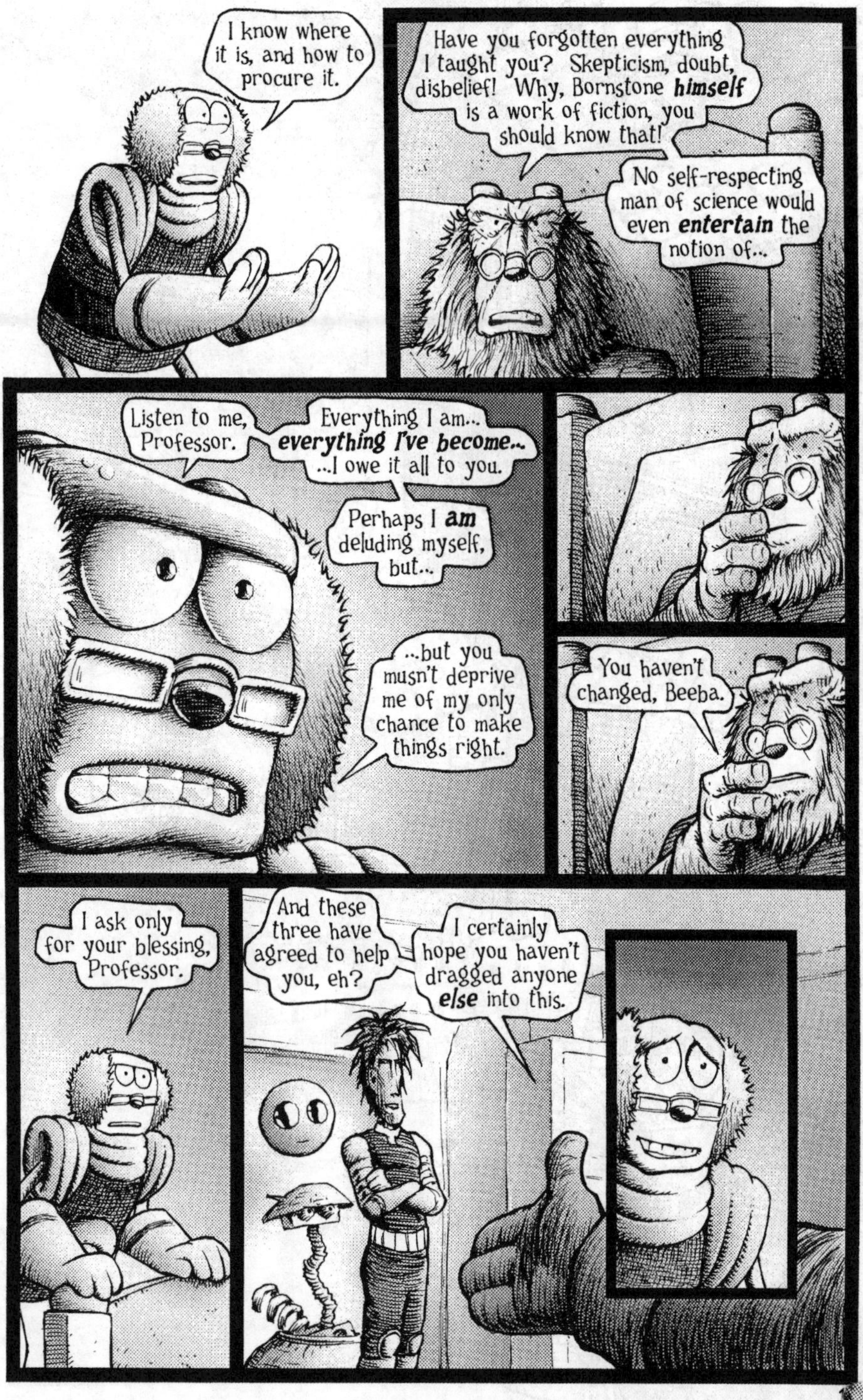
I know where it is, and how to procure it.
Have you forgotten everything I taught you? Skepticism, doubt, disbelief! Why, Bornstone **himself** is a work of fiction, you should know that!
No self-respecting man of science would even **entertain** the notion of...
Listen to me, Professor.
Everything I am... **everything I've become...** ...I owe it all to you.
Perhaps I **am** deluding myself, but...
...but you musn't deprive me of my only chance to make things right.
You haven't changed, Beeba.
I ask only for your blessing, Professor.
And these three have agreed to help you, eh?
I certainly hope you haven't dragged anyone **else** into this.

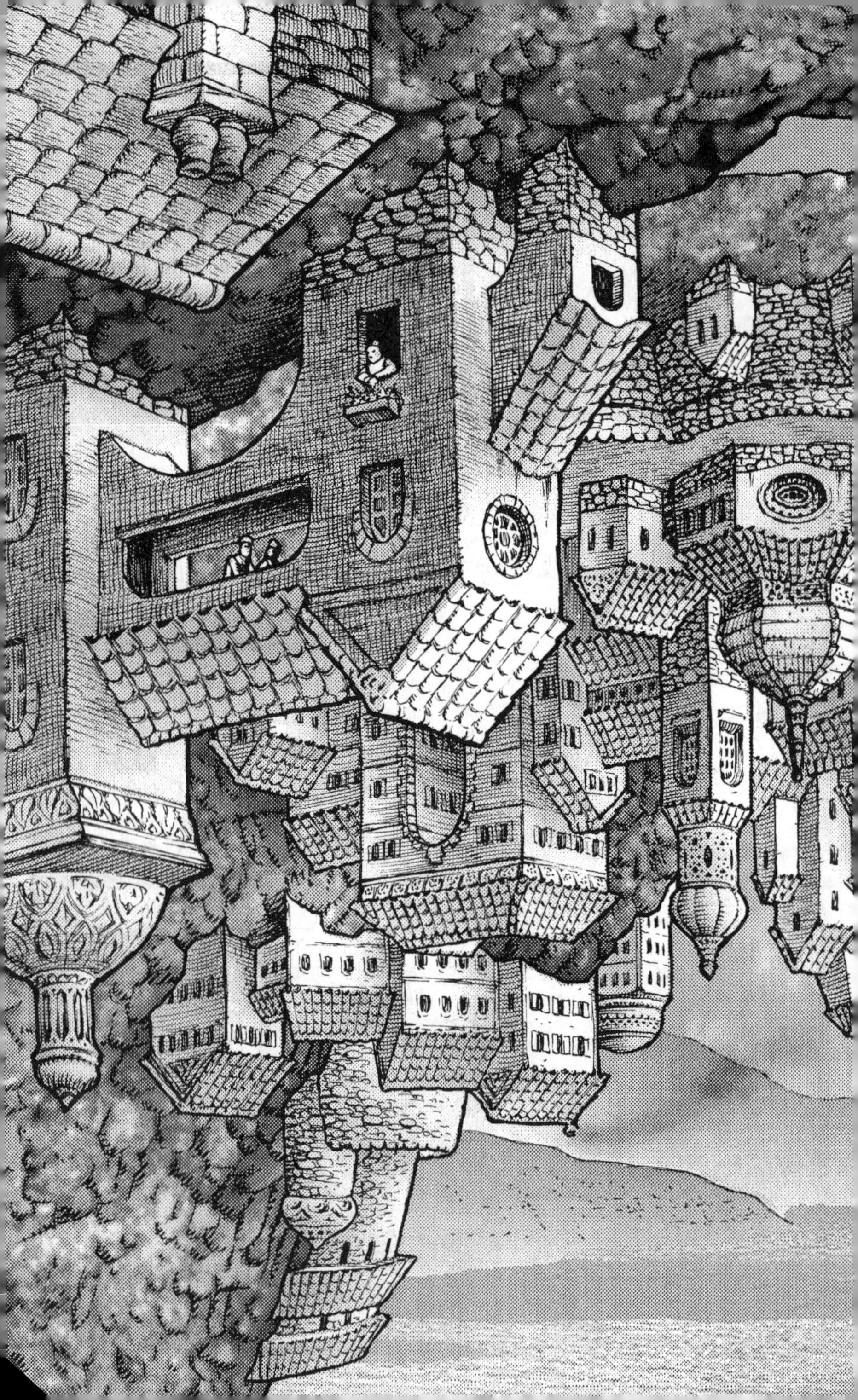

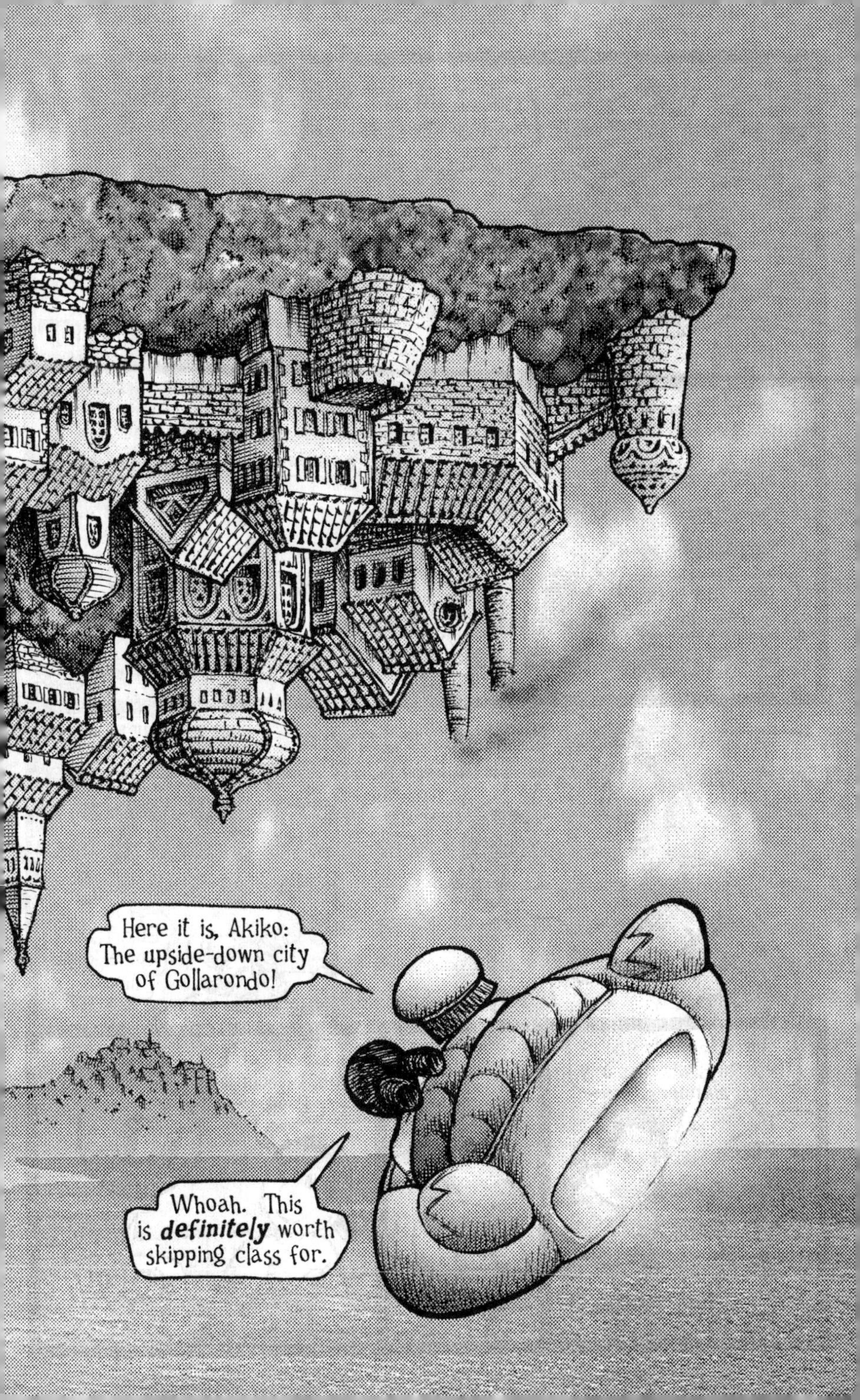
Here it is, Akiko: The upside-down city of Gollarondo!
Whoah. This is ***definitely*** worth skipping class for.

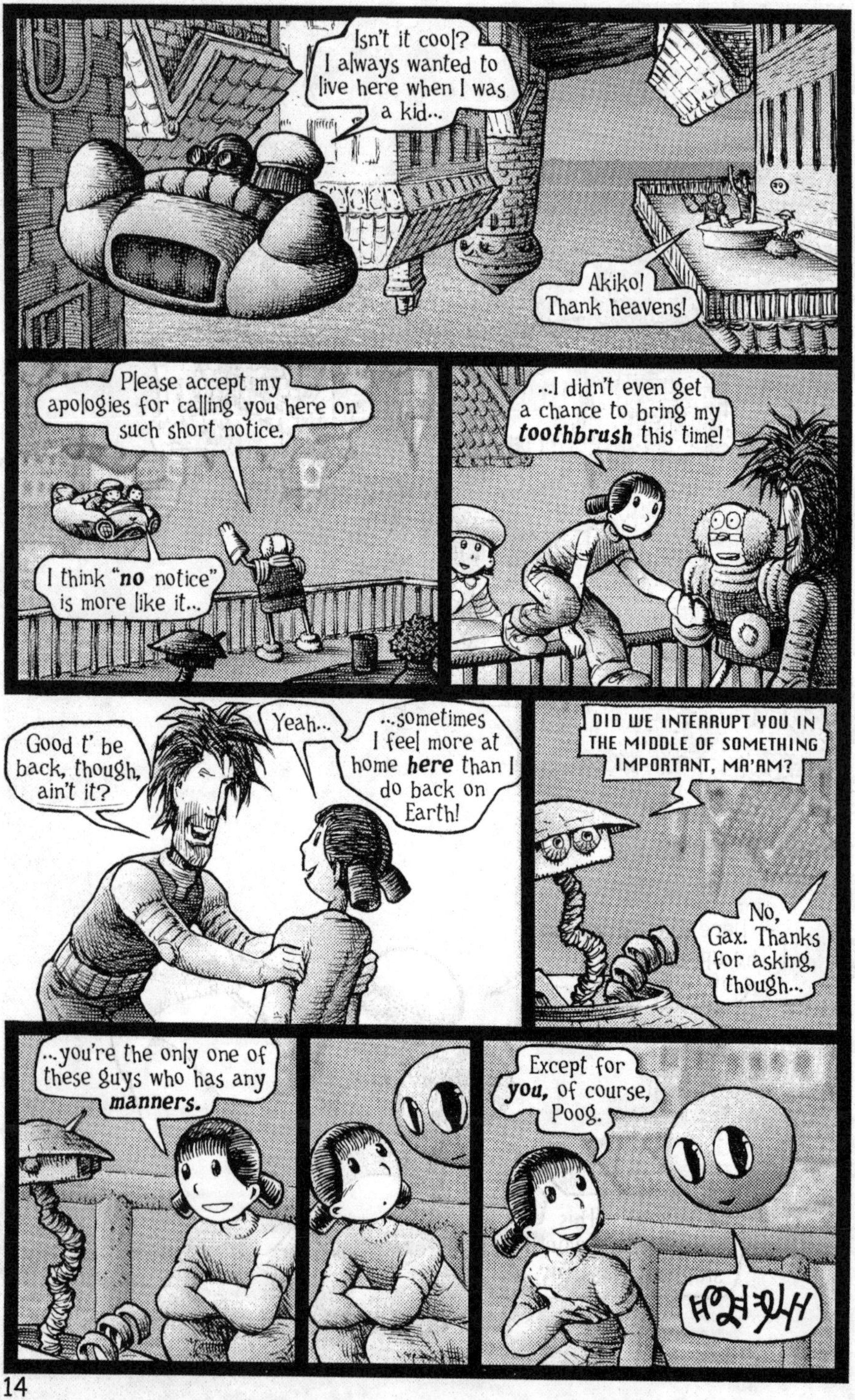
Isn't it cool? I always wanted to live here when I was a kid...
Akiko! Thank heavens!
Please accept my apologies for calling you here on such short notice.
I think "**no** notice" is more like it...
...I didn't even get a chance to bring my ***toothbrush*** this time!
Good t' be back, though, ain't it?
Yeah...
...sometimes I feel more at home ***here*** than I do back on Earth!
DID WE INTERRUPT YOU IN THE MIDDLE OF SOMETHING IMPORTANT, MA'AM?
No, Gax. Thanks for asking, though...
...you're the only one of these guys who has any ***manners.***
Except for ***you,*** of course, Poog.

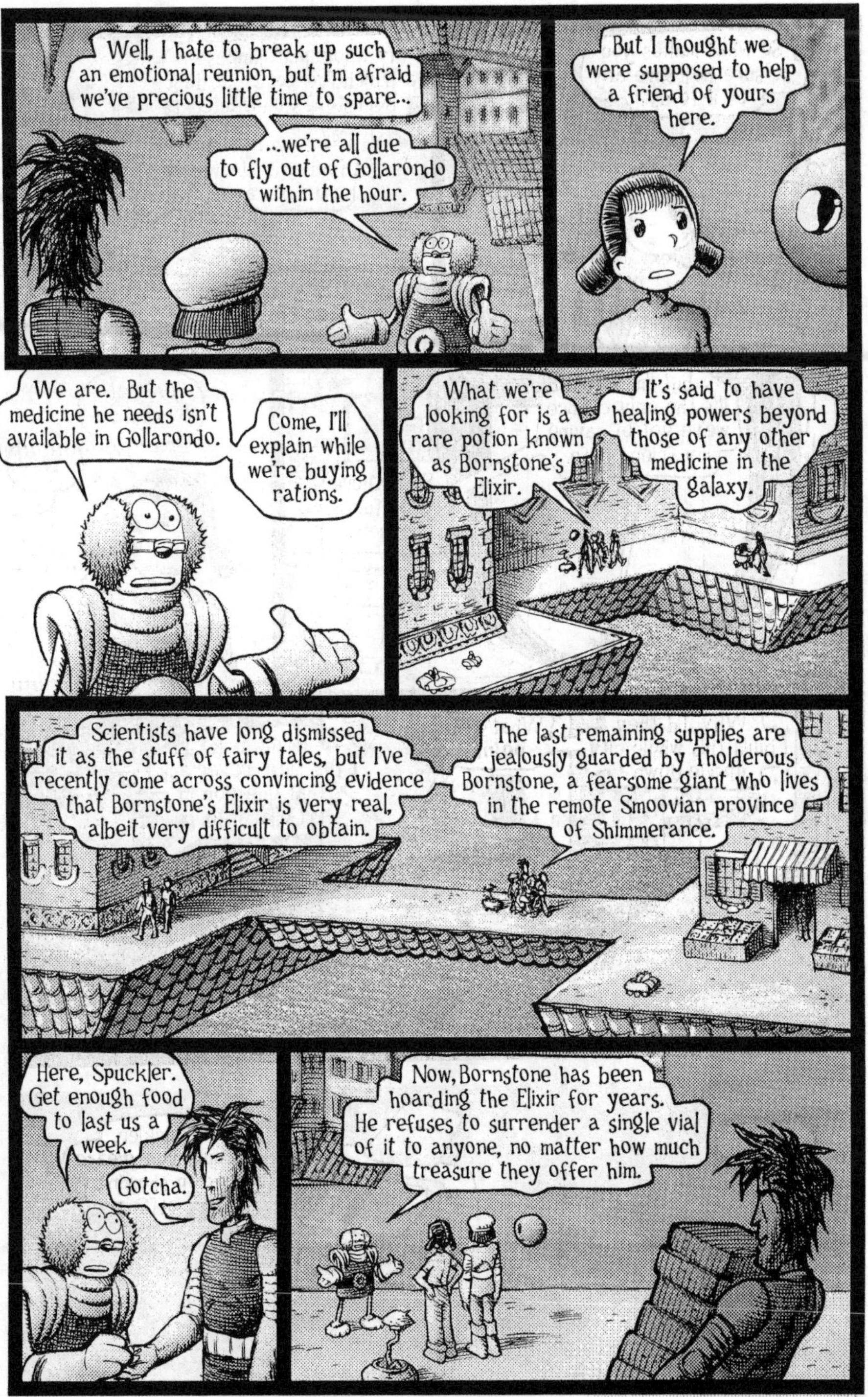

Well, I hate to break up such an emotional reunion, but I'm afraid we've precious little time to spare...
...we're all due to fly out of Gollarondo within the hour.
But I thought we were supposed to help a friend of yours here.
We are. But the medicine he needs isn't available in Gollarondo.
Come, I'll explain while we're buying rations.
What we're looking for is a rare potion known as Bornstone's Elixir.
It's said to have healing powers beyond those of any other medicine in the galaxy.
Scientists have long dismissed it as the stuff of fairy tales, but I've recently come across convincing evidence that Bornstone's Elixir is very real, albeit very difficult to obtain.
The last remaining supplies are jealously guarded by Tholderous Bornstone, a fearsome giant who lives in the remote Smoovian province of Shimmerance.
Here, Spuckler. Get enough food to last us a week.
Gotcha.
Now, Bornstone has been hoarding the Elixir for years. He refuses to surrender a single vial of it to anyone, no matter how much treasure they offer him.

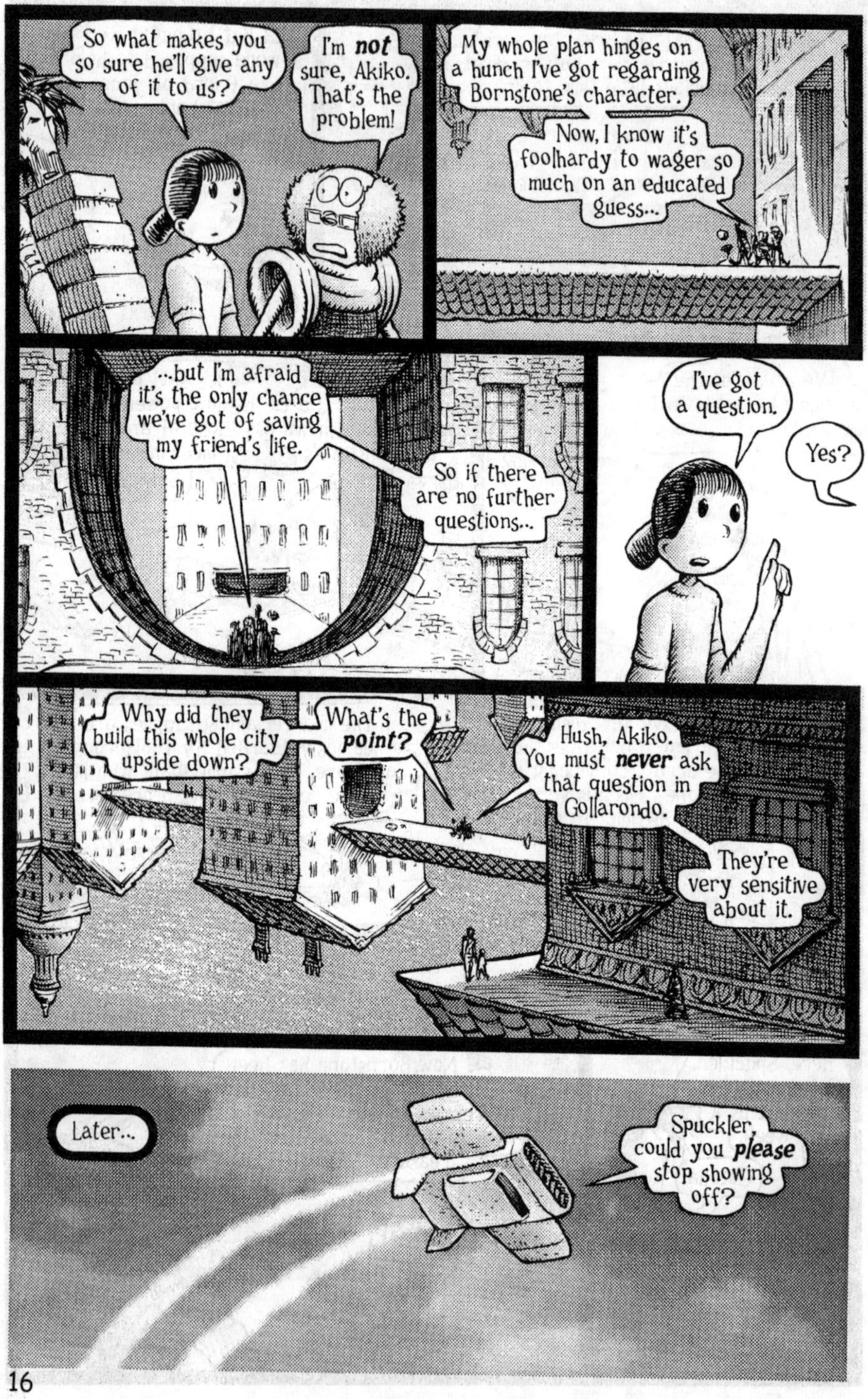

So what makes you so sure he'll give any of it to us?
I'm not sure, Akiko. That's the problem!
My whole plan hinges on a hunch I've got regarding Bornstone's character.
Now, I know it's foolhardy to wager so much on an educated guess...
...but I'm afraid it's the only chance we've got of saving my friend's life.
So if there are no further questions...
I've got a question.
Yes?
Why did they build this whole city upside down?
What's the point?
Hush, Akiko. You must never ask that question in Gollarondo.
They're very sensitive about it.
Later...
Spuckler, could you please stop showing off?

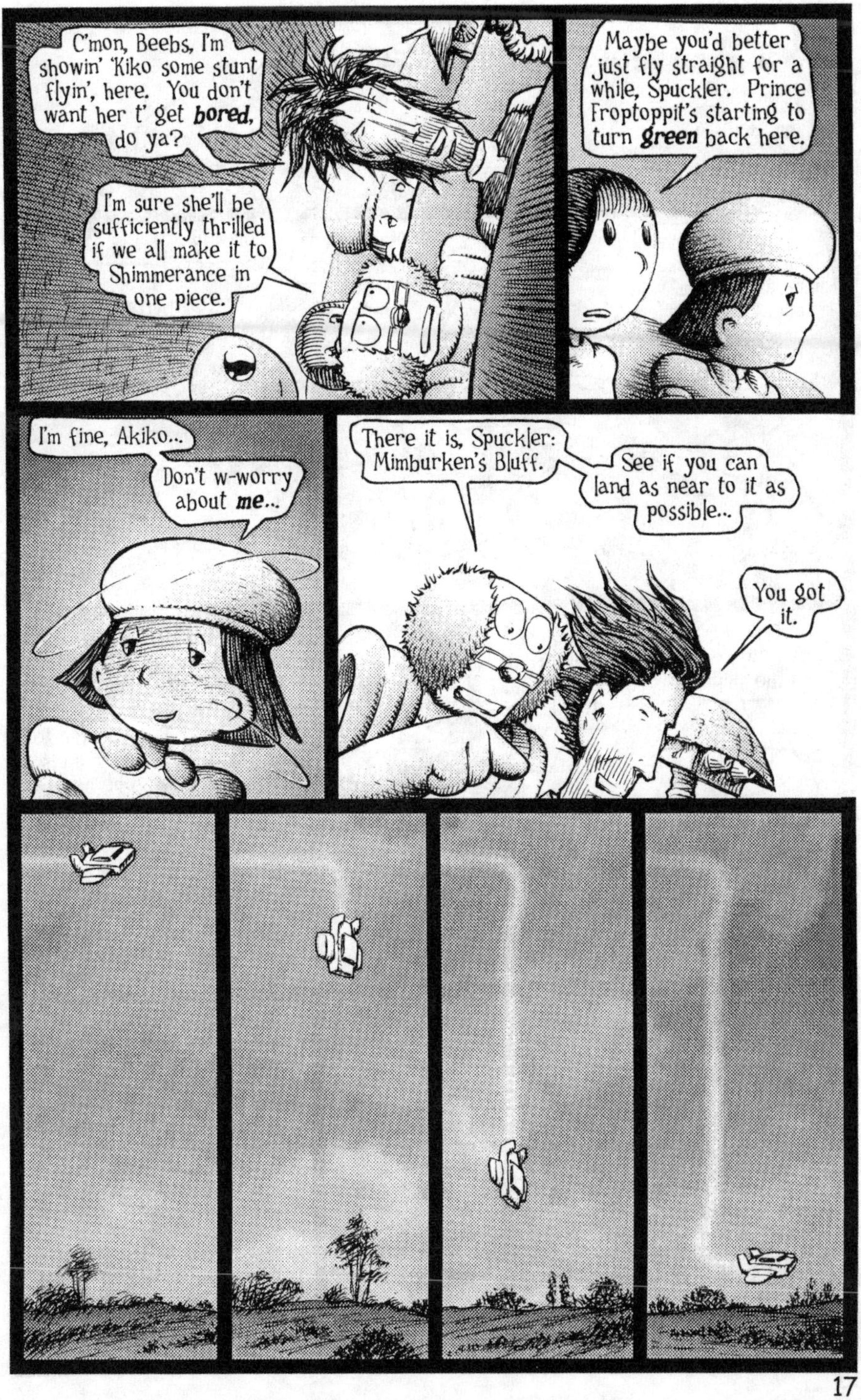

C'mon, Beebs, I'm showin' 'Kiko some stunt flyin', here. You don't want her t' get **bored**, do ya?
I'm sure she'll be sufficiently thrilled if we all make it to Shimmerance in one piece.
Maybe you'd better just fly straight for a while, Spuckler. Prince Froptoppit's starting to turn **green** back here.
I'm fine, Akiko...
Don't w-worry about **me**...
There it is, Spuckler: Mimburken's Bluff.
See if you can land as near to it as possible...
You got it.

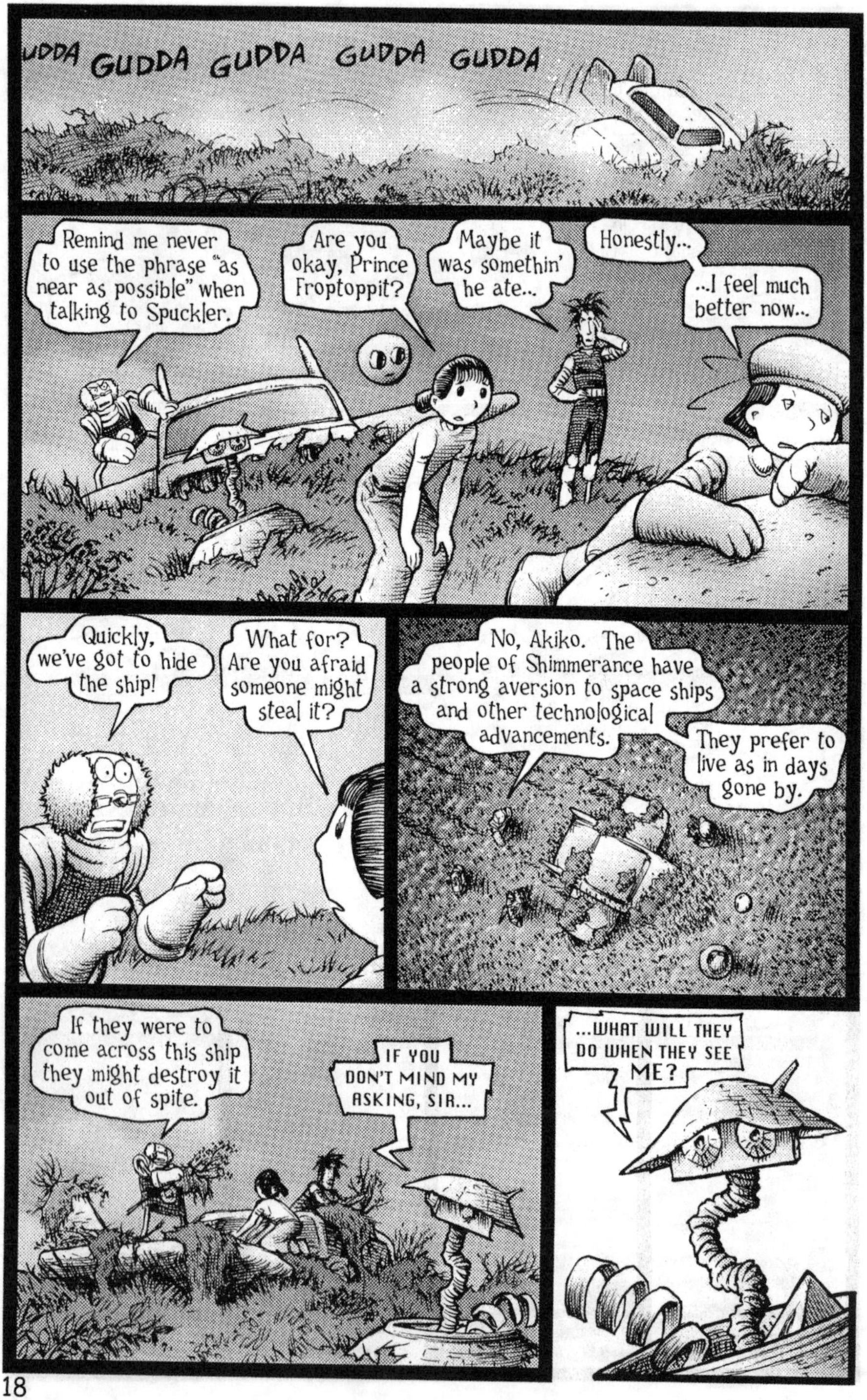
UDDA GUDDA GUDDA GUDDA GUDDA
Remind me never to use the phrase "as near as possible" when talking to Spuckler.
Are you okay, Prince Froptoppit?
Maybe it was somethin' he ate..
Honestly...
...I feel much better now...
Quickly, we've got to hide the ship!
What for? Are you afraid someone might steal it?
No, Akiko. The people of Shimmerance have a strong aversion to space ships and other technological advancements.
They prefer to live as in days gone by.
If they were to come across this ship they might destroy it out of spite.
IF YOU DON'T MIND MY ASKING, SIR...
...WHAT WILL THEY DO WHEN THEY SEE ME?

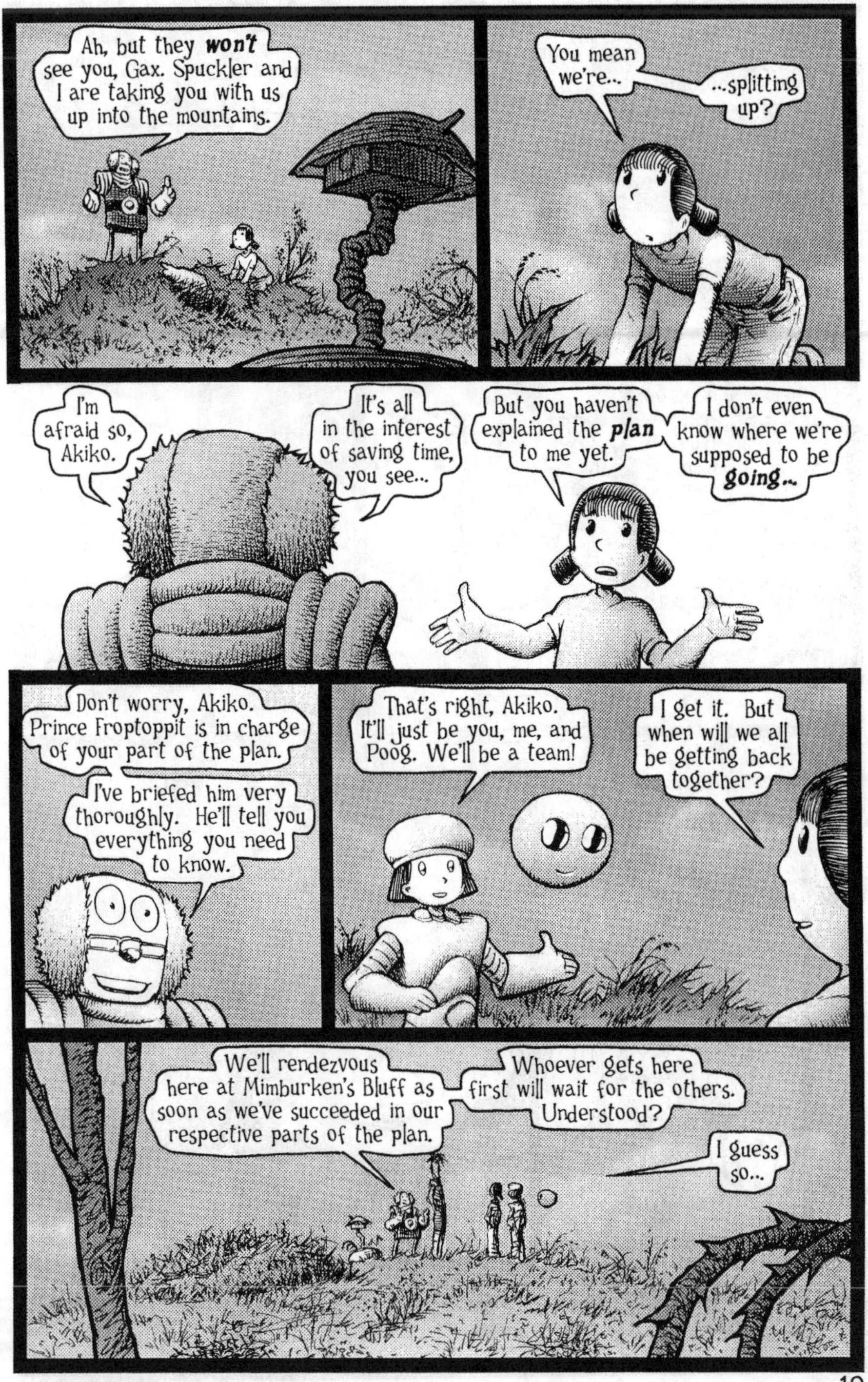

Ah, but they **won't** see you, Gax. Spuckler and I are taking you with us up into the mountains.
You mean we're...
...splitting up?
I'm afraid so, Akiko.
It's all in the interest of saving time, you see...
But you haven't explained the **plan** to me yet.
I don't even know where we're supposed to be **going**...
Don't worry, Akiko. Prince Froptoppit is in charge of your part of the plan.
I've briefed him very thoroughly. He'll tell you everything you need to know.
That's right, Akiko. It'll just be you, me, and Poog. We'll be a team!
I get it. But when will we all be getting back together?
We'll rendezvous here at Mimburken's Bluff as soon as we've succeeded in our respective parts of the plan.
Whoever gets here first will wait for the others. Understood?
I guess so...

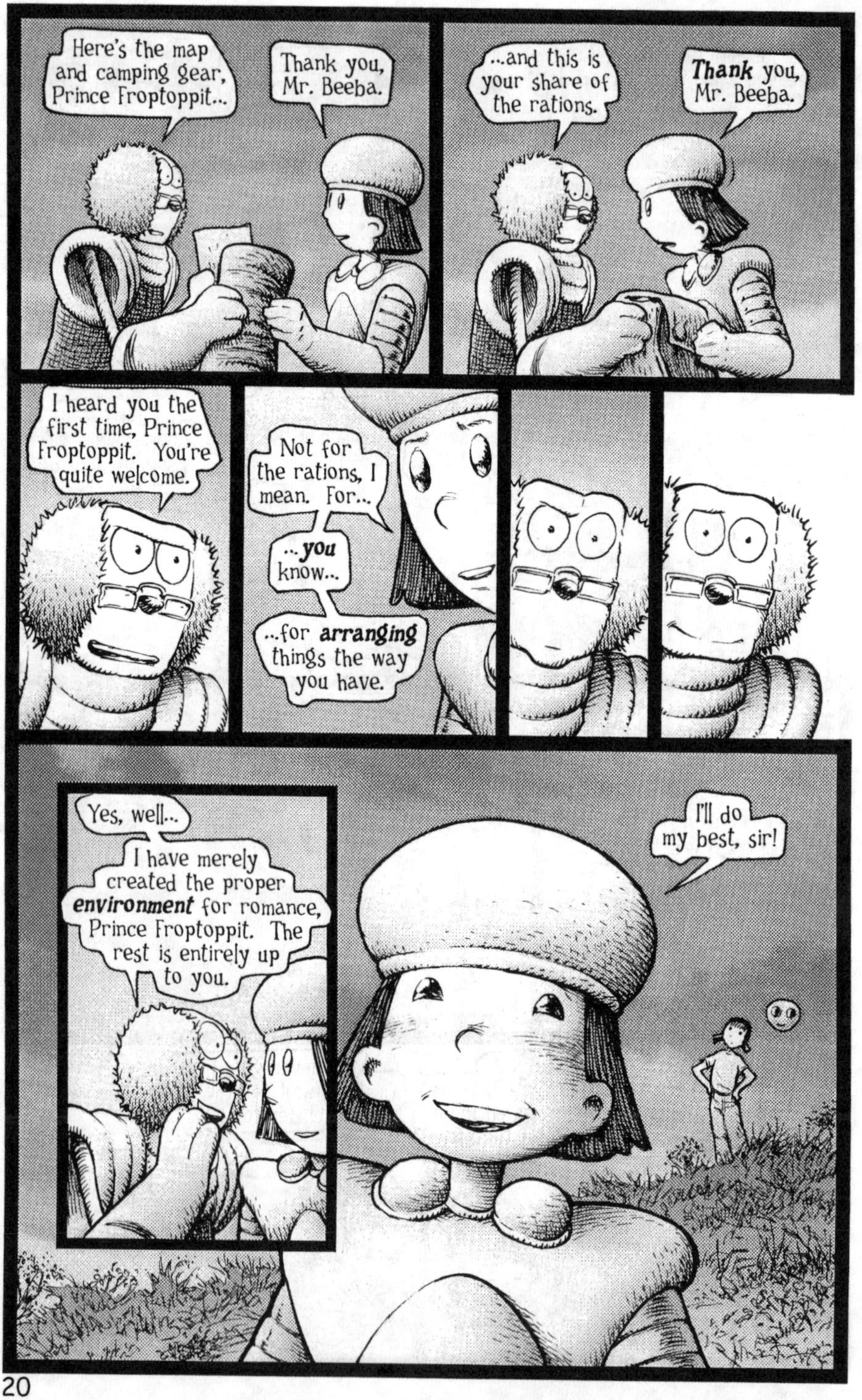
Here's the map and camping gear, Prince Froptoppit...
Thank you, Mr. Beeba.
...and this is your share of the rations.
**Thank** you, Mr. Beeba.
I heard you the first time, Prince Froptoppit. You're quite welcome.
Not for the rations, I mean. For...
...**you** know...
...for **arranging** things the way you have.
Yes, well...
I have merely created the proper **environment** for romance, Prince Froptoppit. The rest is entirely up to you.
I'll do my best, sir!

BORNSTONE'S
ELIXIR

*Chapter 2*

# Up In the Mountains, Deep In the Woods

So let me get this straight...
We're supposed to buy a barrel of Bornstone's favorite ale?
That's right...

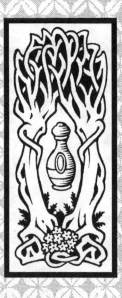

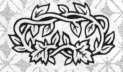

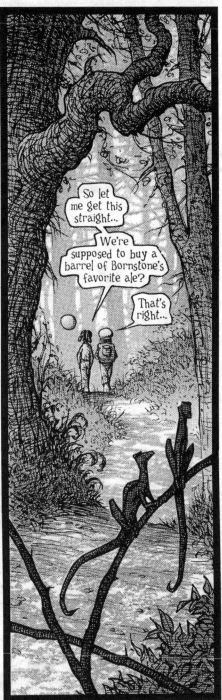

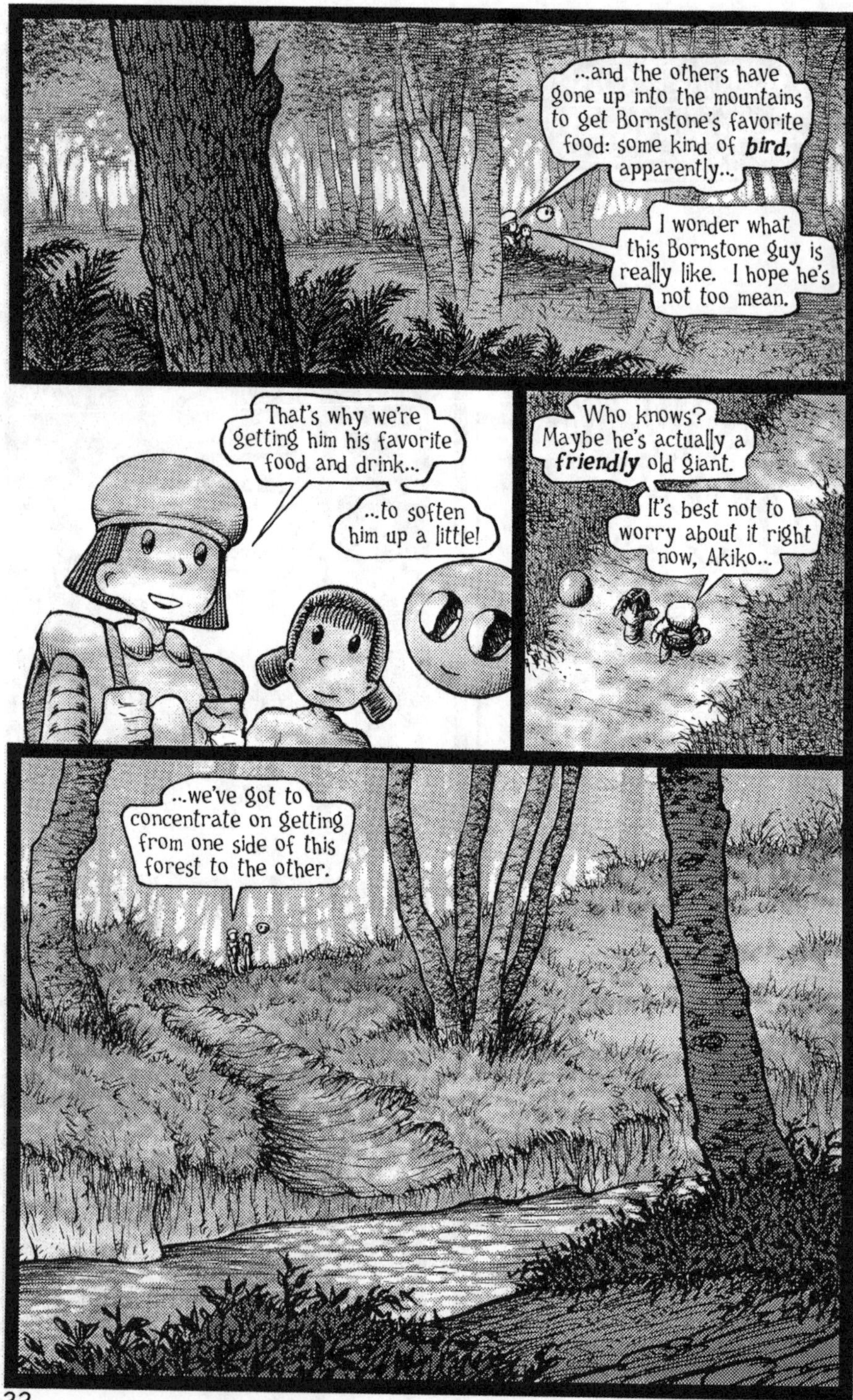
...and the others have gone up into the mountains to get Bornstone's favorite food: some kind of **bird,** apparently...
I wonder what this Bornstone guy is really like. I hope he's not too mean.
That's why we're getting him his favorite food and drink...
...to soften him up a little!
Who knows? Maybe he's actually a ***friendly*** old giant.
It's best not to worry about it right now, Akiko...
...we've got to concentrate on getting from one side of this forest to the other.

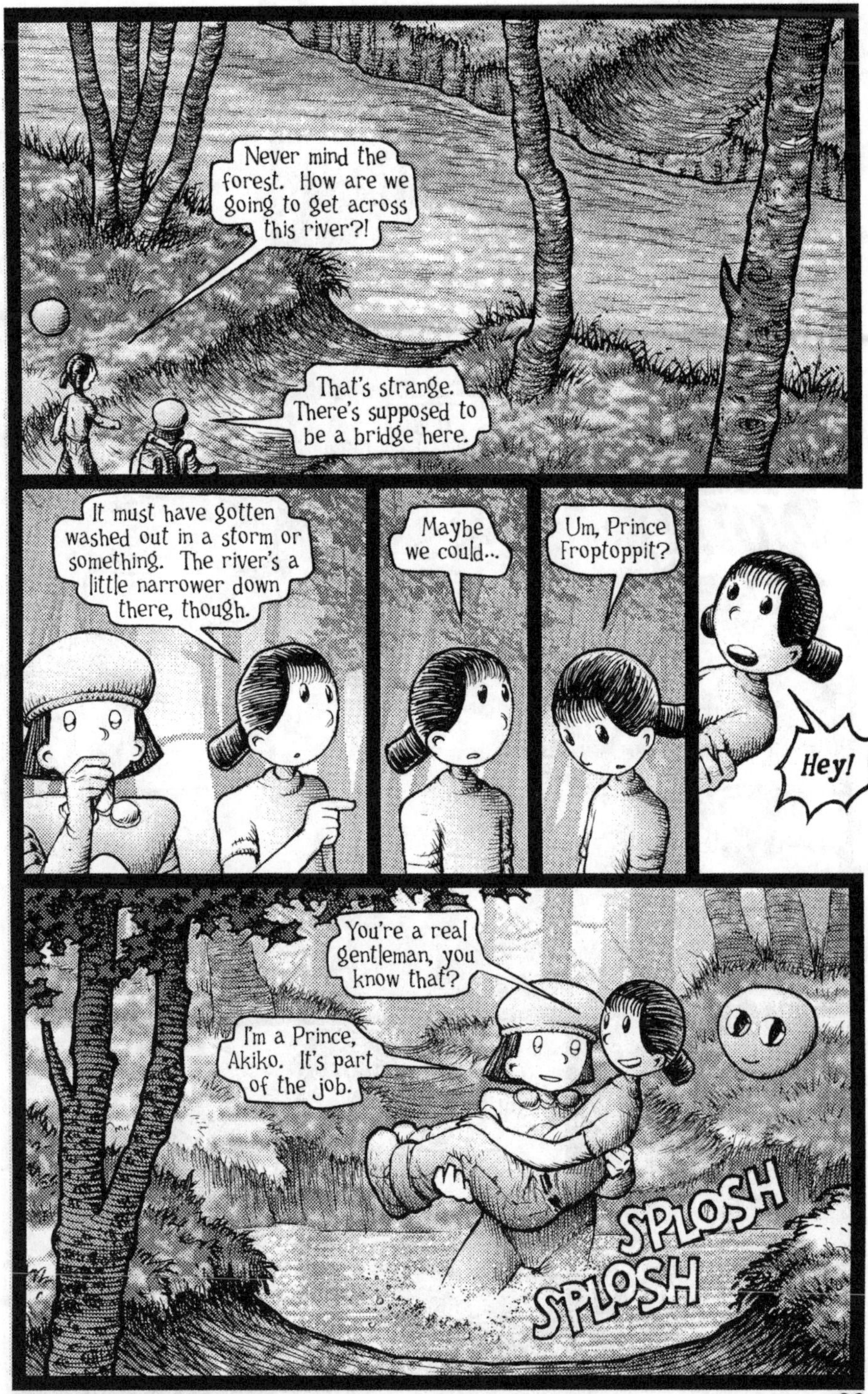
Never mind the forest. How are we going to get across this river?!
That's strange. There's supposed to be a bridge here.
It must have gotten washed out in a storm or something. The river's a little narrower down there, though.
Maybe we could...
Um, Prince Froptoppit?
Hey!
You're a real gentleman, you know that?
I'm a Prince, Akiko. It's part of the job.
SPLOSH
SPLOSH

I wonder how Spuckler and Mr. Beeba are getting along...

"Getting along?"

You don't know them very well, do you?

SPUCKLER YOU *IDIOT!!!*

I *told* you we should have taken the low road!

Quit squirmin', Beebs...

...you're gonna lose your grip!

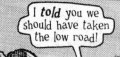

SHALL I THROW HIM A LINE, SIR?

Naw, Gax. I got this under control.

Here, Beeba. Gimme your hand, an' let go of the log.

24

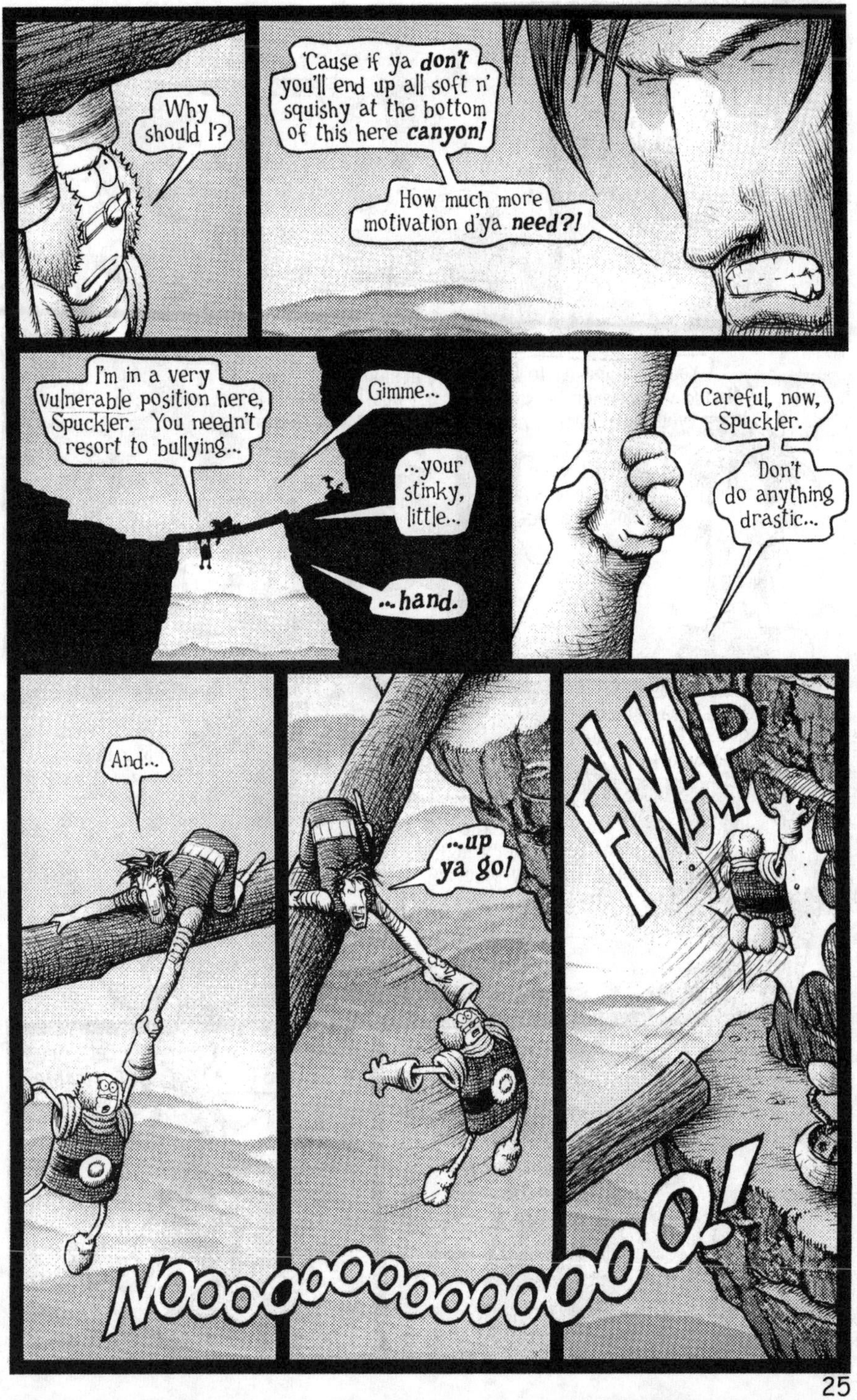
Why should I?
'Cause if ya **don't** you'll end up all soft n' squishy at the bottom of this here **canyon!**
How much more motivation d'ya **need?!**
I'm in a very vulnerable position here, Spuckler. You needn't resort to bullying...
Gimme...
...your stinky, little...
**...hand.**
Careful, now, Spuckler.
Don't do anything drastic...
And...
**...up ya go!**
FWAP
NOOOOOOOOOOOOOOOOO!

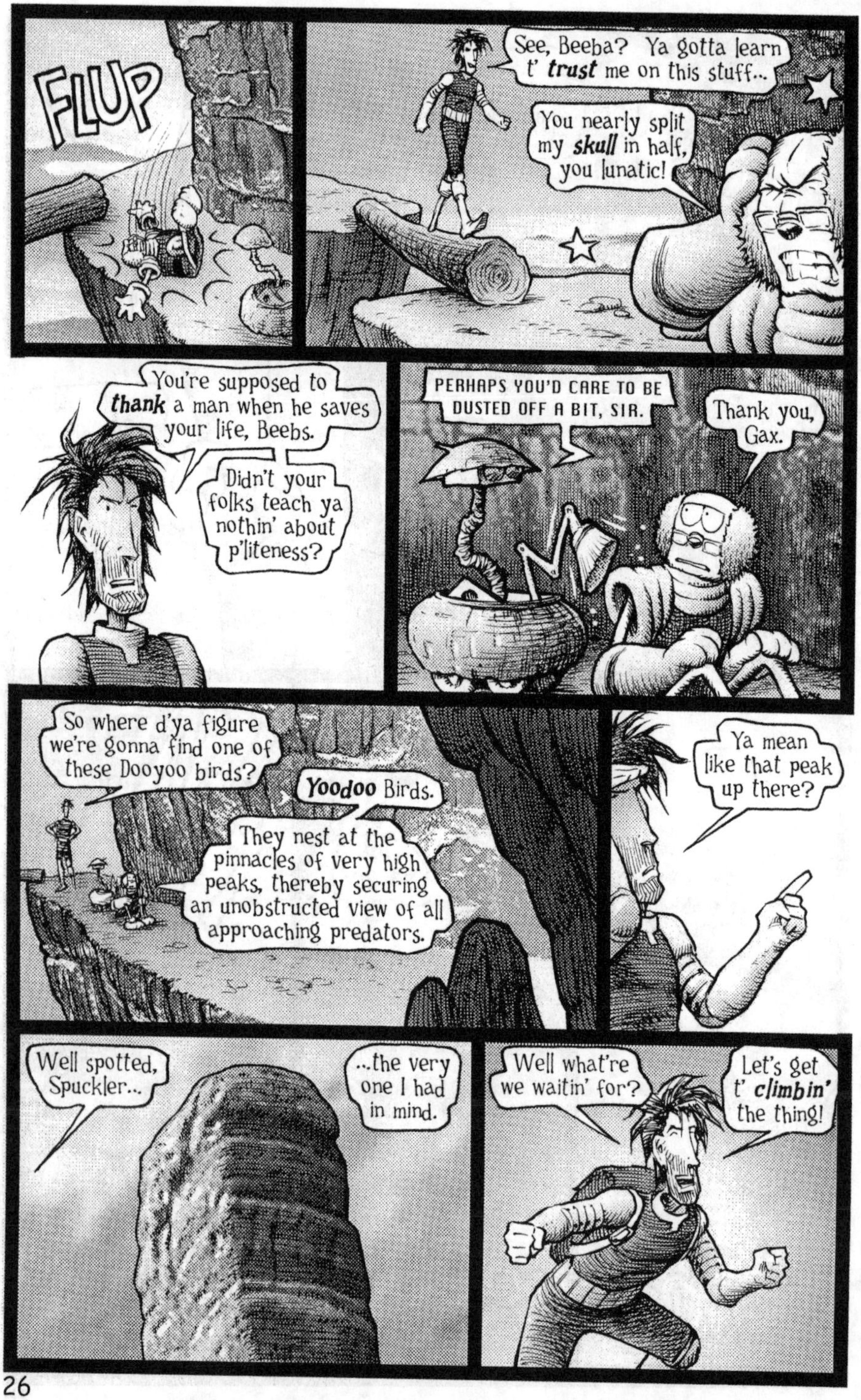

FLUP
See, Beeba? Ya gotta learn t' *trust* me on this stuff...
You nearly split my *skull* in half, you lunatic!
You're supposed to *thank* a man when he saves your life, Beebs.
Didn't your folks teach ya nothin' about p'liteness?
PERHAPS YOU'D CARE TO BE DUSTED OFF A BIT, SIR.
Thank you, Gax.
So where d'ya figure we're gonna find one of these Dooyoo birds?
*Yoodoo* Birds.
They nest at the pinnacles of very high peaks, thereby securing an unobstructed view of all approaching predators.
Ya mean like that peak up there?
Well spotted, Spuckler...
...the very one I had in mind.
Well what're we waitin' for?
Let's get t' *climbin'* the thing!

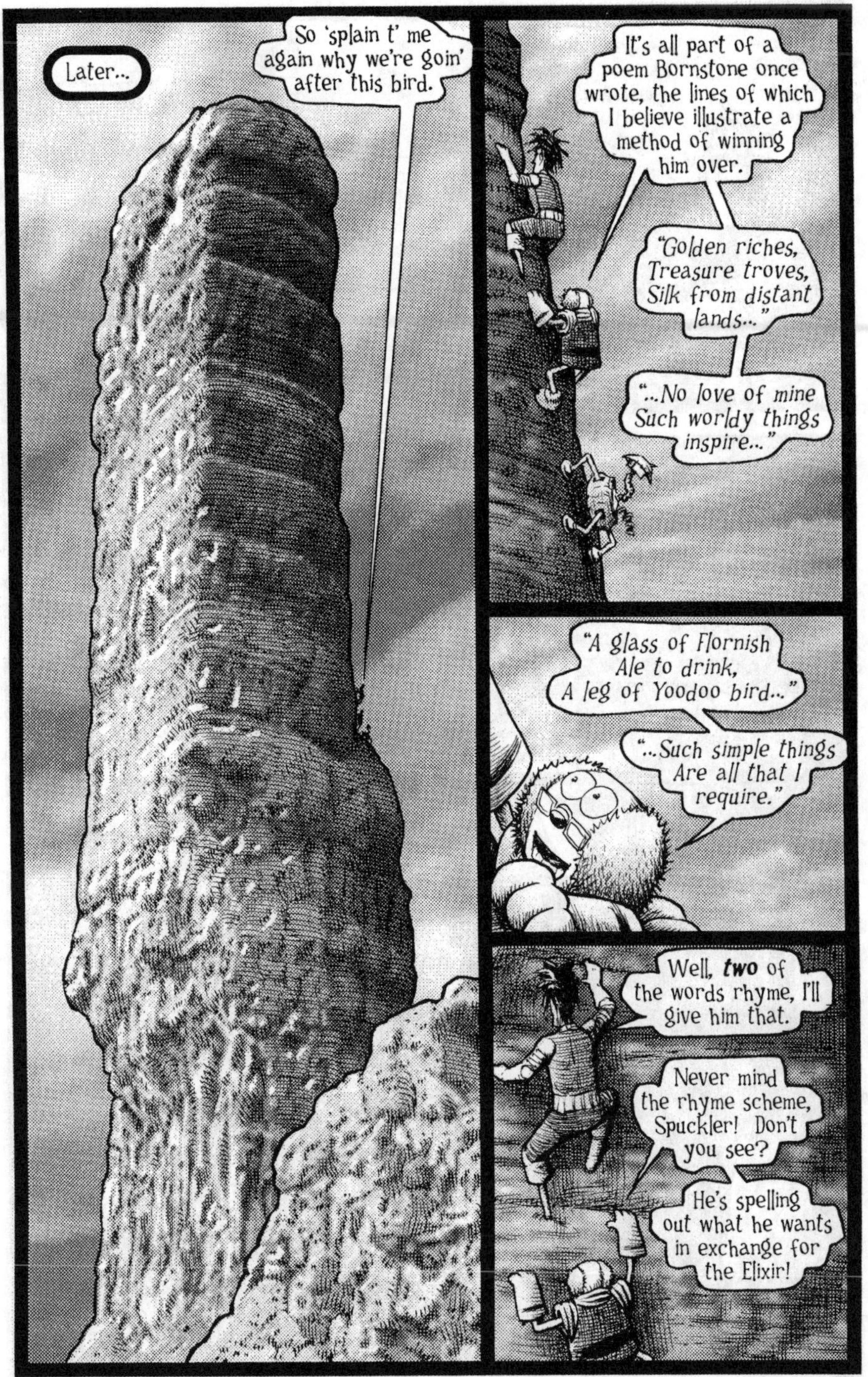
Later...
So 'splain t' me again why we're goin' after this bird.
It's all part of a poem Bornstone once wrote, the lines of which I believe illustrate a method of winning him over.
"Golden riches, Treasure troves, Silk from distant lands..."
"...No love of mine Such worldy things inspire..."
"A glass of Flornish Ale to drink, A leg of Yoodoo bird..."
"...Such simple things Are all that I require."
Well, **two** of the words rhyme, I'll give him that.
Never mind the rhyme scheme, Spuckler! Don't you see?
He's spelling out what he wants in exchange for the Elixir!

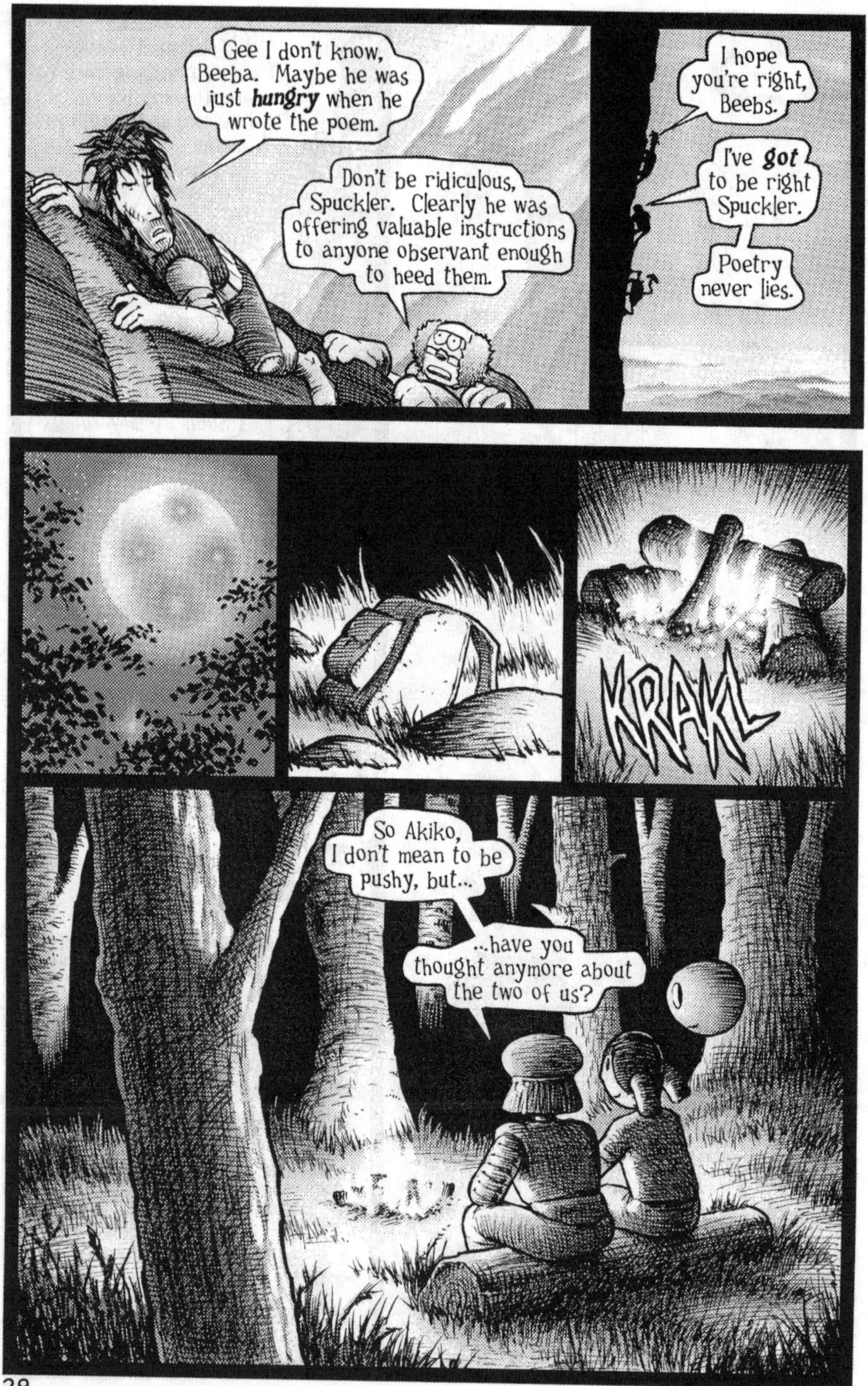
Gee I don't know, Beeba. Maybe he was just **hungry** when he wrote the poem.
Don't be ridiculous, Spuckler. Clearly he was offering valuable instructions to anyone observant enough to heed them.
I hope you're right, Beebs.
I've **got** to be right Spuckler.
Poetry never lies.
KRAKL
So Akiko, I don't mean to be pushy, but...
...have you thought anymore about the two of us?

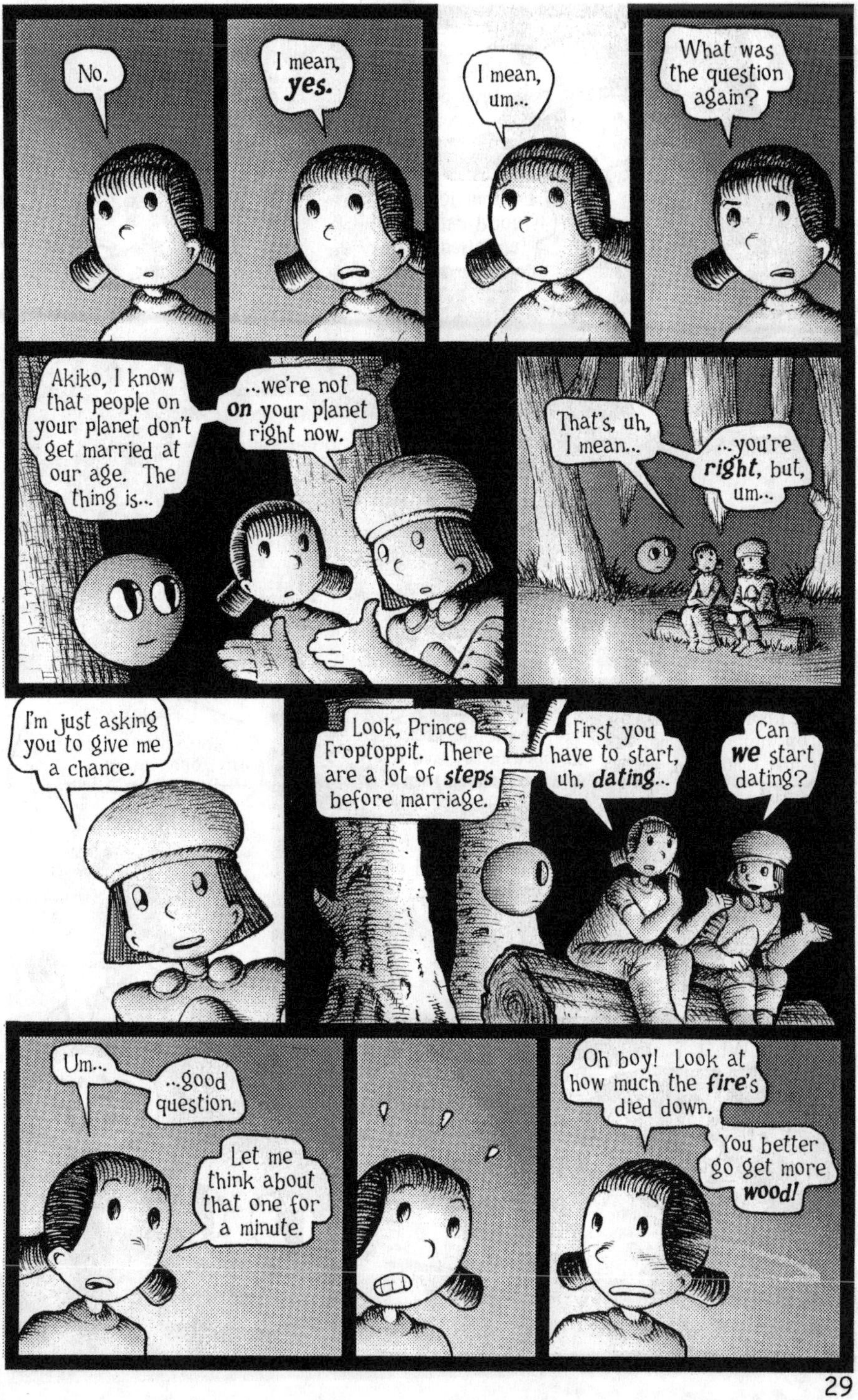
No.
I mean, yes.
I mean, um...
What was the question again?
Akiko, I know that people on your planet don't get married at our age. The thing is...
...we're not on your planet right now.
That's, uh, I mean...
...you're right, but, um...
I'm just asking you to give me a chance.
Look, Prince Froptoppit. There are a lot of steps before marriage.
First you have to start, uh, dating...
Can we start dating?
Um...
...good question.
Let me think about that one for a minute.
Oh boy! Look at how much the fire's died down.
You better go get more wood!

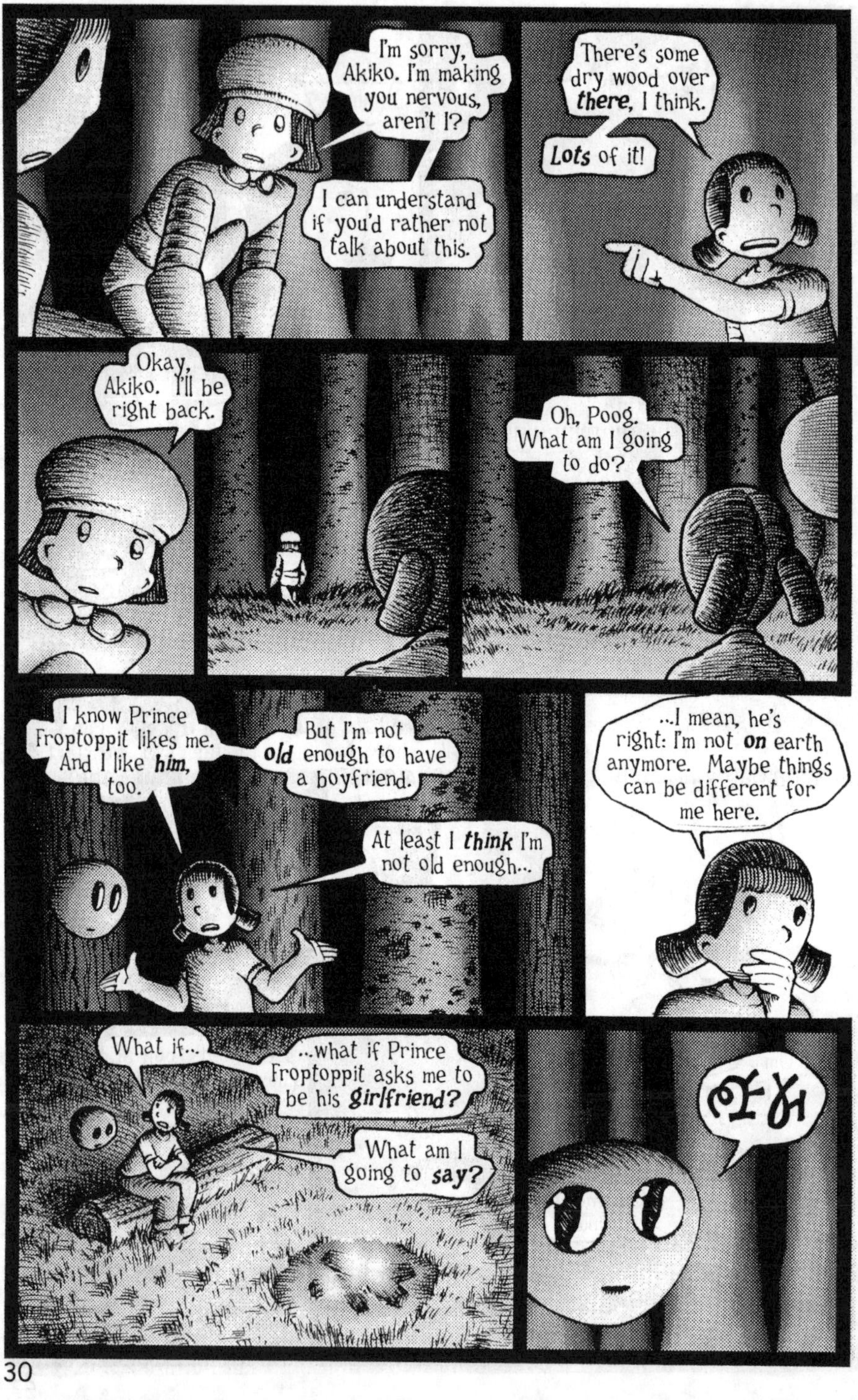
I'm sorry, Akiko. I'm making you nervous, aren't I?
I can understand if you'd rather not talk about this.
There's some dry wood over **there**, I think.
**Lots** of it!
Okay, Akiko. I'll be right back.
Oh, Poog. What am I going to do?
I know Prince Froptoppit likes me. And I like **him**, too.
But I'm not **old** enough to have a boyfriend.
At least I **think** I'm not old enough...
...I mean, he's right: I'm not **on** earth anymore. Maybe things can be different for me here.
What if...
...what if Prince Froptoppit asks me to be his **girlfriend?**
What am I going to **say?**

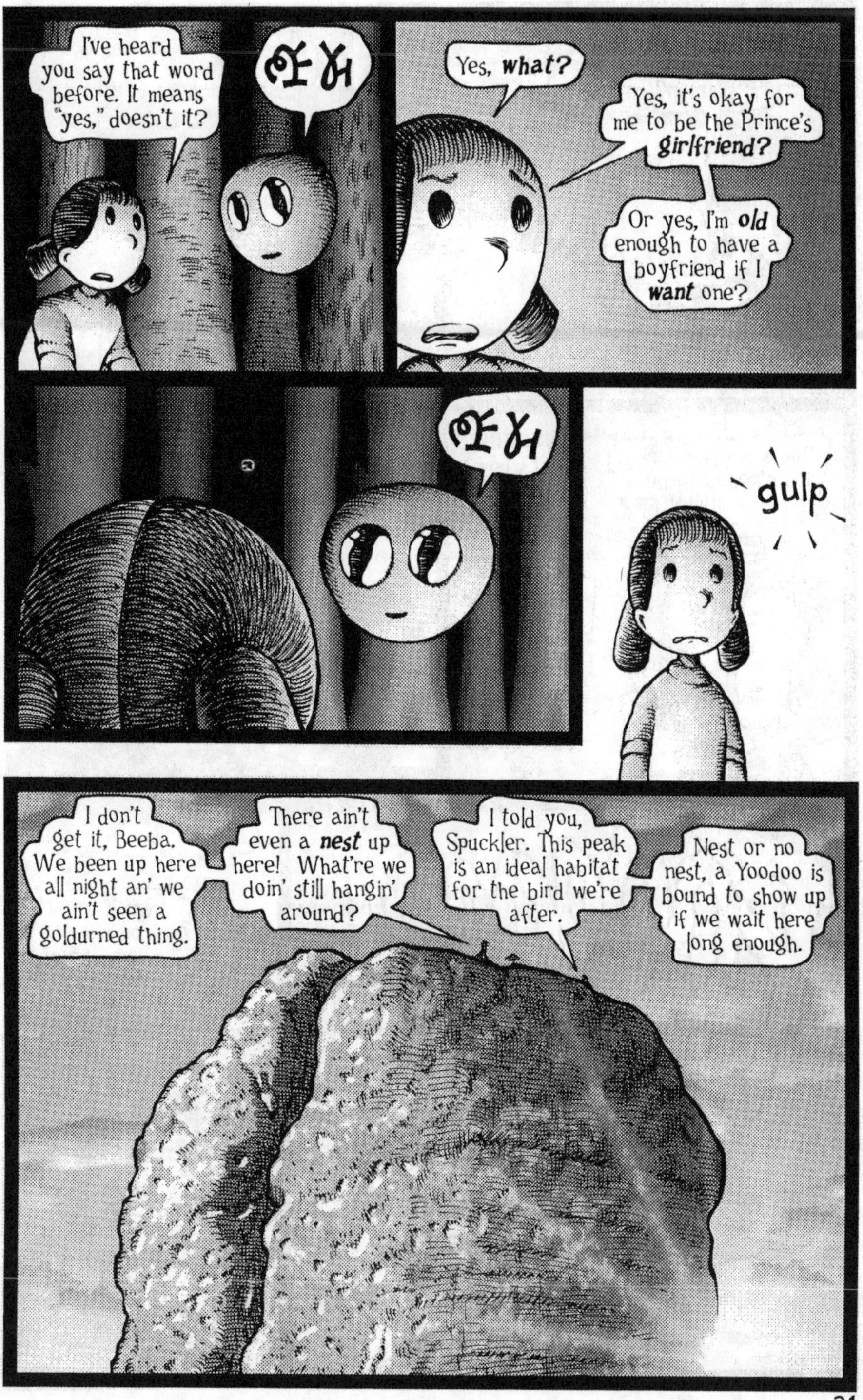
I've heard you say that word before. It means "yes," doesn't it?
Yes, **what?**
Yes, it's okay for me to be the Prince's **girlfriend?**
Or yes, I'm **old** enough to have a boyfriend if I **want** one?
gulp
I don't get it, Beeba. We been up here all night an' we ain't seen a goldurned thing.
There ain't even a **nest** up here! What're we doin' still hangin' around?
I told you, Spuckler. This peak is an ideal habitat for the bird we're after.
Nest or no nest, a Yoodoo is bound to show up if we wait here long enough.

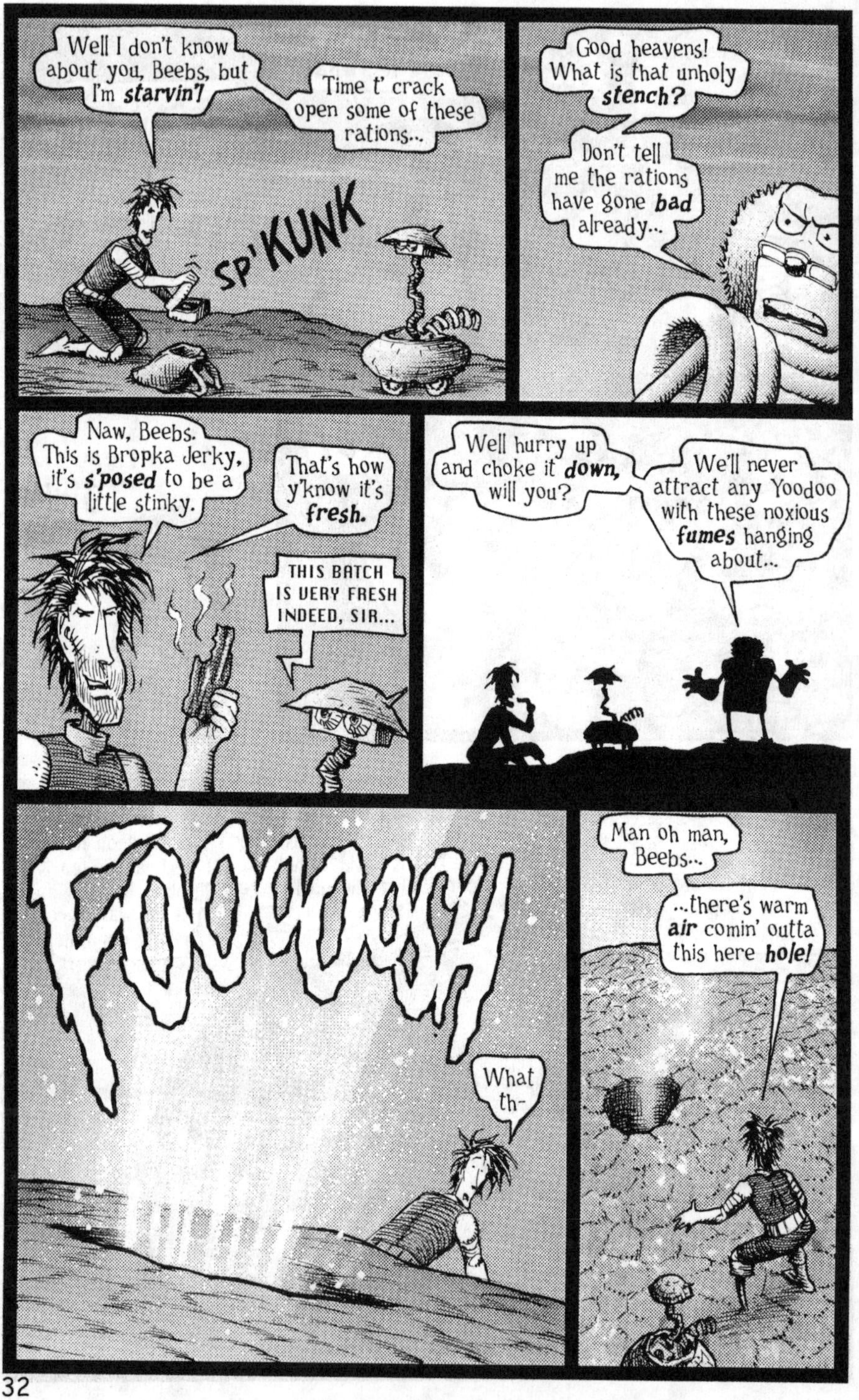
Well I don't know about you, Beebs, but I'm starvin'!
Time t' crack open some of these rations...
SP'KUNK
Good heavens! What is that unholy stench?
Don't tell me the rations have gone bad already...
Naw, Beebs. This is Bropka Jerky, it's s'posed to be a little stinky.
That's how y'know it's fresh.
THIS BATCH IS VERY FRESH INDEED, SIR...
Well hurry up and choke it down, will you?
We'll never attract any Yoodoo with these noxious fumes hanging about...
FOOOOOCH
What th-
Man oh man, Beebs...
...there's warm air comin' outta this here hole!

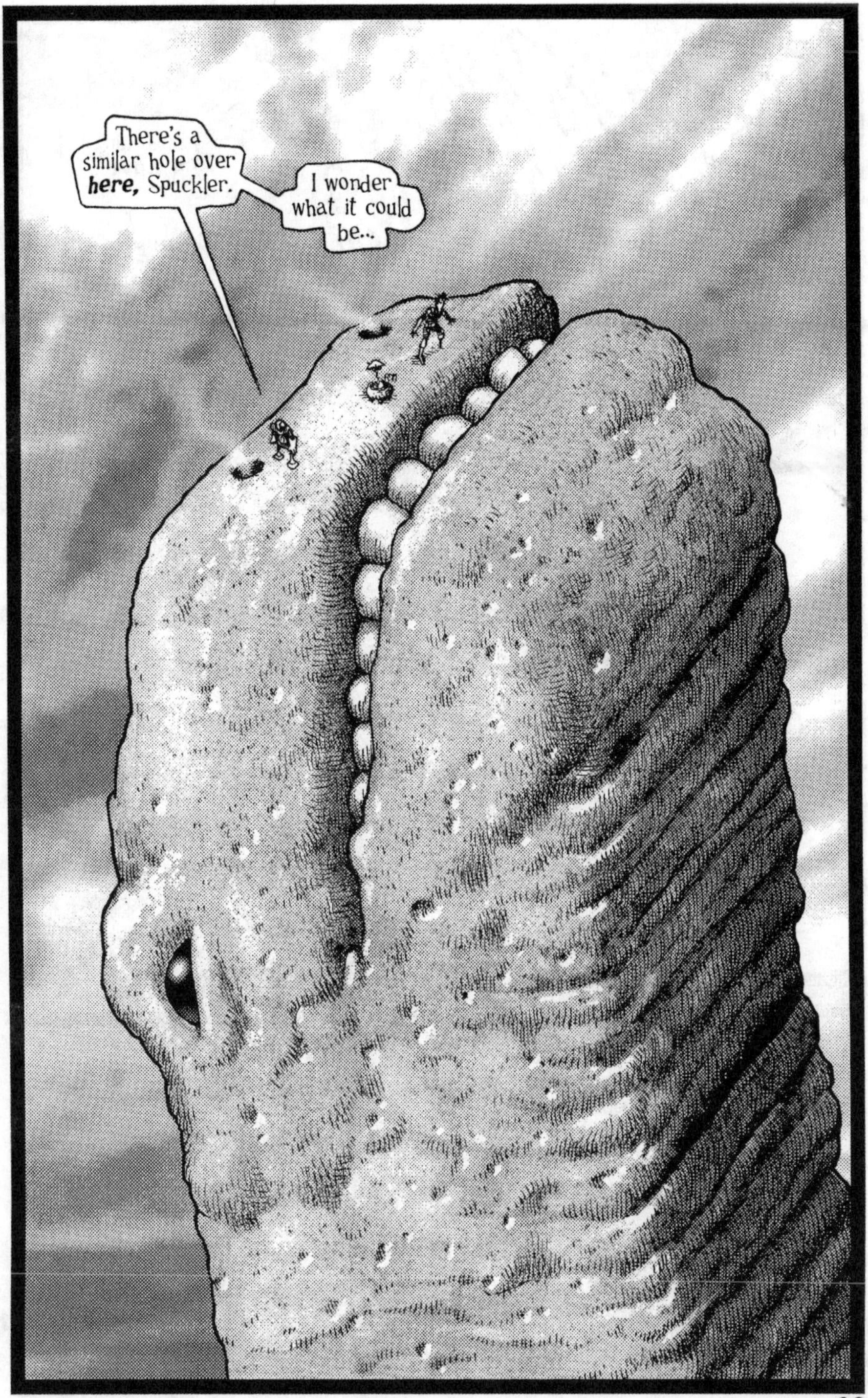
There's a similar hole over **here,** Spuckler.
I wonder what it could be...

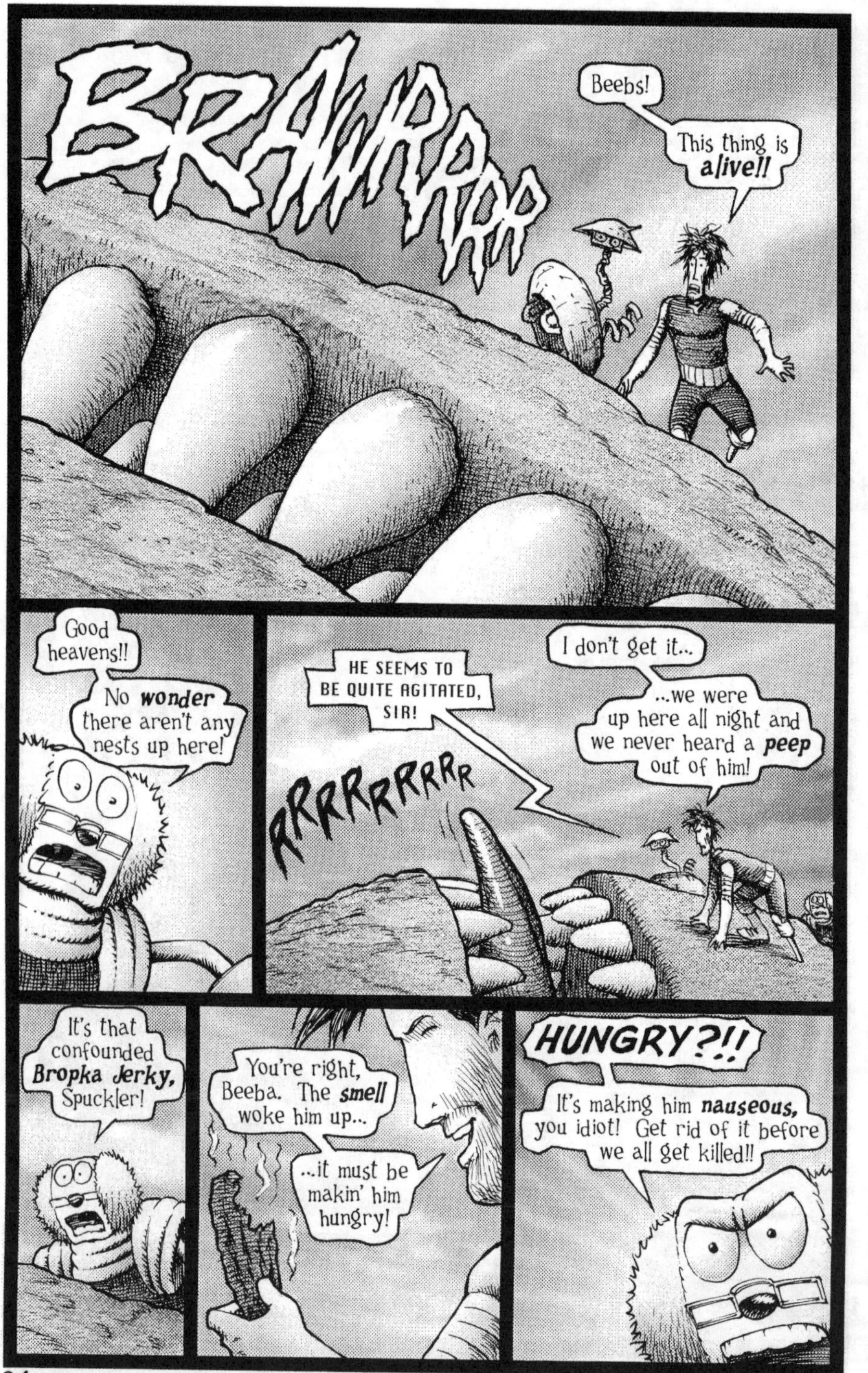
BRAWRRRRR
Beebs!
This thing is alive!!
Good heavens!!
No wonder there aren't any nests up here!
HE SEEMS TO BE QUITE AGITATED, SIR!
I don't get it...
...we were up here all night and we never heard a peep out of him!
RRRRRRRRR
It's that confounded Bropka Jerky, Spuckler!
You're right, Beeba. The smell woke him up...
...it must be makin' him hungry!
HUNGRY?!!
It's making him nauseous, you idiot! Get rid of it before we all get killed!!

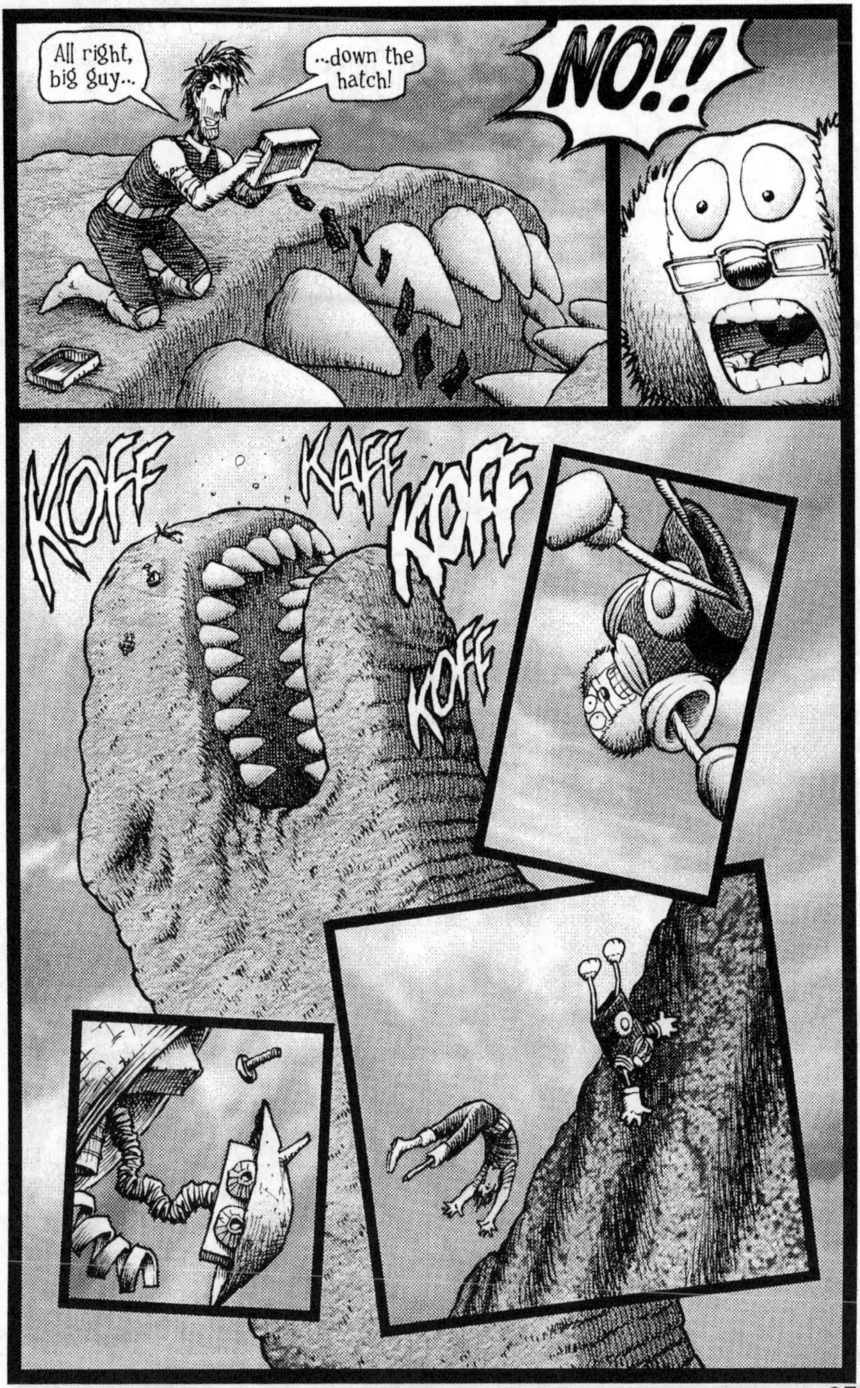

All right, big guy...
...down the hatch!
NO!!
KOFF
KAFF
KOFF
KOFF

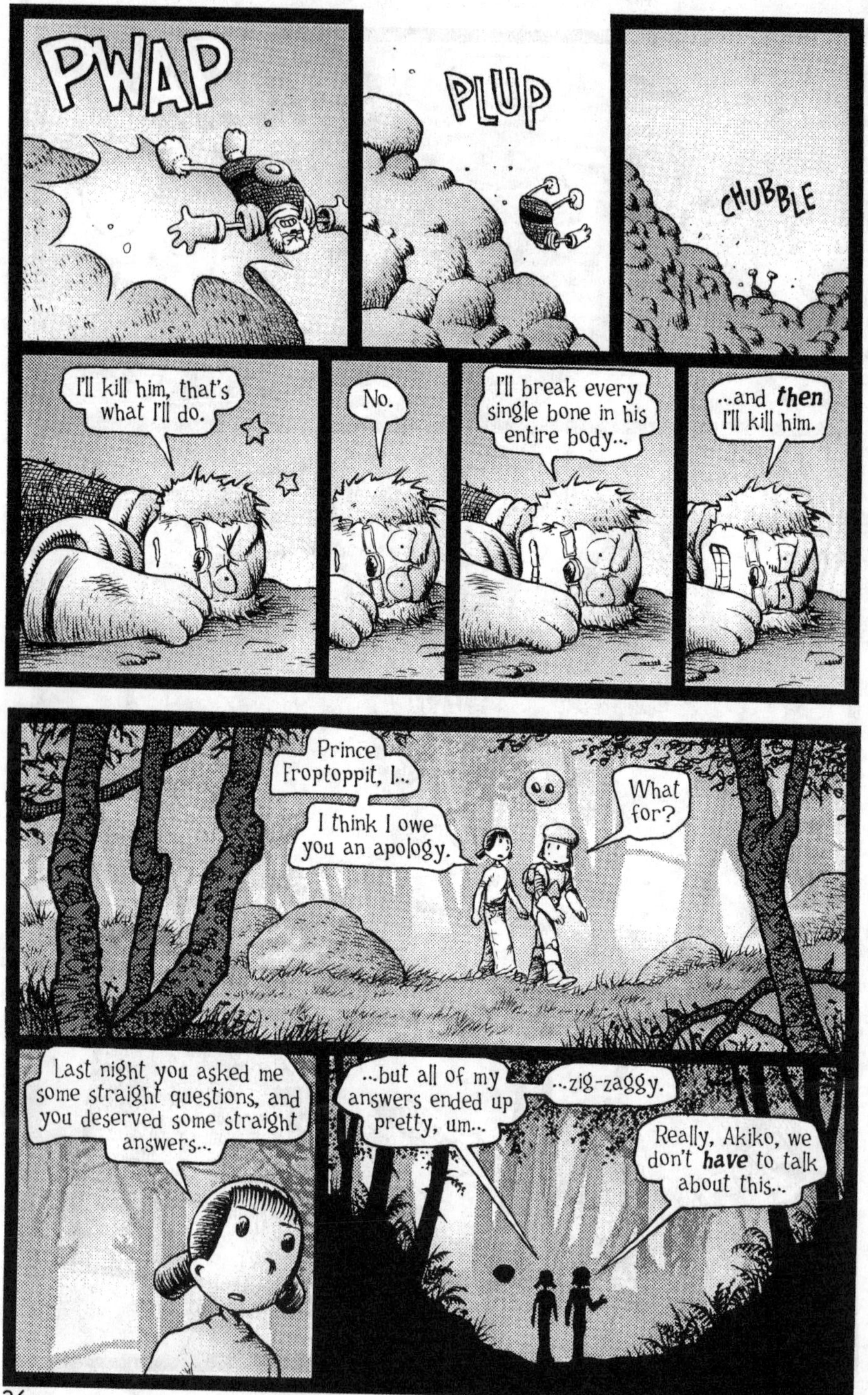
PWAP
PLUP
CHUBBLE
I'll kill him, that's what I'll do.
No.
I'll break every single bone in his entire body...
...and *then* I'll kill him.
Prince Froptoppit, I...
I think I owe you an apology.
What for?
Last night you asked me some straight questions, and you deserved some straight answers...
...but all of my answers ended up pretty, um...
...zig-zaggy.
Really, Akiko, we don't **have** to talk about this...

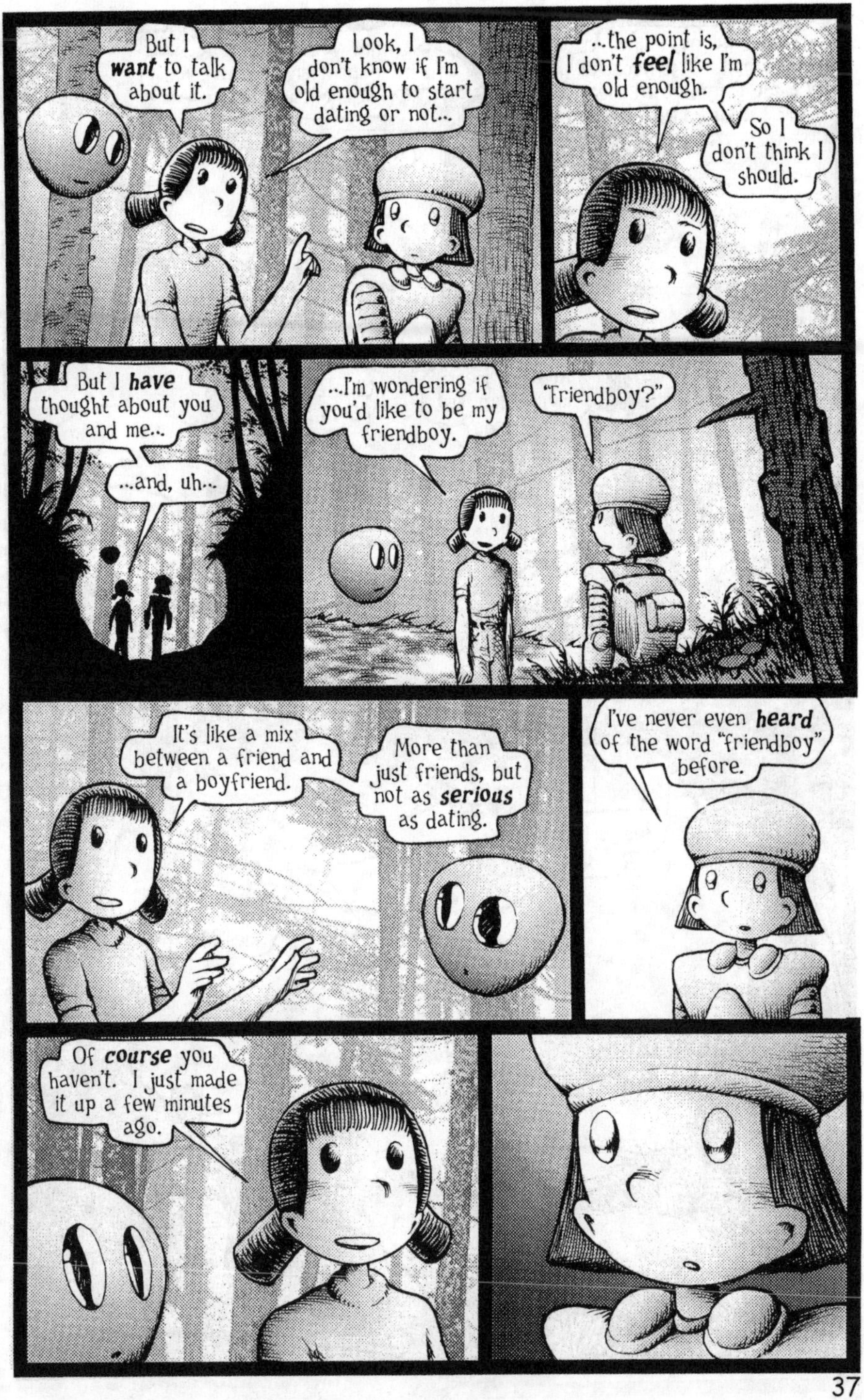
But I want to talk about it.
Look, I don't know if I'm old enough to start dating or not...
...the point is, I don't feel like I'm old enough.
So I don't think I should.
But I have thought about you and me...
...and, uh...
...I'm wondering if you'd like to be my friendboy.
"Friendboy?"
It's like a mix between a friend and a boyfriend.
More than just friends, but not as serious as dating.
I've never even heard of the word "friendboy" before.
Of course you haven't. I just made it up a few minutes ago.

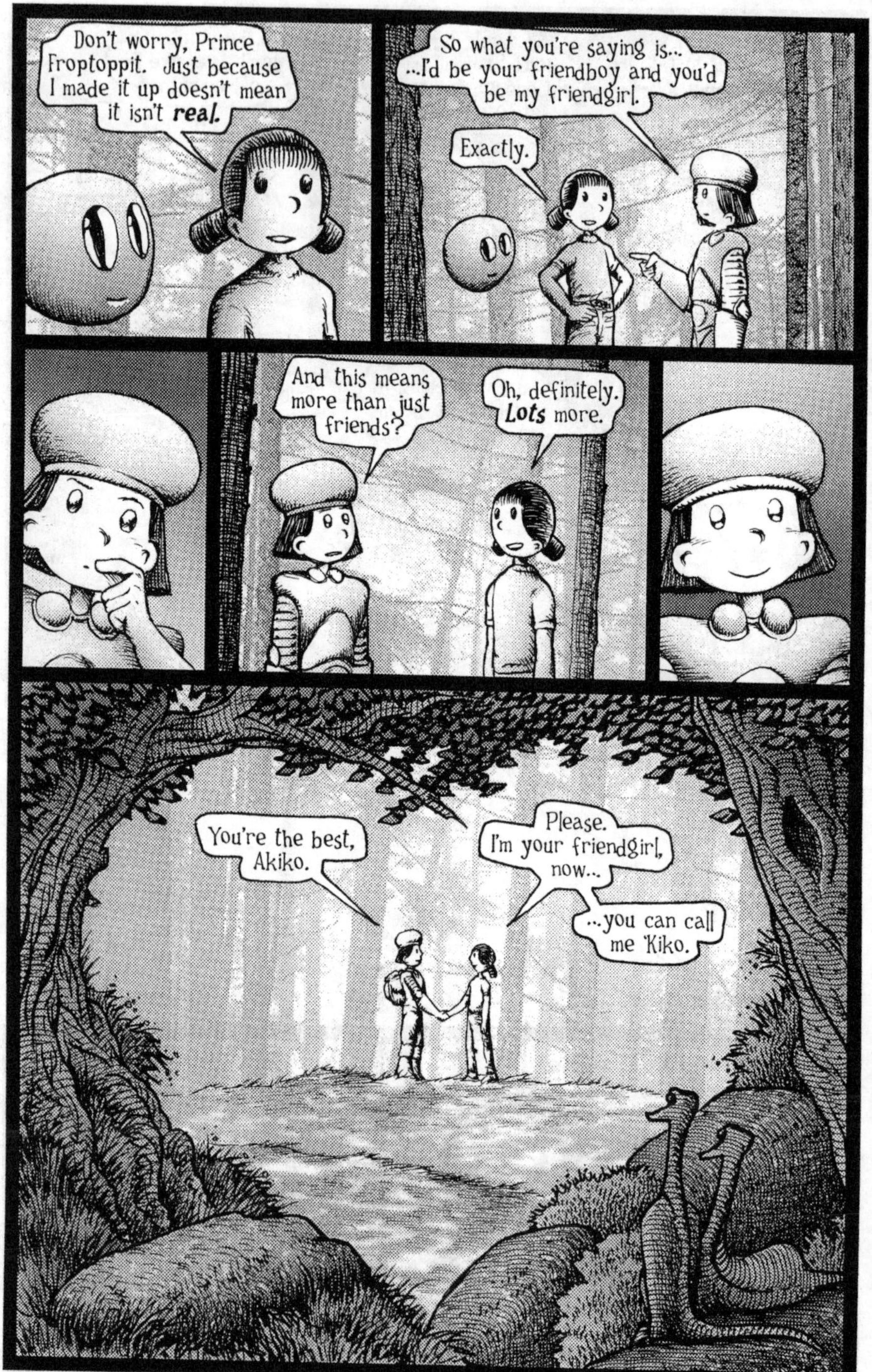
Don't worry, Prince Froptoppit. Just because I made it up doesn't mean it isn't ***real.***
So what you're saying is... ...I'd be your friendboy and you'd be my friendgirl.
Exactly.
And this means more than just friends?
Oh, definitely. ***Lots*** more.
You're the best, Akiko.
Please. I'm your friendgirl, now...
...you can call me 'Kiko.

# BORNSTONE'S ELIXIR

*Chapter 3*

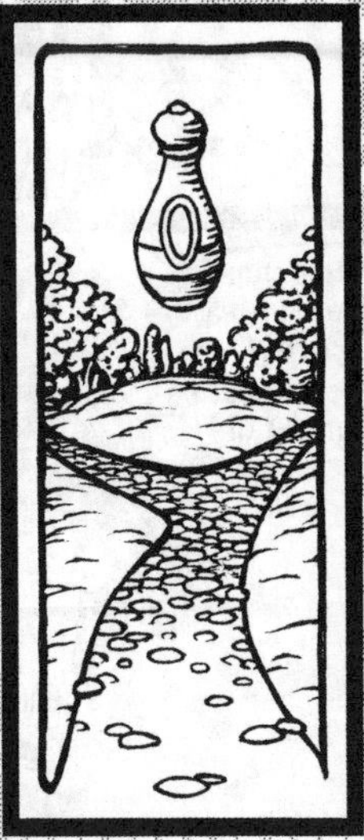

## A Fork In the Road

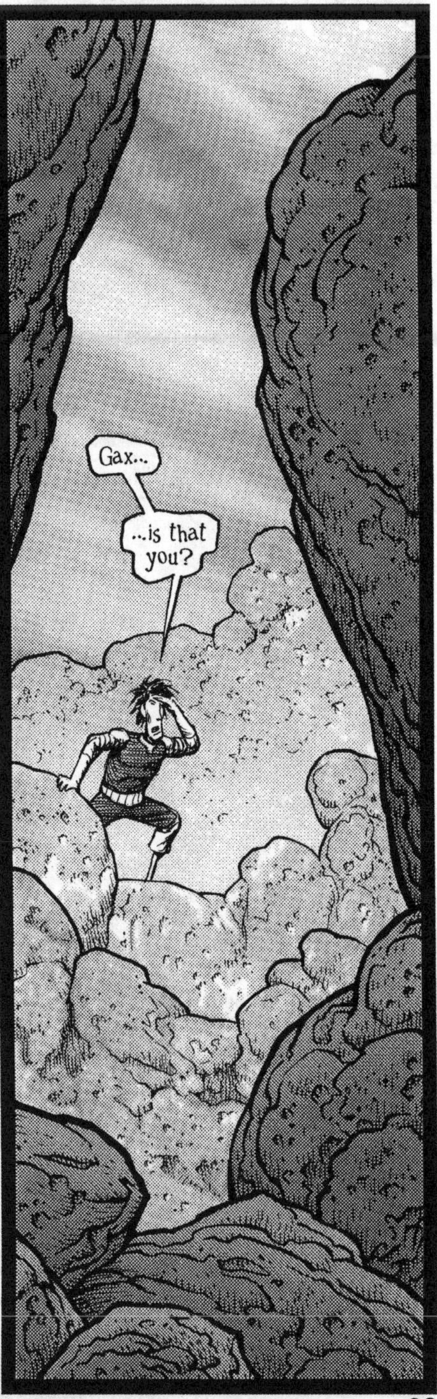

Gax...
...is that you?

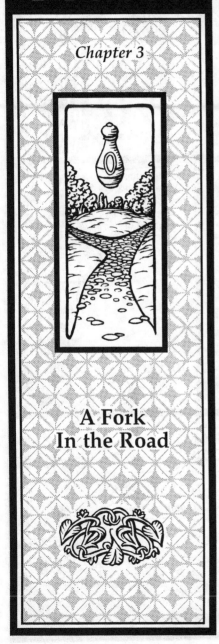

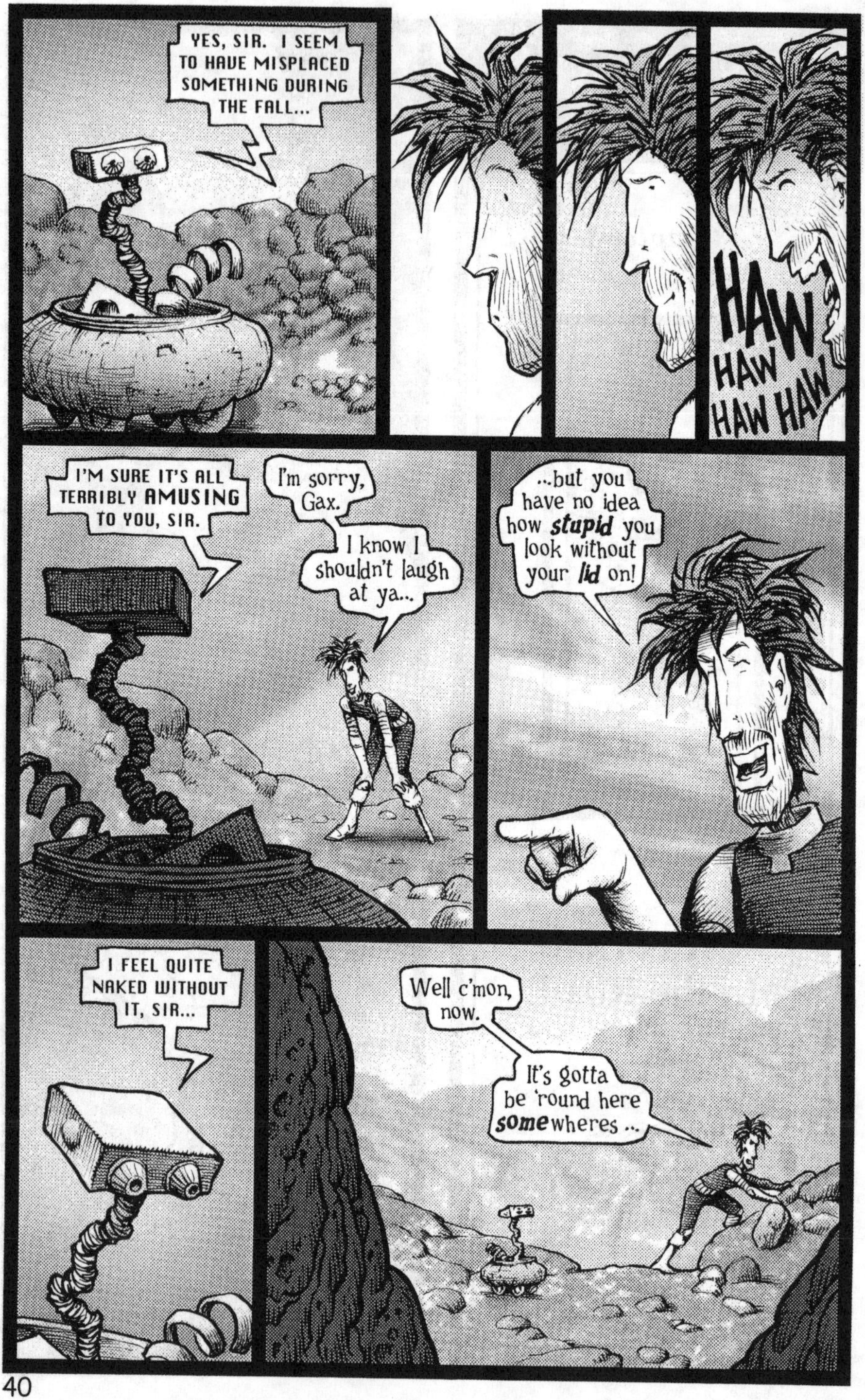
YES, SIR. I SEEM TO HAVE MISPLACED SOMETHING DURING THE FALL...
HAW HAW HAW HAW
I'M SURE IT'S ALL TERRIBLY AMUSING TO YOU, SIR.
I'm sorry, Gax.
I know I shouldn't laugh at ya...
...but you have no idea how stupid you look without your lid on!
I FEEL QUITE NAKED WITHOUT IT, SIR...
Well c'mon, now.
It's gotta be 'round here somewheres ...

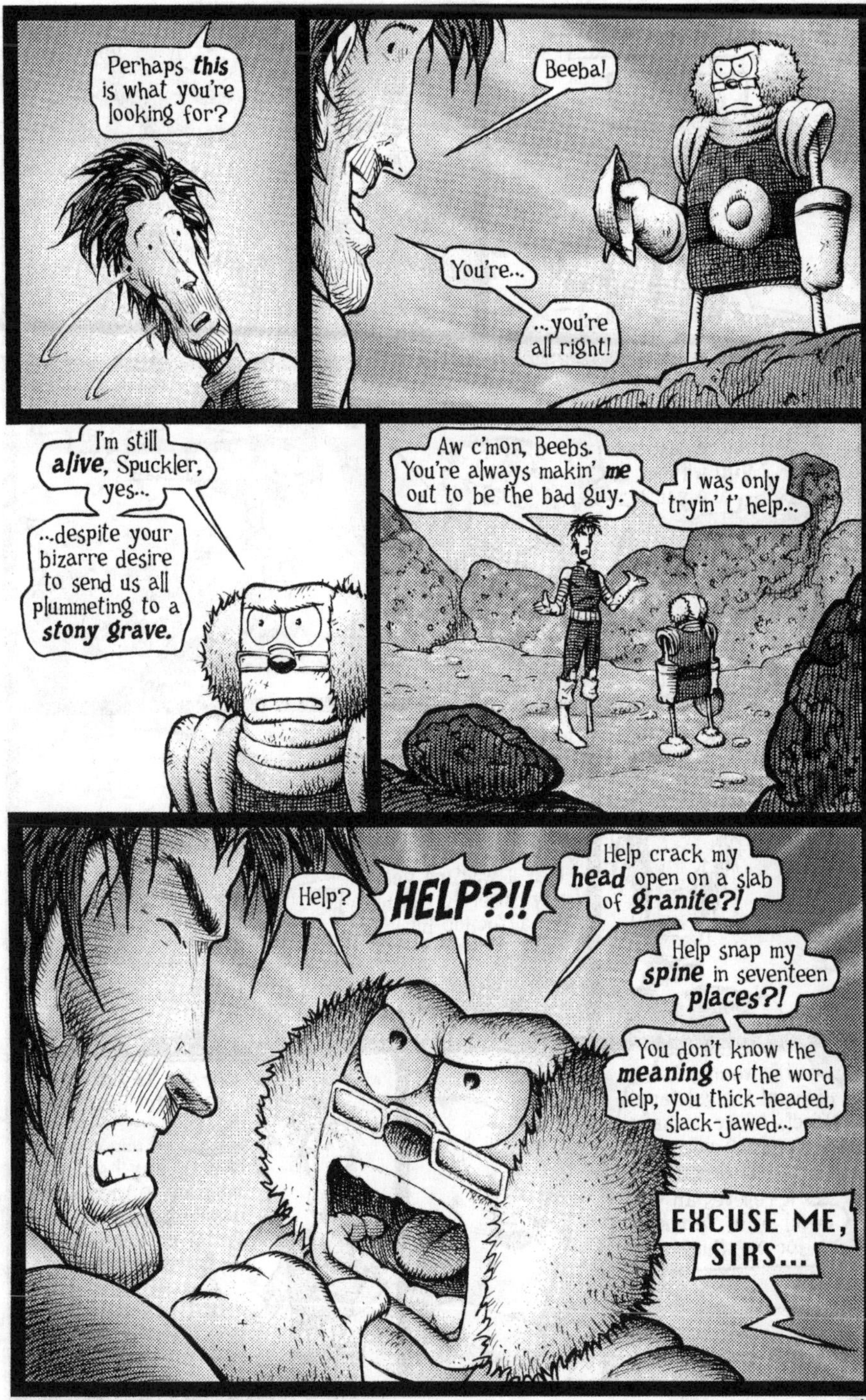
Perhaps **this** is what you're looking for?
Beeba!
You're...
...you're all right!
I'm still **alive**, Spuckler, yes...
...despite your bizarre desire to send us all plummeting to a **stony grave.**
Aw c'mon, Beebs. You're always makin' **me** out to be the bad guy.
I was only tryin' t' help...
Help?
**HELP?!!**
Help crack my **head** open on a slab of **granite?!**
Help snap my **spine** in seventeen **places?!**
You don't know the **meaning** of the word help, you thick-headed, slack-jawed...
EXCUSE ME, SIRS...

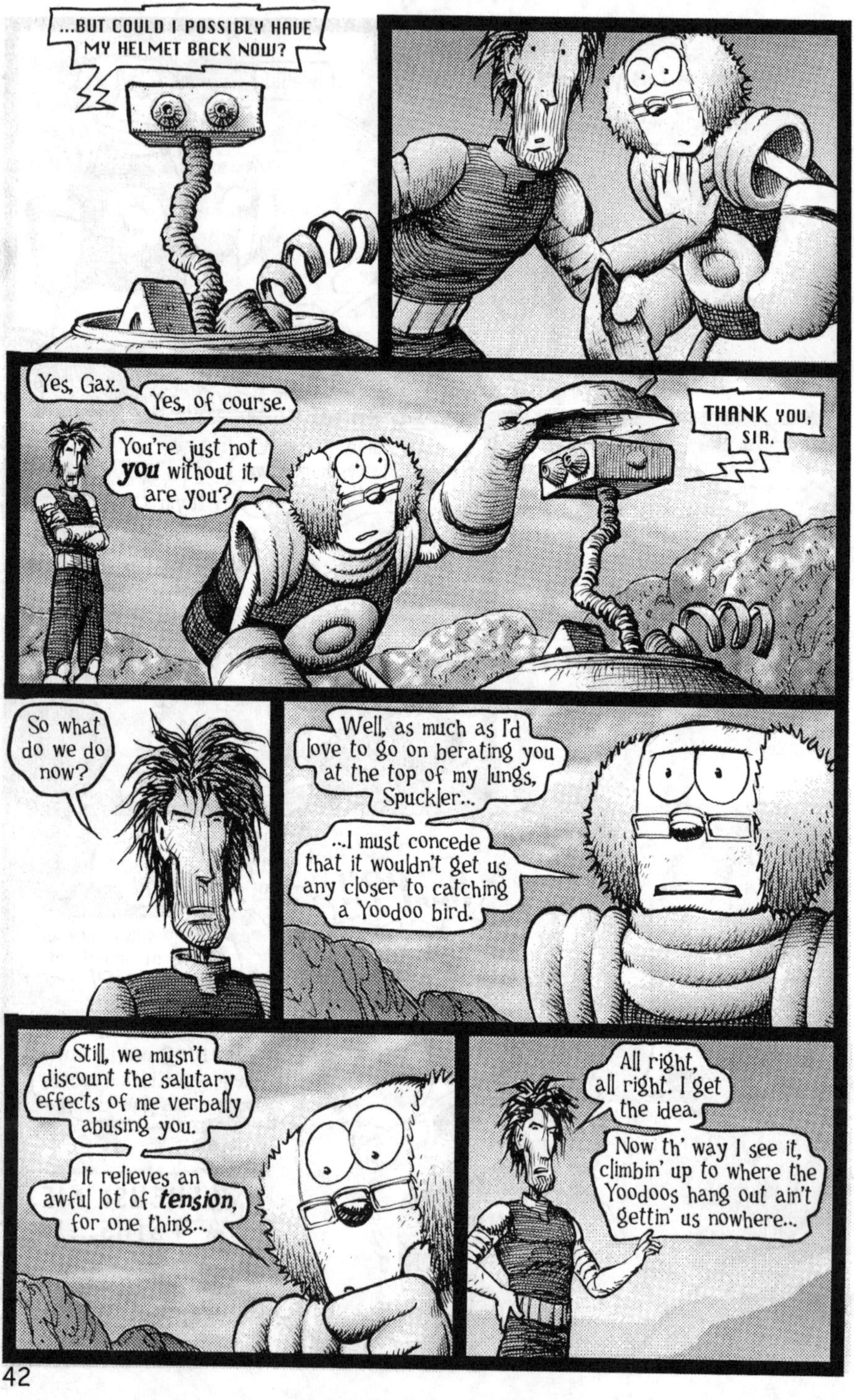
...BUT COULD I POSSIBLY HAVE MY HELMET BACK NOW?
Yes, Gax.
Yes, of course.
You're just not **you** without it, are you?
THANK YOU, SIR.
So what do we do now?
Well, as much as I'd love to go on berating you at the top of my lungs, Spuckler...
...I must concede that it wouldn't get us any closer to catching a Yoodoo bird.
Still, we musn't discount the salutary effects of me verbally abusing you.
It relieves an awful lot of ***tension***, for one thing...
All right, all right. I get the idea.
Now th' way I see it, climbin' up to where the Yoodoos hang out ain't gettin' us nowhere..

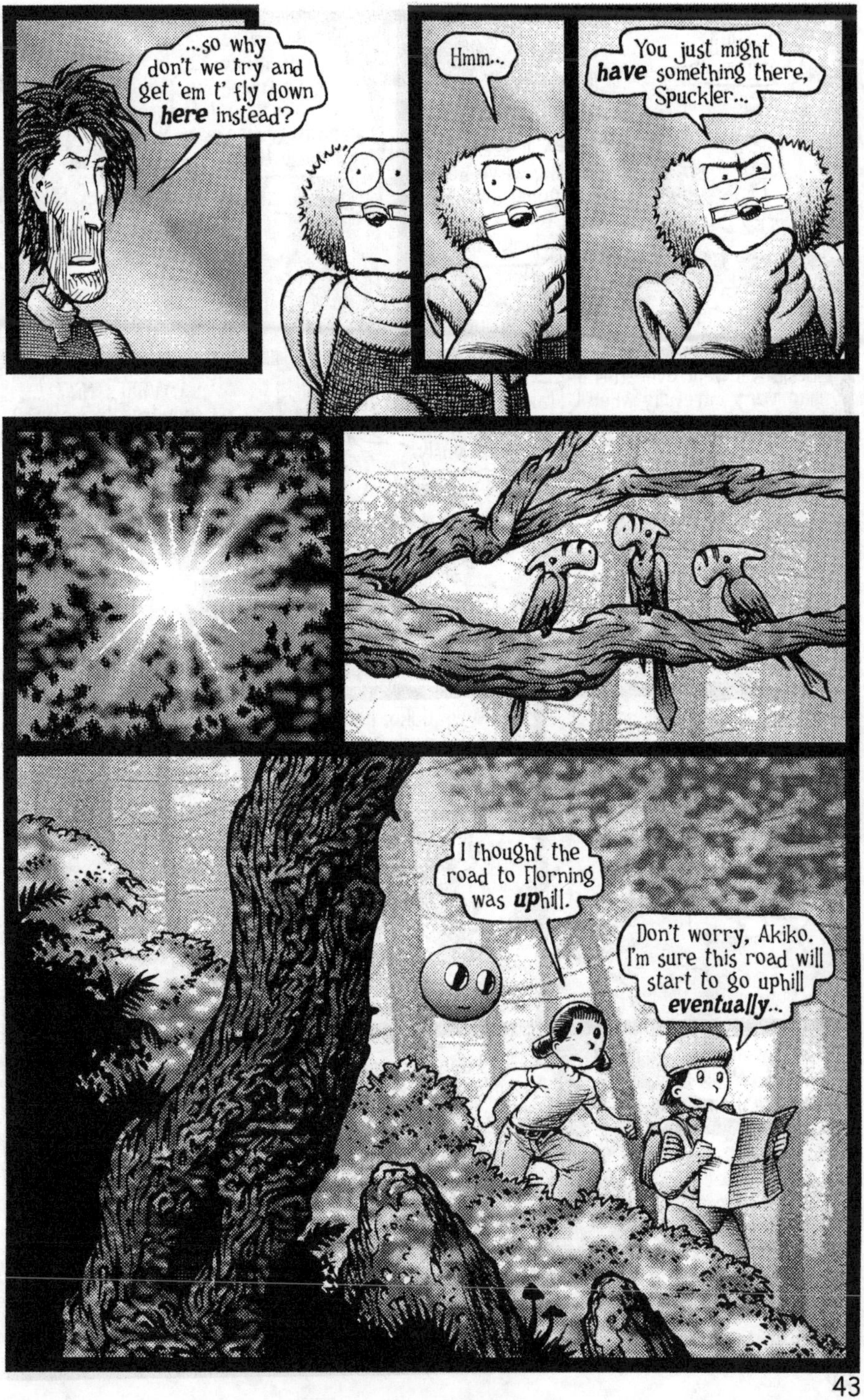
...so why don't we try and get 'em t' fly down **here** instead?
Hmm...
You just might **have** something there, Spuckler...
I thought the road to Florning was **up**hill.
Don't worry, Akiko. I'm sure this road will start to go uphill ***eventually***...

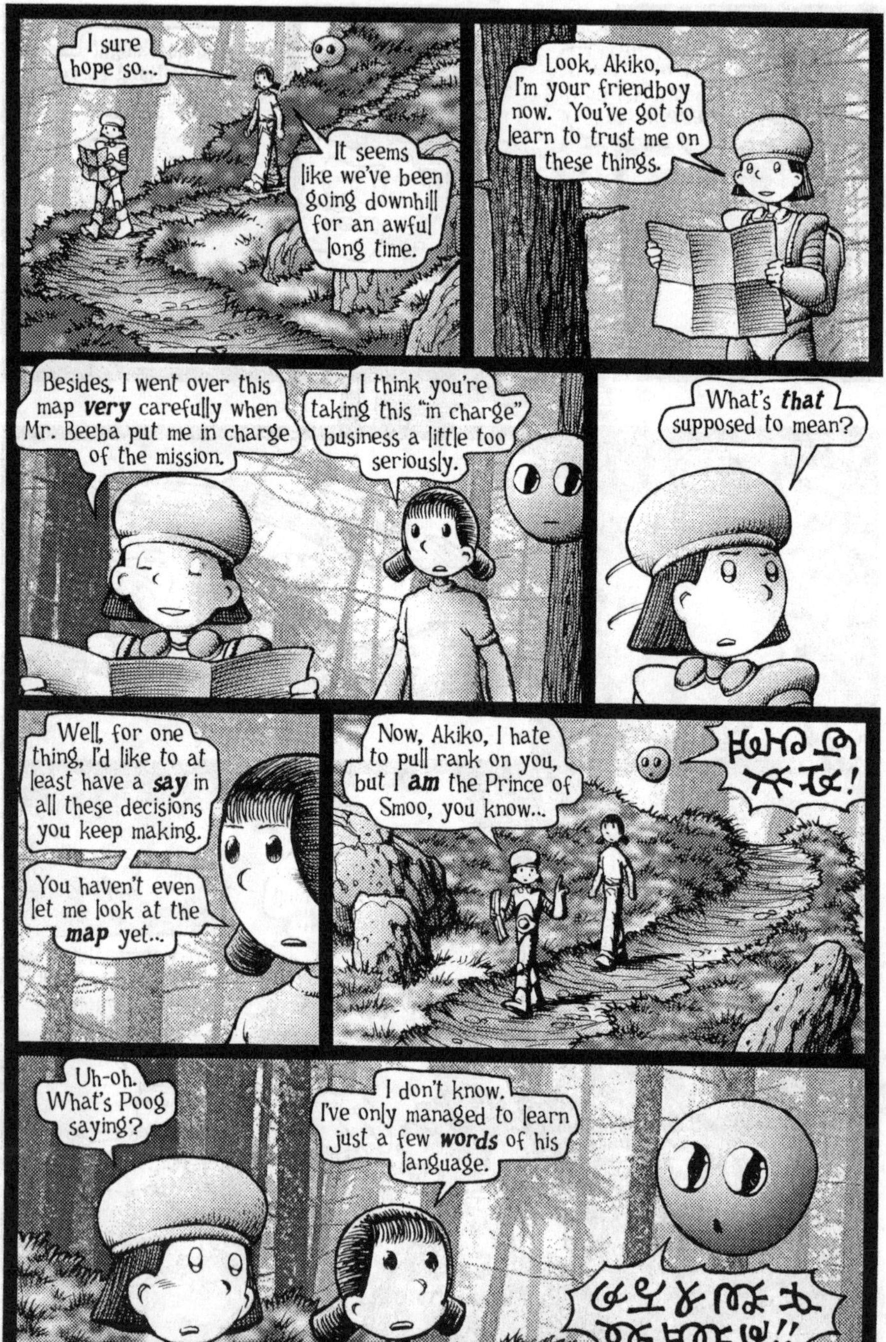
I sure hope so...
It seems like we've been going downhill for an awful long time.
Look, Akiko, I'm your friendboy now. You've got to learn to trust me on these things.
Besides, I went over this map **very** carefully when Mr. Beeba put me in charge of the mission.
I think you're taking this "in charge" business a little too seriously.
What's **that** supposed to mean?
Well, for one thing, I'd like to at least have a **say** in all these decisions you keep making.
You haven't even let me look at the **map** yet...
Now, Akiko, I hate to pull rank on you, but I **am** the Prince of Smoo, you know...
Uh-oh. What's Poog saying?
I don't know. I've only managed to learn just a few **words** of his language.

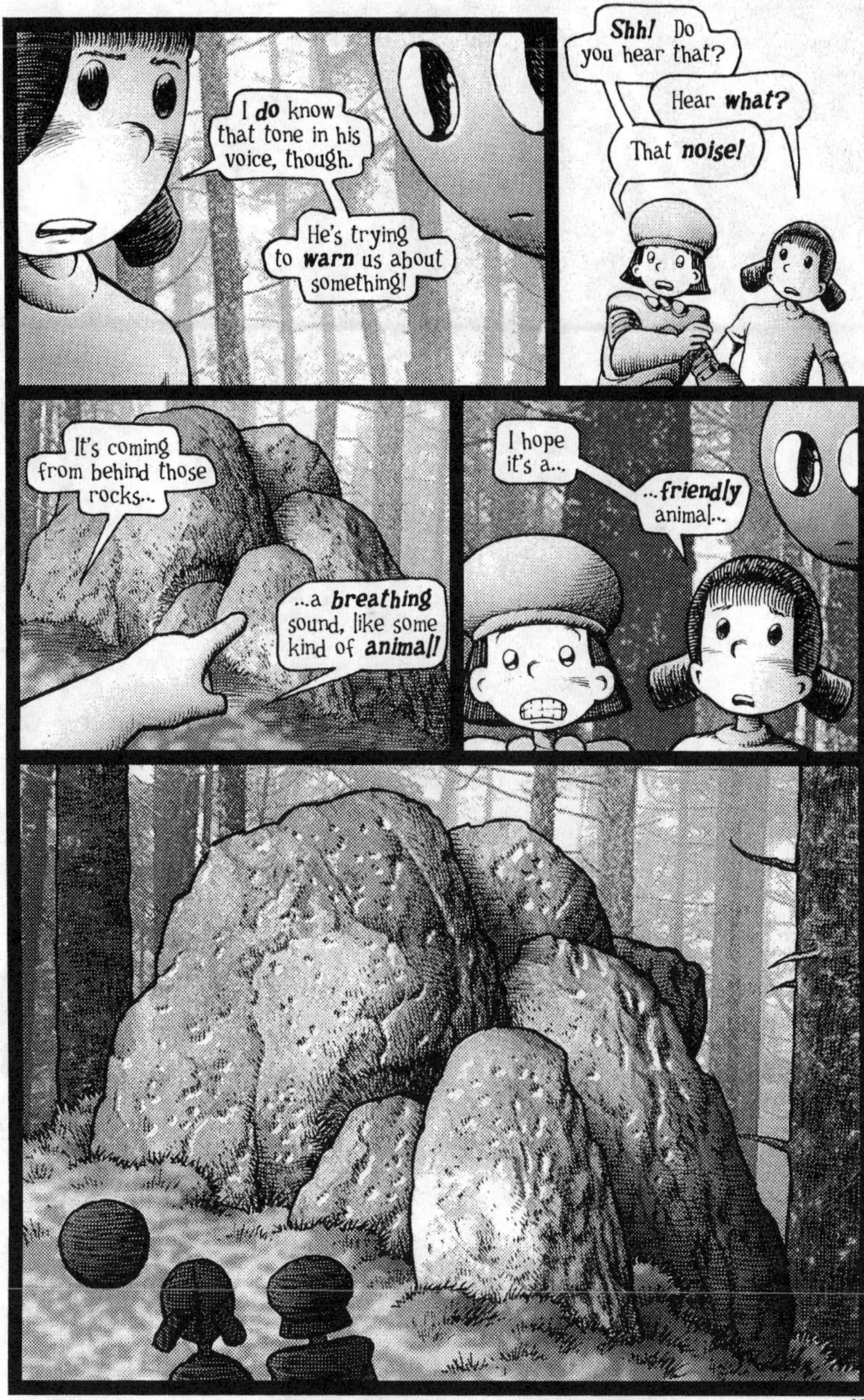
I **do** know that tone in his voice, though.
He's trying to **warn** us about something!
**Shh!** Do you hear that?
Hear **what?**
That **noise!**
It's coming from behind those rocks...
...a **breathing** sound, like some kind of **animal!**
I hope it's a...
...**friendly** animal...

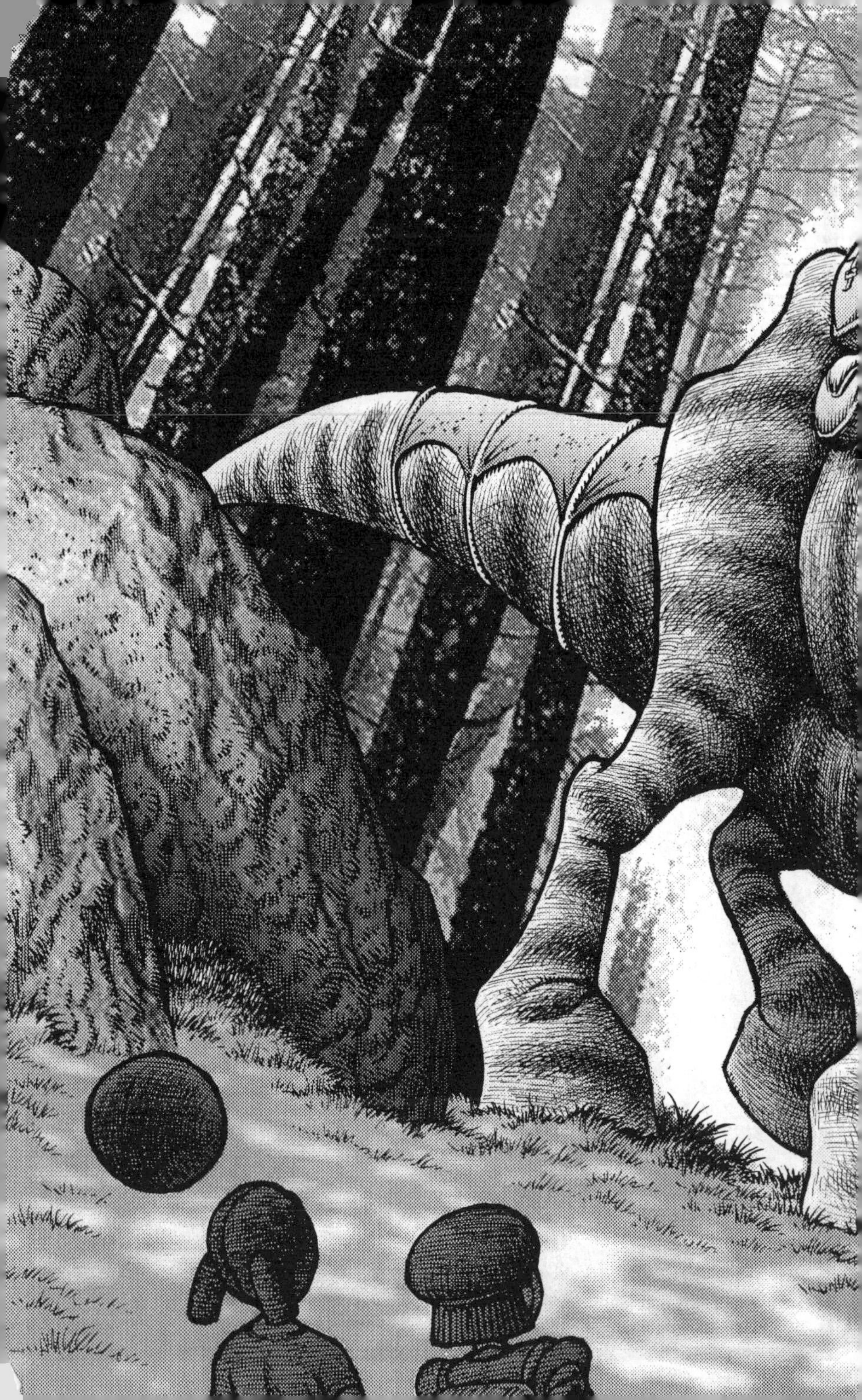

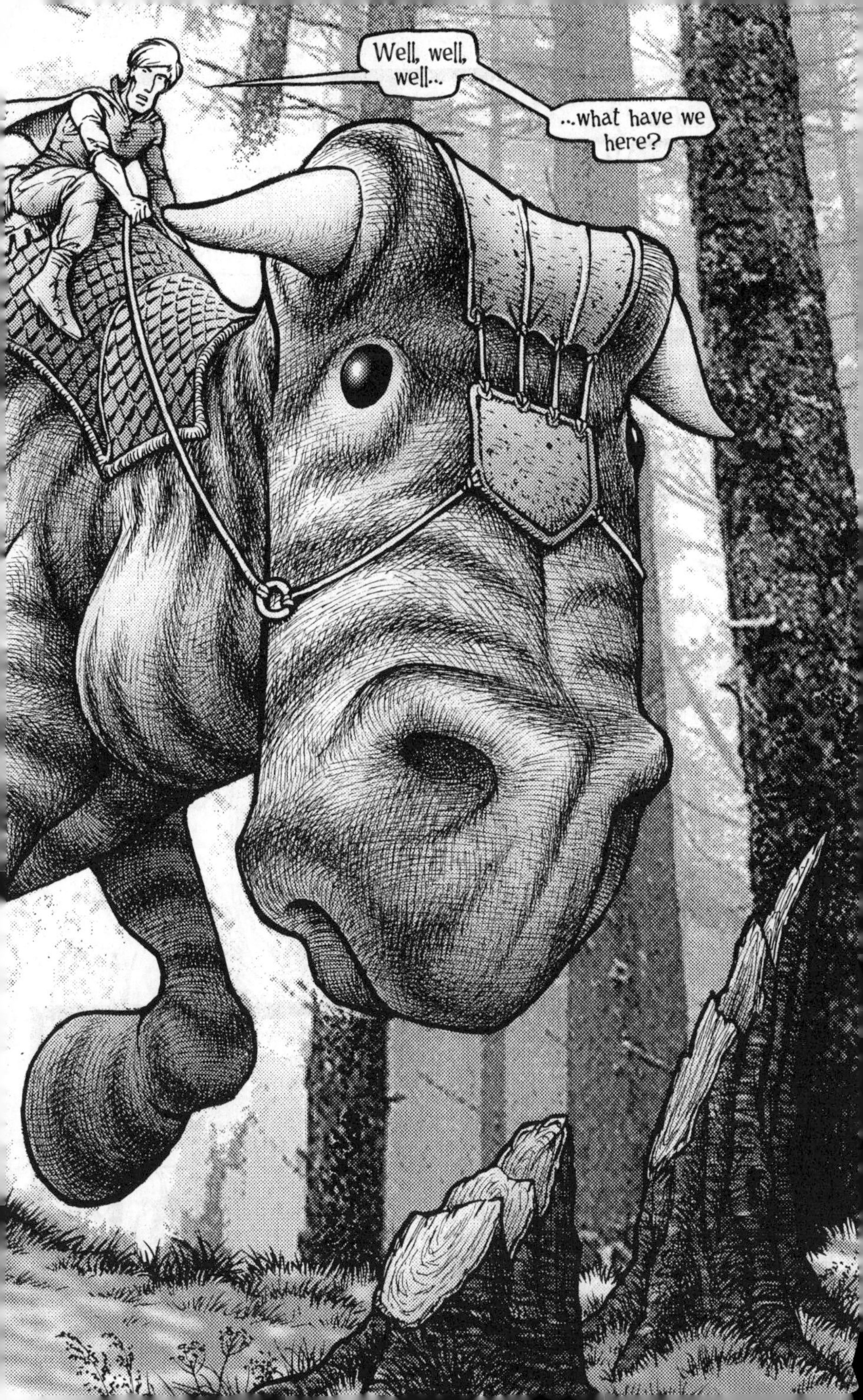
Well, well, well...
...what have we here?

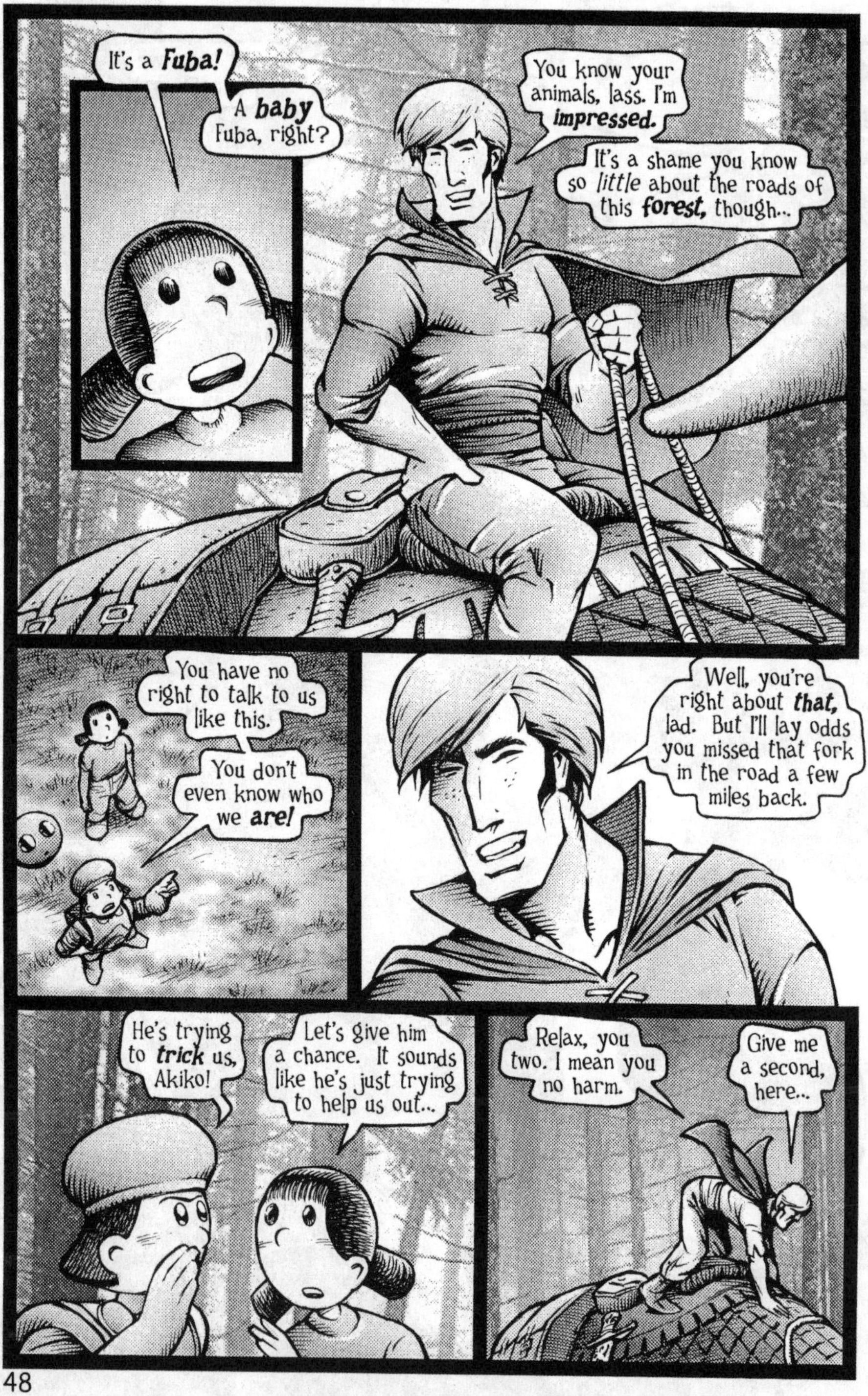
It's a **Fuba!**
A **baby** Fuba, right?
You know your animals, lass. I'm **impressed.**
It's a shame you know so *little* about the roads of this **forest,** though...
You have no right to talk to us like this.
You don't even know who we **are!**
Well, you're right about **that,** lad. But I'll lay odds you missed that fork in the road a few miles back.
He's trying to **trick** us, Akiko!
Let's give him a chance. It sounds like he's just trying to help us out...
Relax, you two. I mean you no harm.
Give me a second, here...

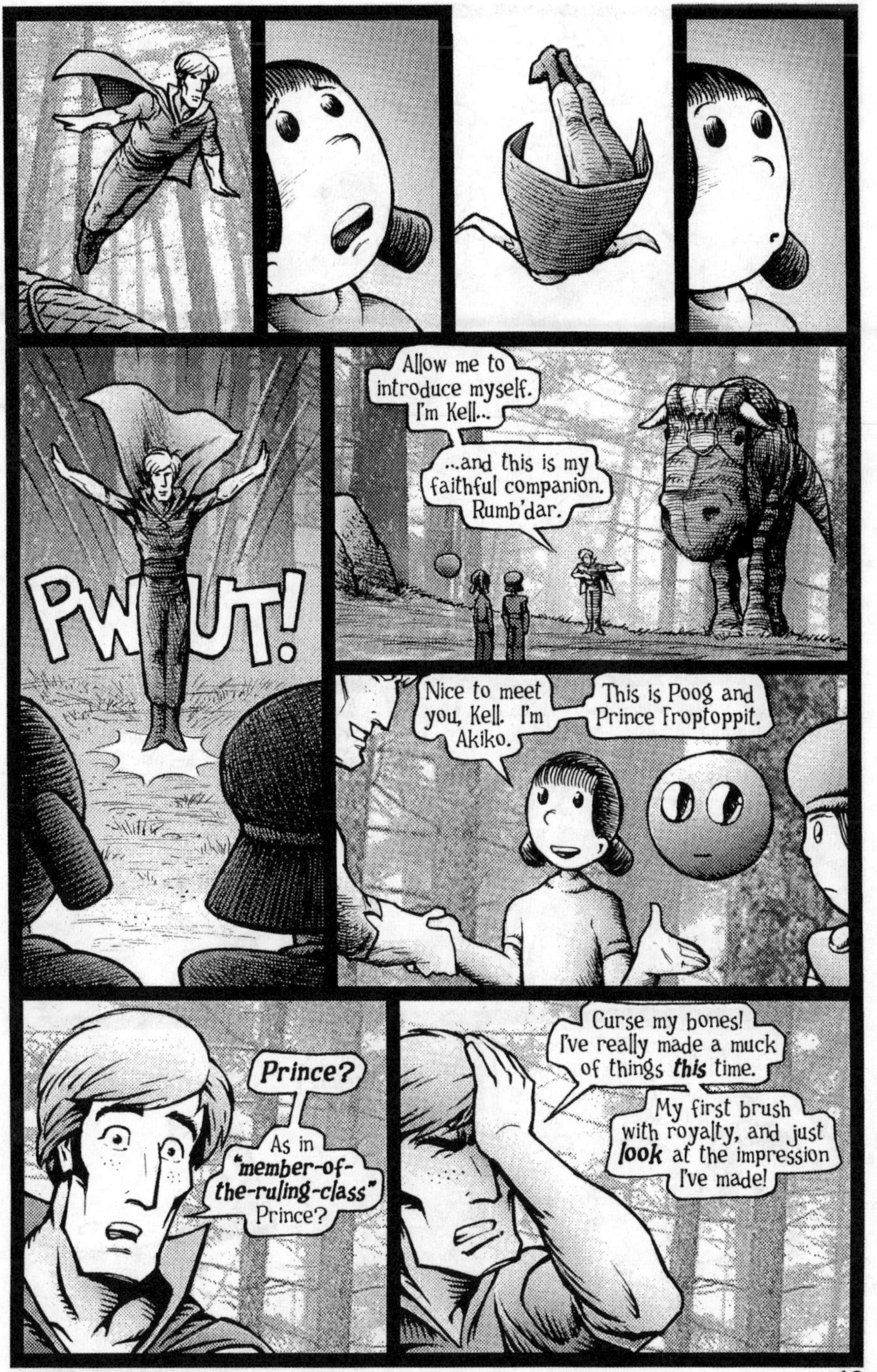
PWUT!
Allow me to introduce myself. I'm Kell...
...and this is my faithful companion. Rumb'dar.
Nice to meet you, Kell. I'm Akiko.
This is Poog and Prince Froptoppit.
Prince?
As in "member-of-the-ruling-class" Prince?
Curse my bones! I've really made a muck of things this time.
My first brush with royalty, and just look at the impression I've made!

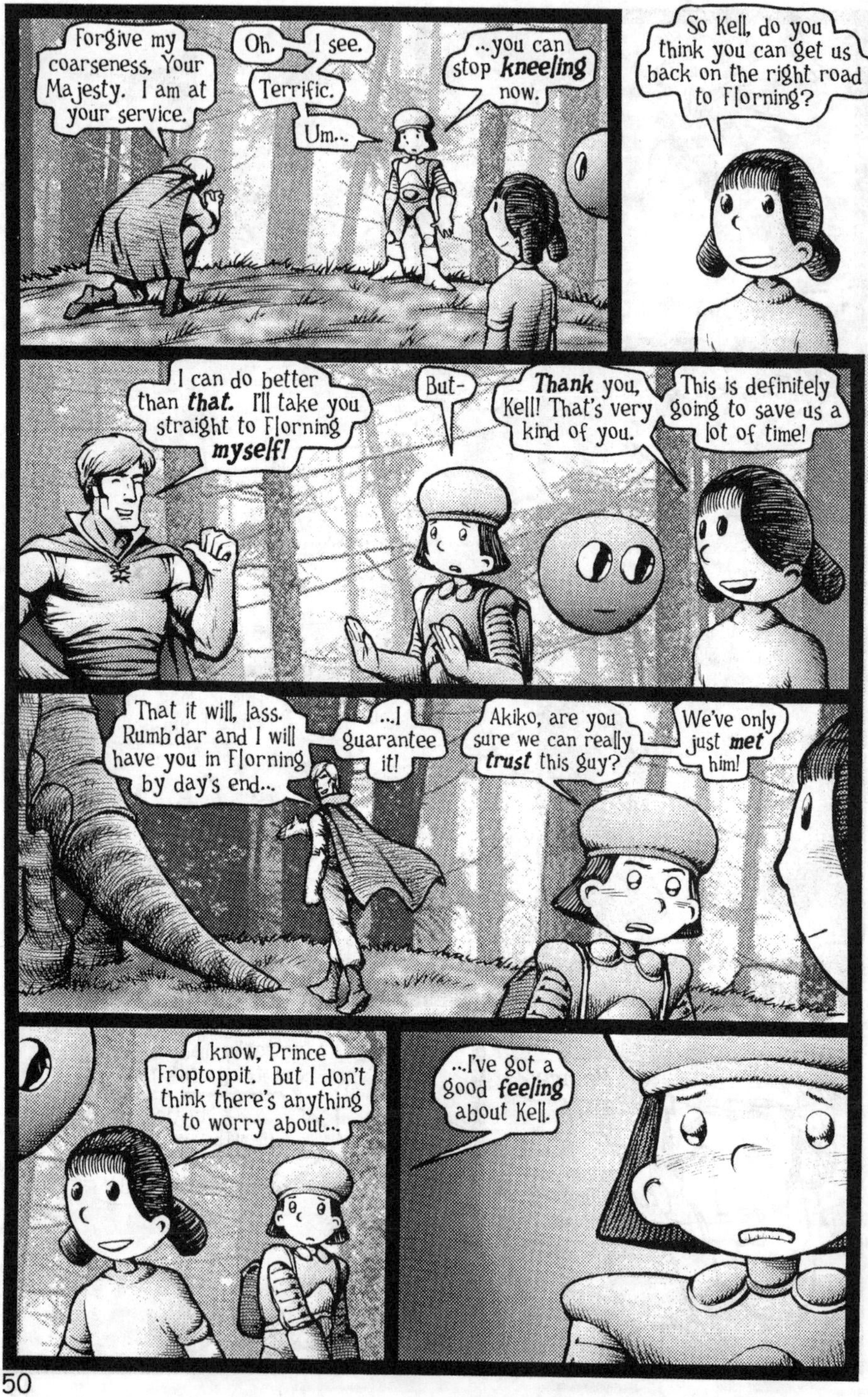

Forgive my coarseness, Your Majesty. I am at your service.
Oh.
I see.
Terrific.
Um...
...you can stop **kneeling** now.
So Kell, do you think you can get us back on the right road to Florning?
I can do better than **that.** I'll take you straight to Florning **myself!**
But-
**Thank** you, Kell! That's very kind of you.
This is definitely going to save us a lot of time!
That it will, lass. Rumb'dar and I will have you in Florning by day's end...
...I guarantee it!
Akiko, are you sure we can really **trust** this guy?
We've only just **met** him!
I know, Prince Froptoppit. But I don't think there's anything to worry about...
...I've got a good **feeling** about Kell.

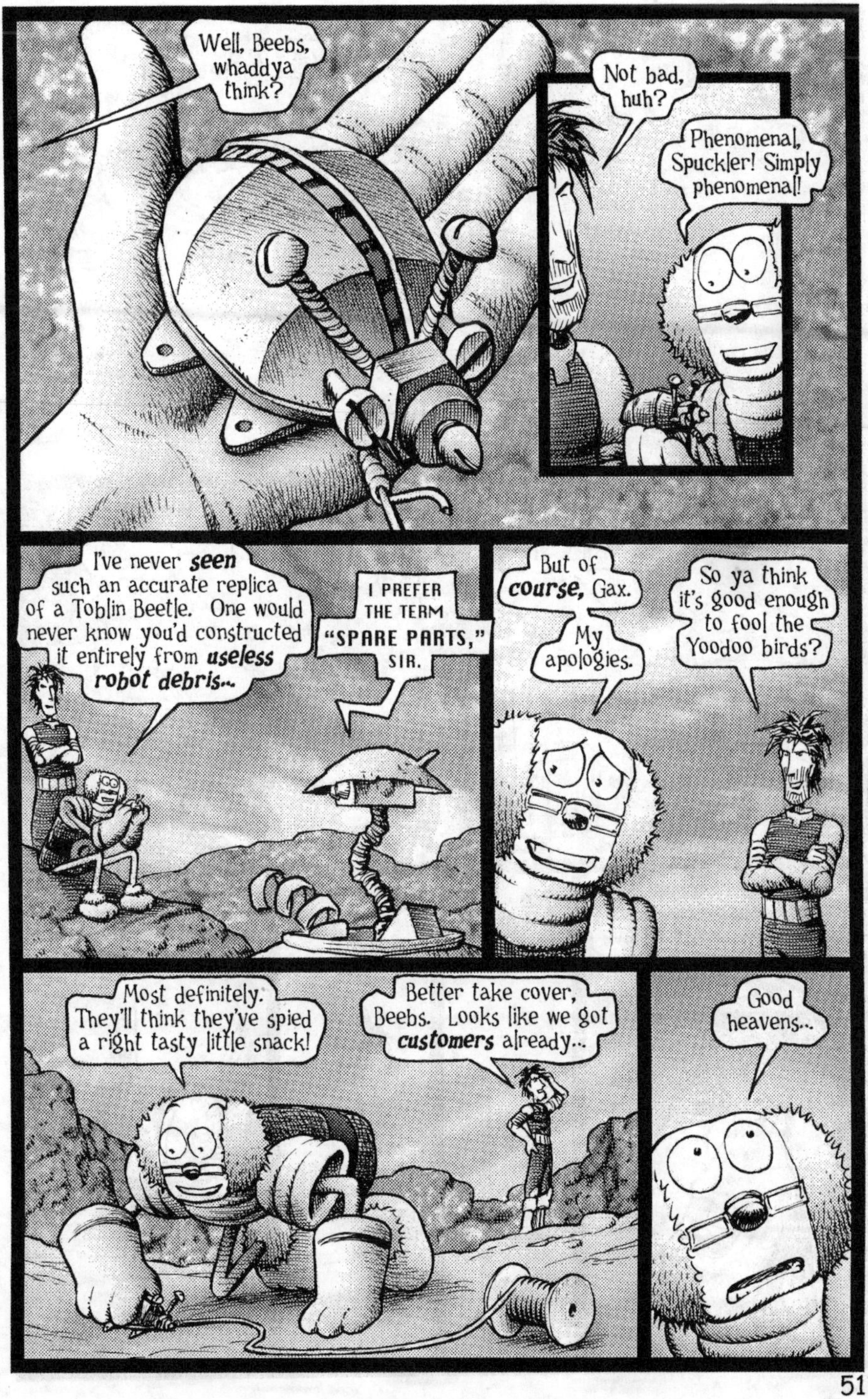
Well, Beebs, whaddya think?
Not bad, huh?
Phenomenal, Spuckler! Simply phenomenal!
I've never **seen** such an accurate replica of a Toblin Beetle. One would never know you'd constructed it entirely from **useless robot debris...**
I PREFER THE TERM "SPARE PARTS," SIR.
But of **course,** Gax.
My apologies.
So ya think it's good enough to fool the Yoodoo birds?
Most definitely. They'll think they've spied a right tasty little snack!
Better take cover, Beebs. Looks like we got **customers** already...
Good heavens...

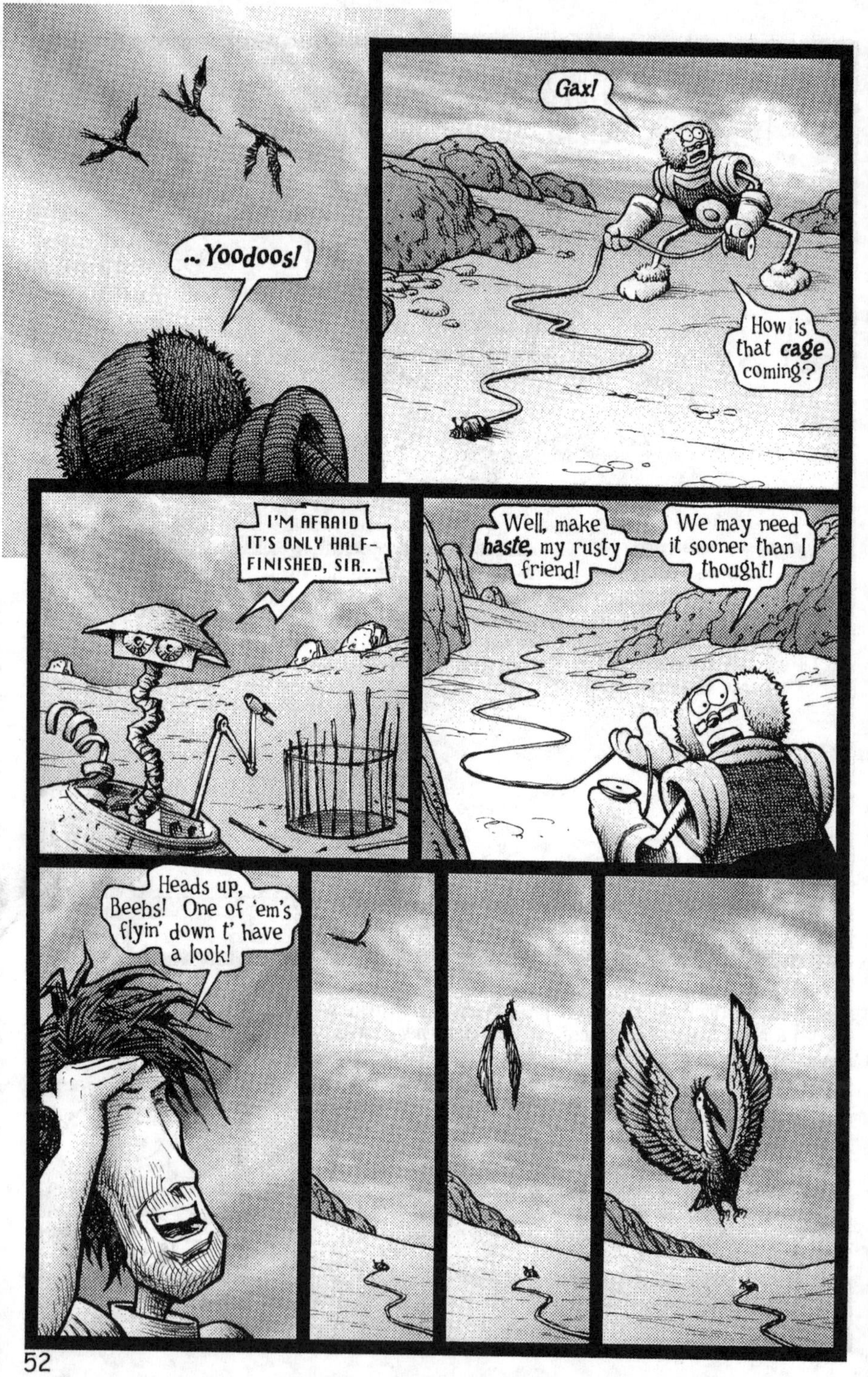
...Yoodoos!
Gax!
How is that cage coming?
I'M AFRAID IT'S ONLY HALF-FINISHED, SIR...
Well, make haste, my rusty friend!
We may need it sooner than I thought!
Heads up, Beebs! One of 'em's flyin' down t' have a look!

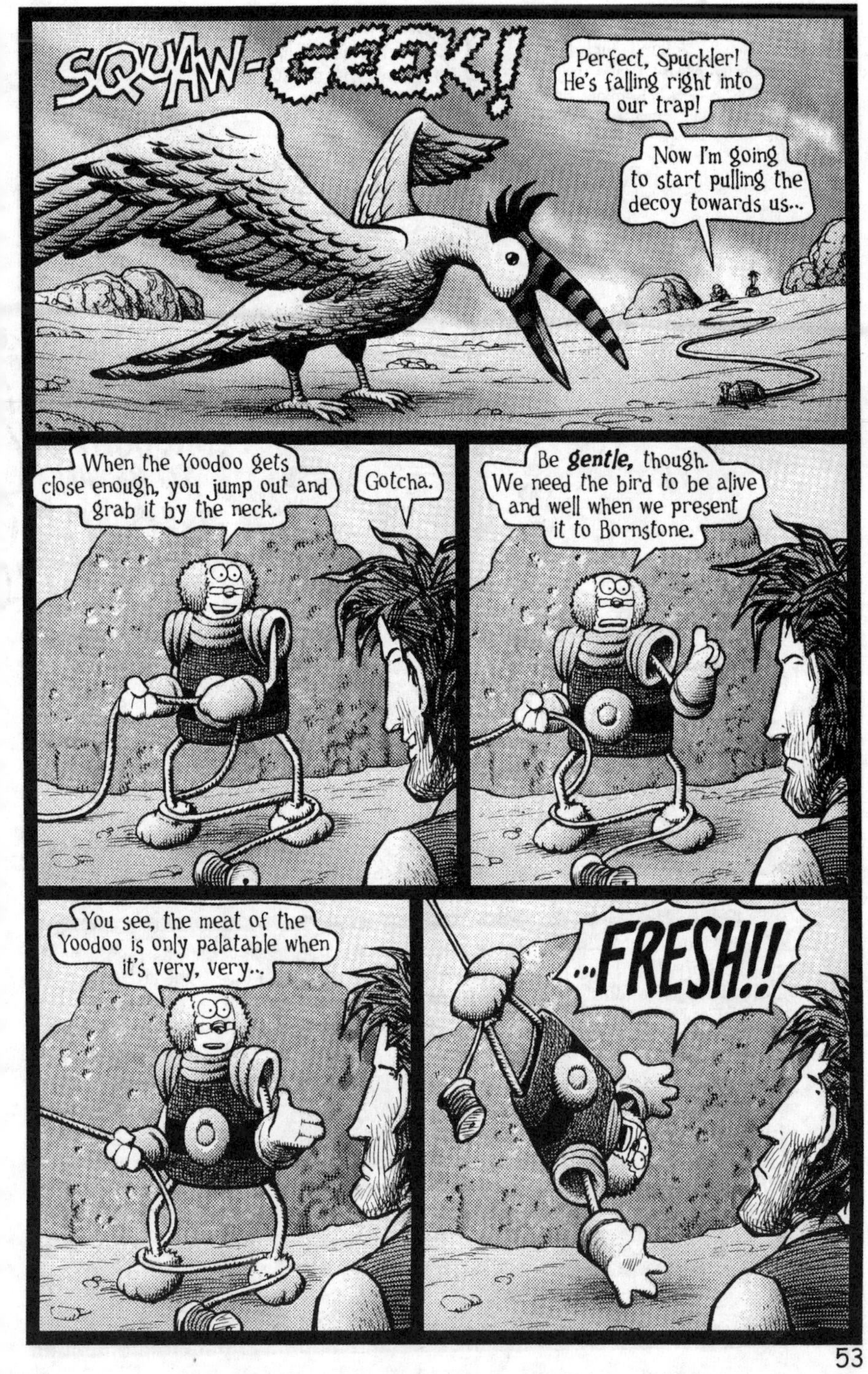
SQUAW-GEEK!
Perfect, Spuckler! He's falling right into our trap!
Now I'm going to start pulling the decoy towards us...
When the Yoodoo gets close enough, you jump out and grab it by the neck.
Gotcha.
Be *gentle,* though. We need the bird to be alive and well when we present it to Bornstone.
You see, the meat of the Yoodoo is only palatable when it's very, very...
...FRESH!!

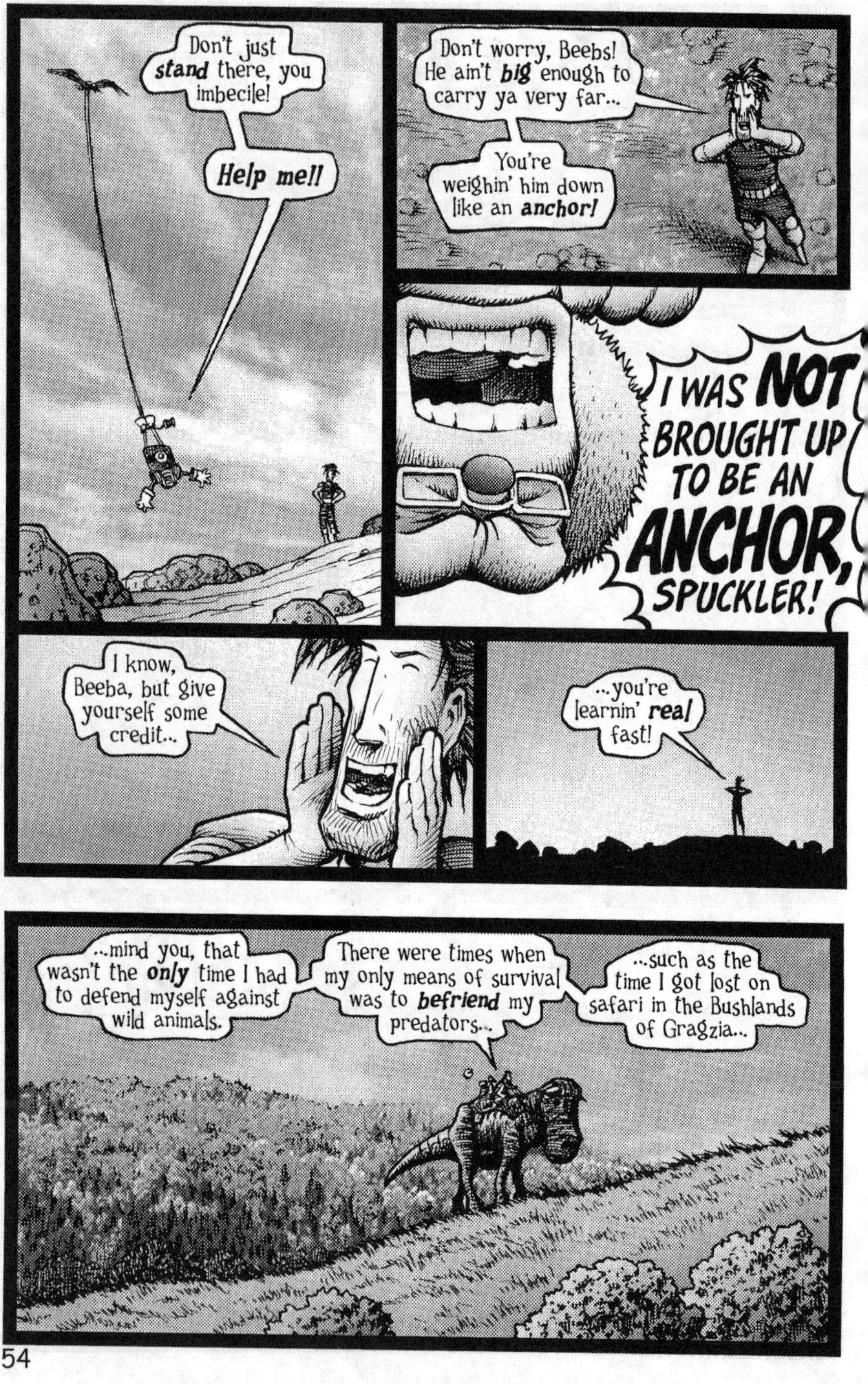

Don't just **stand** there, you imbecile!
**Help me!!**
Don't worry, Beebs! He ain't **big** enough to carry ya very far...
You're weighin' him down like an **anchor!**
I WAS **NOT** BROUGHT UP TO BE AN **ANCHOR,** SPUCKLER!
I know, Beeba, but give yourself some credit...
...you're learnin' **real** fast!
...mind you, that wasn't the **only** time I had to defend myself against wild animals.
There were times when my only means of survival was to **befriend** my predators...
...such as the time I got lost on safari in the Bushlands of Gragzia...

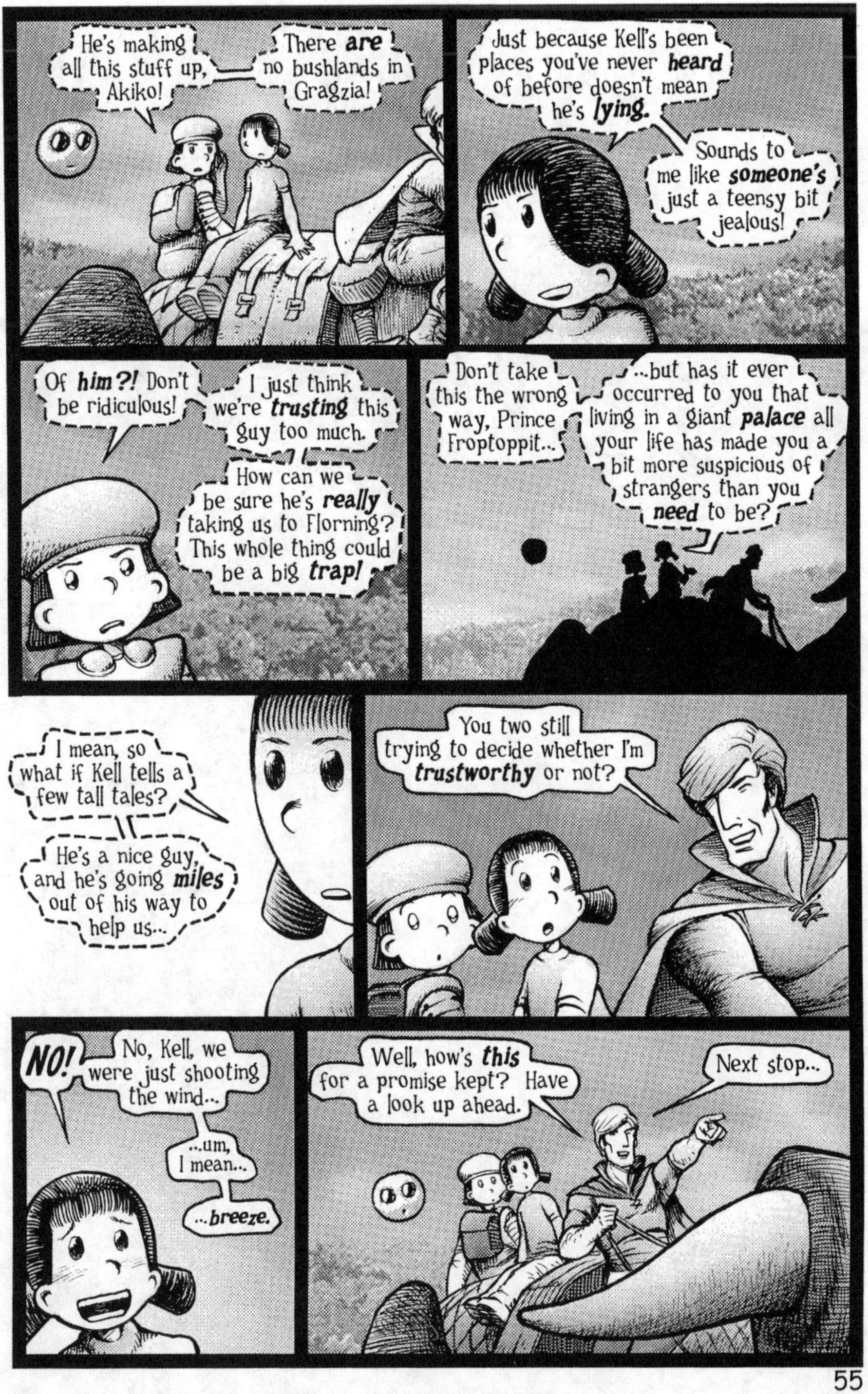
He's making all this stuff up, Akiko!
There **are** no bushlands in Gragzia!
Just because Kell's been places you've never **heard** of before doesn't mean he's ***lying.***
Sounds to me like **someone's** just a teensy bit jealous!
Of ***him?!*** Don't be ridiculous!
I just think we're ***trusting*** this guy too much.
How can we be sure he's ***really*** taking us to Florning? This whole thing could be a big ***trap!***
Don't take this the wrong way, Prince Froptoppit...
...but has it ever occurred to you that living in a giant ***palace*** all your life has made you a bit more suspicious of strangers than you ***need*** to be?
I mean, so what if Kell tells a few tall tales?
He's a nice guy, and he's going ***miles*** out of his way to help us...
You two still trying to decide whether I'm ***trustworthy*** or not?
**NO!**
No, Kell, we were just shooting the wind...
...um, I mean...
...***breeze.***
Well, how's ***this*** for a promise kept? Have a look up ahead.
Next stop...

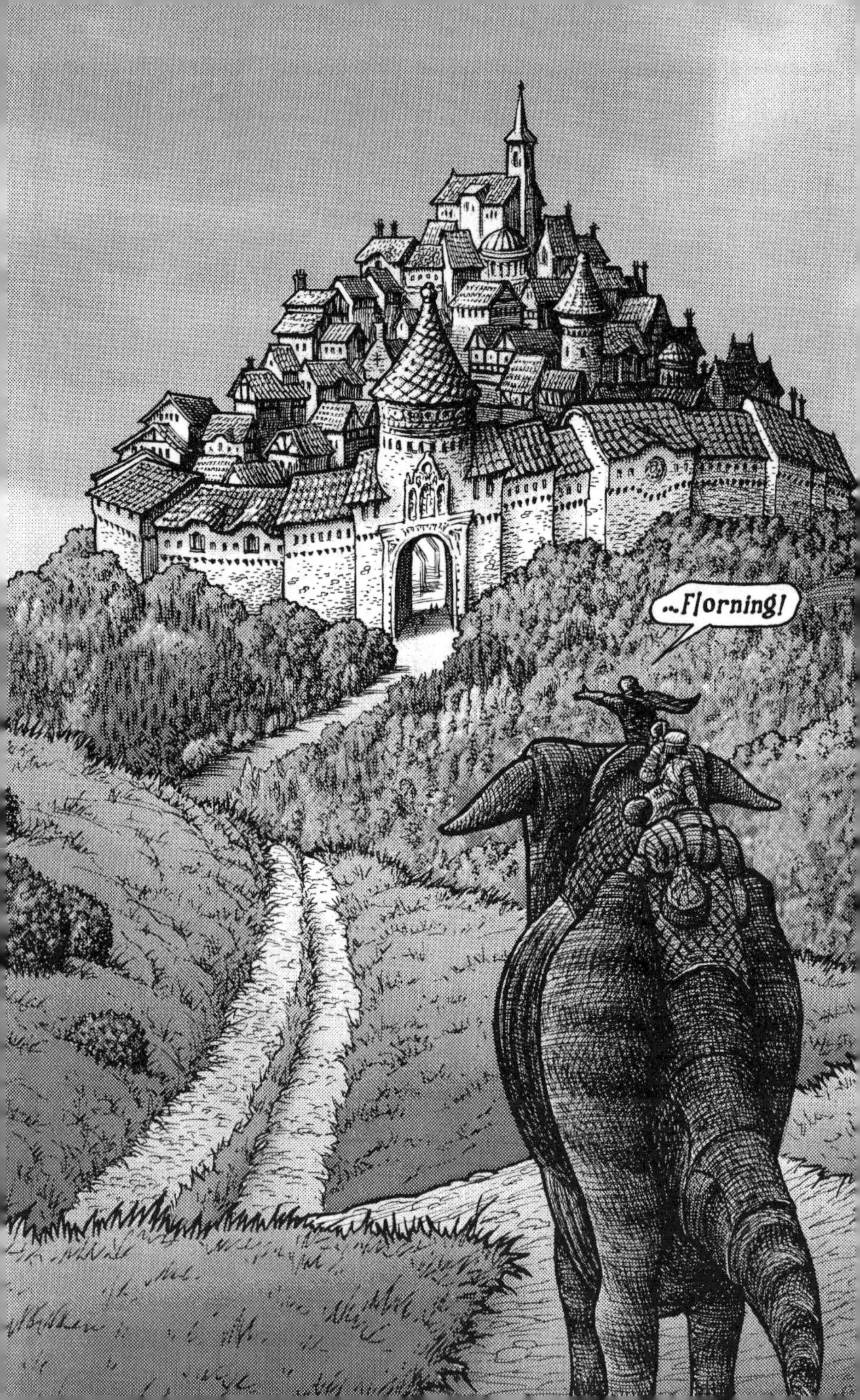
...Florning!

# BORNSTONE'S ELIXIR

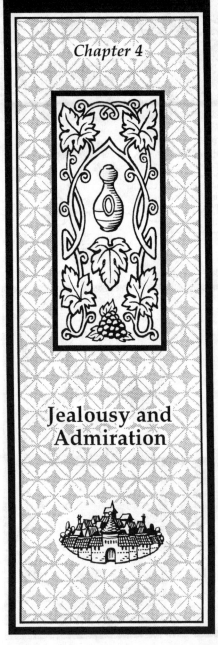

## *Chapter 4*

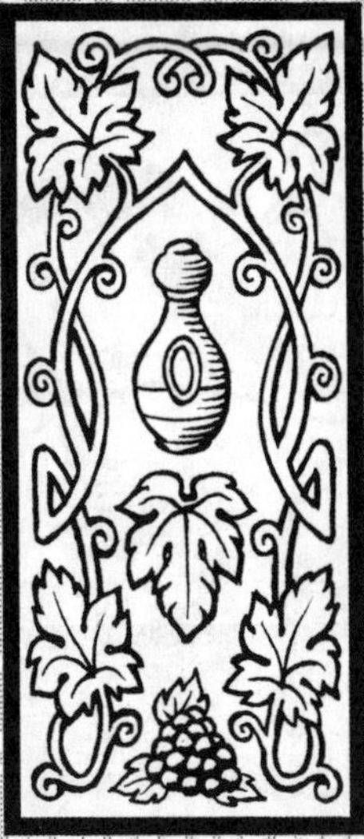

## Jealousy and Admiration

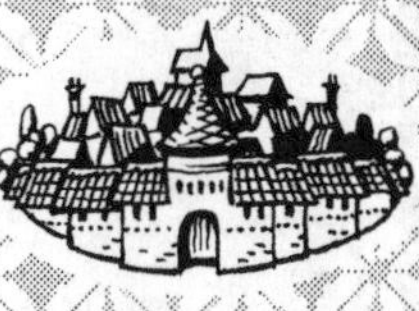

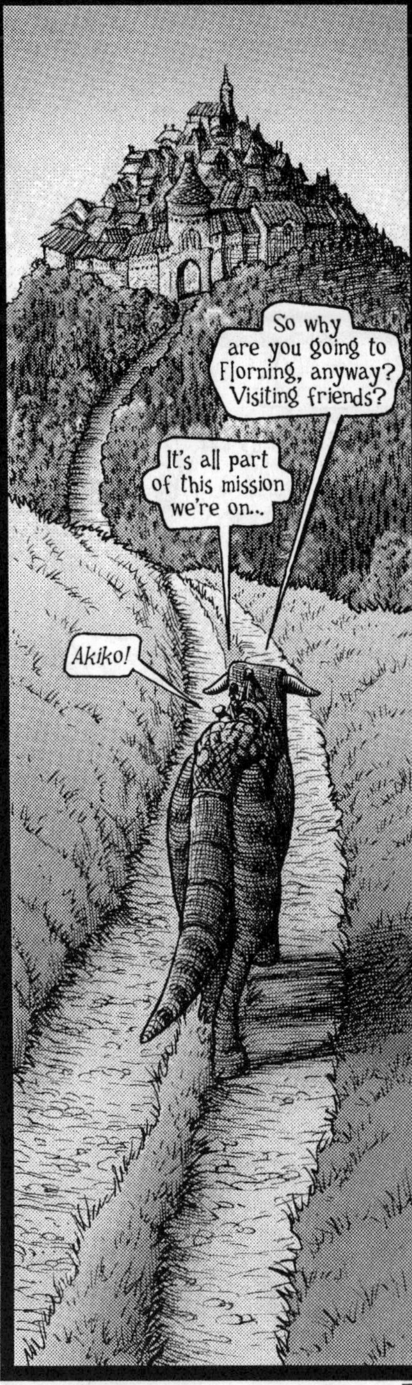
Akiko!
It's all part of this mission we're on...
So why are you going to Florning, anyway? Visiting friends?

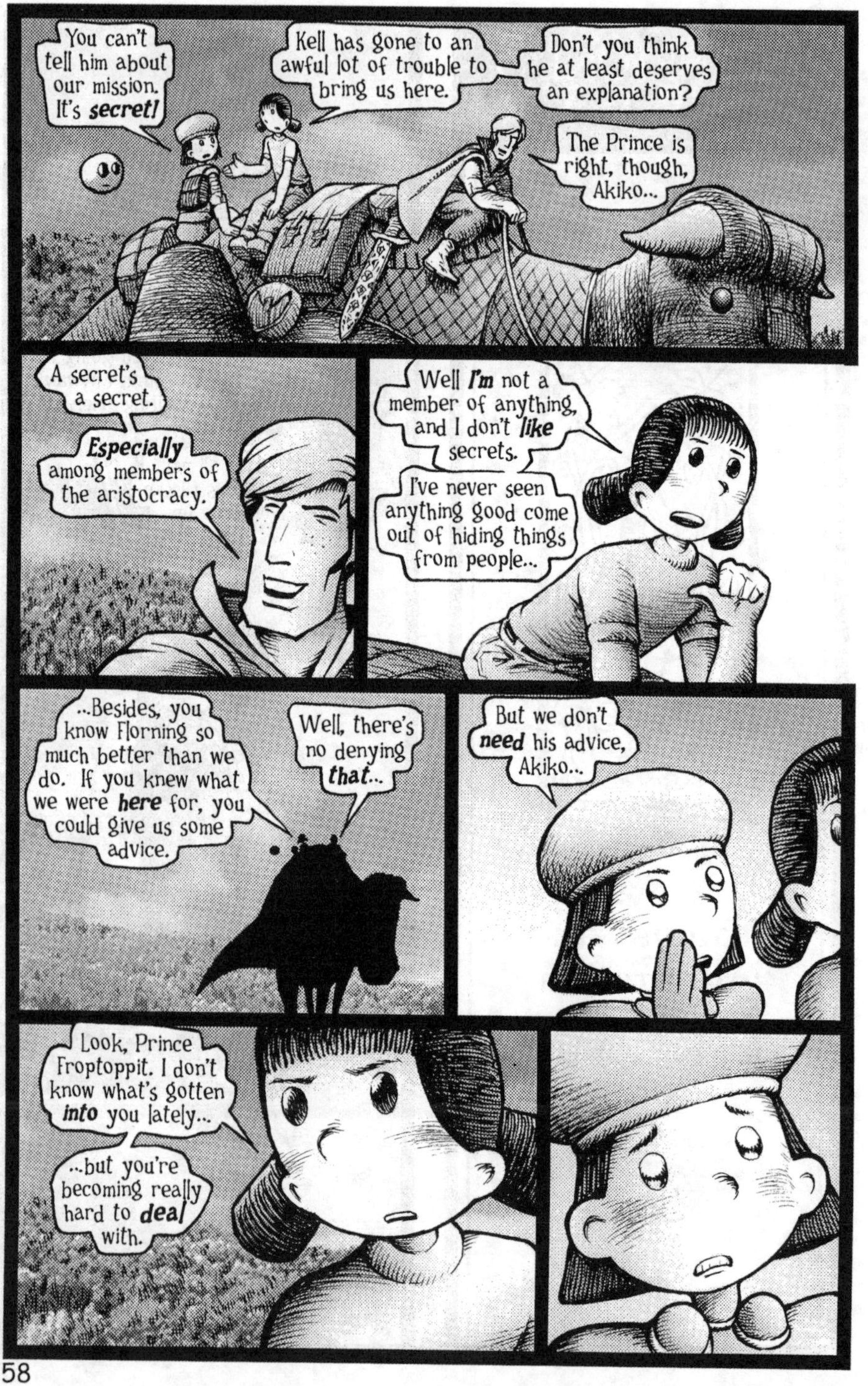
You can't tell him about our mission. It's *secret!*
Kell has gone to an awful lot of trouble to bring us here.
Don't you think he at least deserves an explanation?
The Prince is right, though, Akiko...
A secret's a secret.
*Especially* among members of the aristocracy.
Well *I'm* not a member of anything, and I don't *like* secrets.
I've never seen anything good come out of hiding things from people...
...Besides, you know Florning so much better than we do. If you knew what we were *here* for, you could give us some advice.
Well, there's no denying *that*...
But we don't *need* his advice, Akiko...
Look, Prince Froptoppit. I don't know what's gotten *into* you lately...
...but you're becoming really hard to *deal* with.

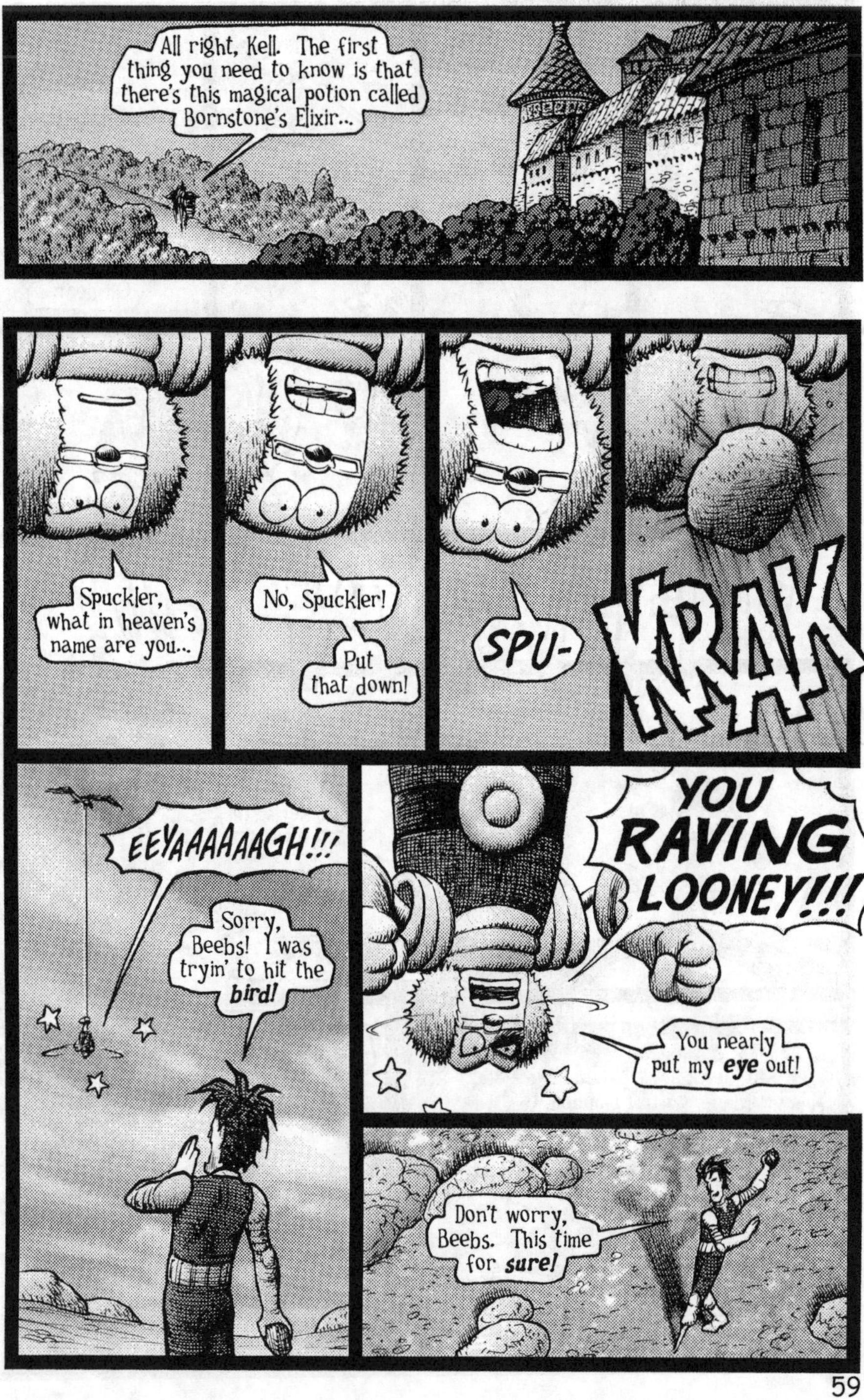
All right, Kell. The first thing you need to know is that there's this magical potion called Bornstone's Elixir...
Spuckler, what in heaven's name are you...
No, Spuckler!
Put that down!
SPU-
KRAK
EEYAAAAAAGH!!!
Sorry, Beebs! I was tryin' to hit the bird!
YOU RAVING LOONEY!!!
You nearly put my eye out!
Don't worry, Beebs. This time for sure!

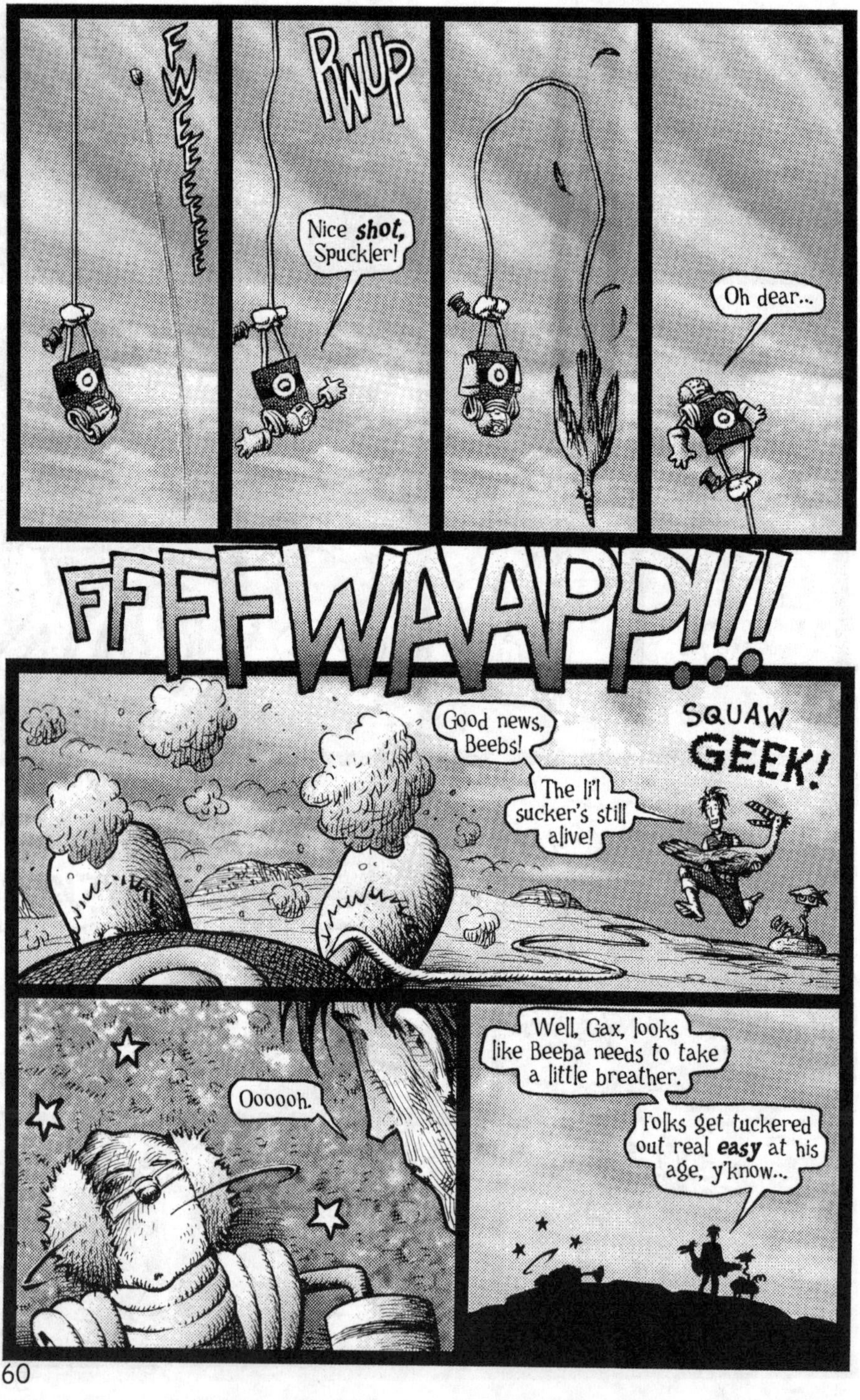
FWEEEEEEE
RWUP
Nice shot, Spuckler!
Oh dear...
FFFFWAAPP!!!
Good news, Beebs!
The li'l sucker's still alive!
SQUAW GEEK!
Ooooh.
Well, Gax, looks like Beeba needs to take a little breather.
Folks get tuckered out real easy at his age, y'know...

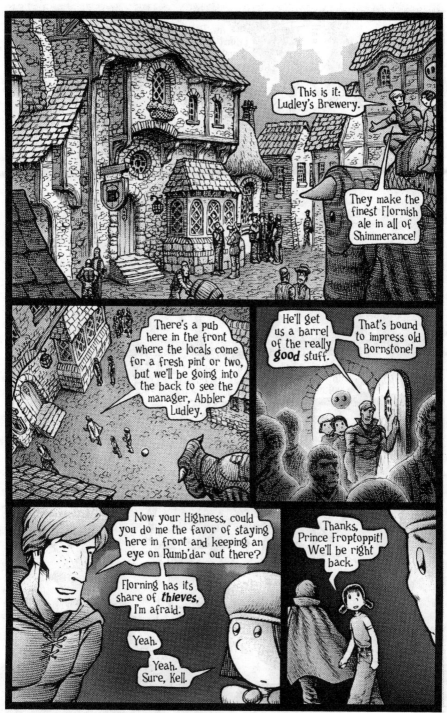

This is it:
Ludley's Brewery.

They make the
finest Flornish
ale in all of
Shimmerance!

There's a pub
here in the front
where the locals come
for a fresh pint or two,
but we'll be going into
the back to see the
manager, Abbler
Ludley.

He'll get
us a barrel
of the really
**good** stuff.

That's bound
to impress old
Bornstone!

Now your Highness, could
you do me the favor of staying
here in front and keeping an
eye on Rumb'dar out there?

Florning has its
share of **thieves**,
I'm afraid.

Yeah.

Yeah.
Sure, Kell.

Thanks,
Prince Froptoppit!
We'll be right
back.

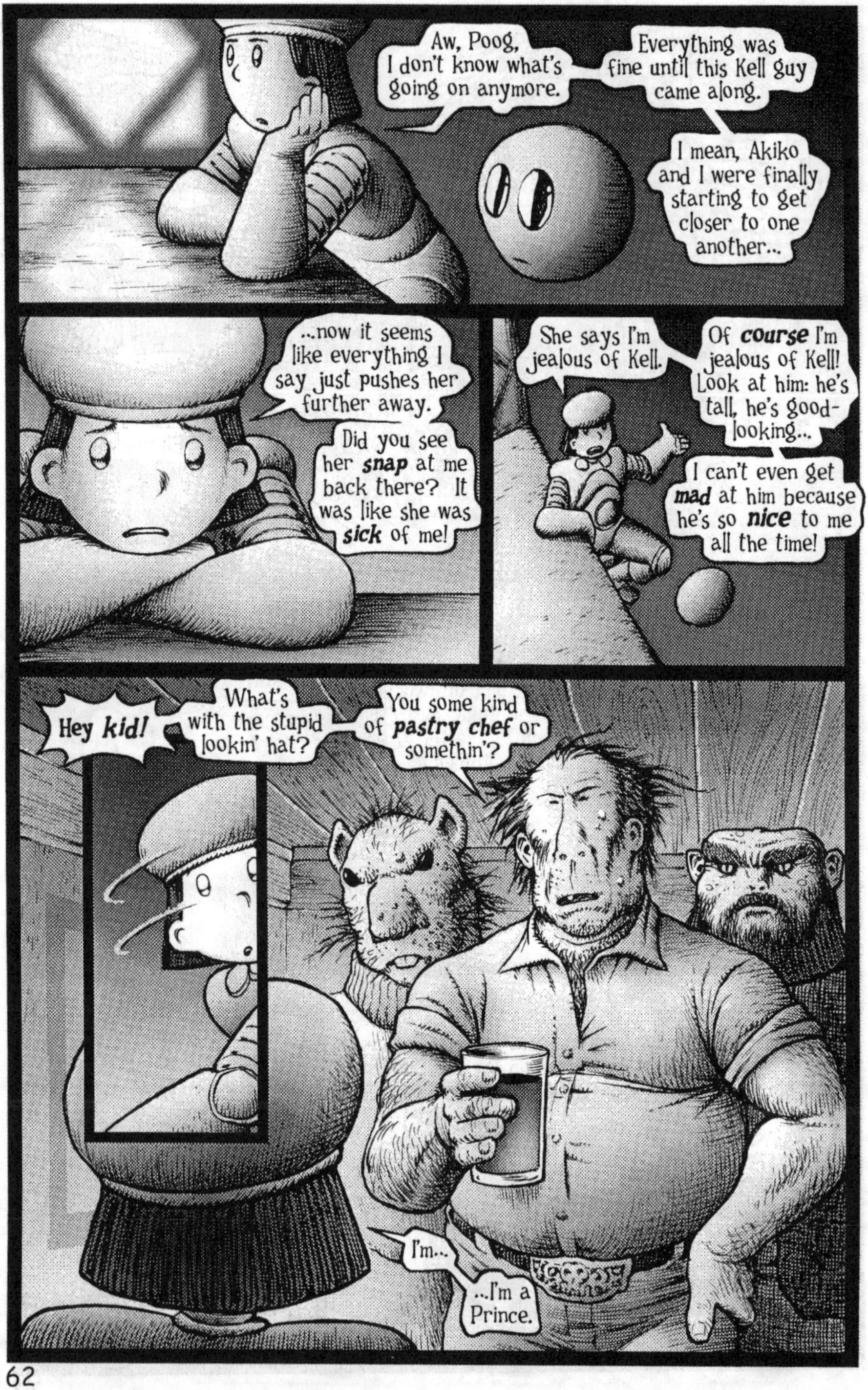
Aw, Poog, I don't know what's going on anymore.
Everything was fine until this Kell guy came along.
I mean, Akiko and I were finally starting to get closer to one another...
...now it seems like everything I say just pushes her further away.
Did you see her snap at me back there? It was like she was sick of me!
She says I'm jealous of Kell.
Of course I'm jealous of Kell! Look at him: he's tall, he's good-looking...
I can't even get mad at him because he's so nice to me all the time!
Hey kid!
What's with the stupid lookin' hat?
You some kind of pastry chef or somethin'?
I'm...
...I'm a Prince.

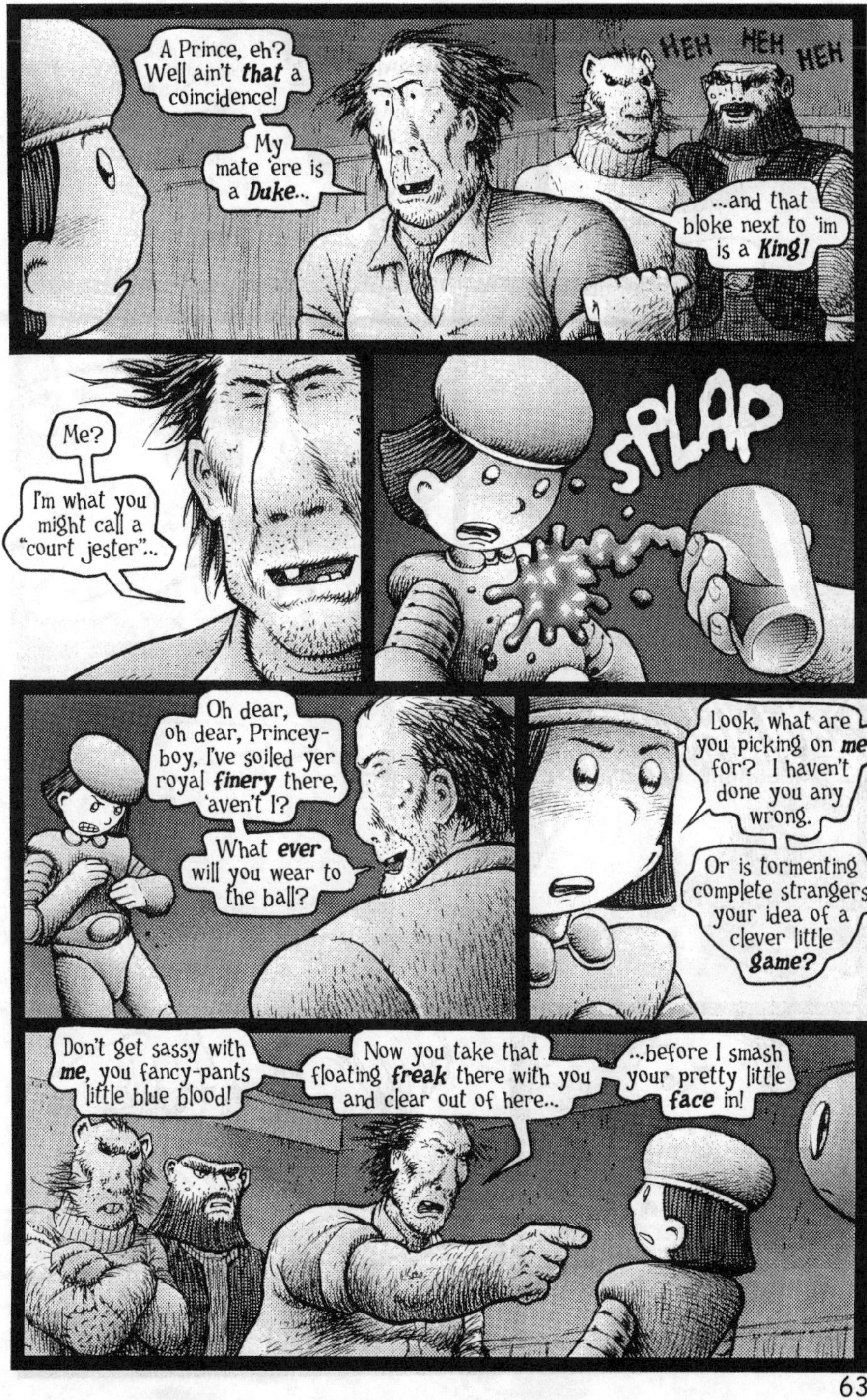
A Prince, eh? Well ain't **that** a coincidence!
My mate 'ere is a **Duke**..
HEH HEH HEH
...and that bloke next to 'im is a **King!**
Me?
I'm what you might call a "court jester"..
SPLAP
Oh dear, oh dear, Princey-boy, I've soiled yer royal **finery** there, 'aven't I?
What **ever** will you wear to the ball?
Look, what are you picking on **me** for? I haven't done you any wrong.
Or is tormenting complete strangers your idea of a clever little **game?**
Don't get sassy with **me**, you fancy-pants little blue blood!
Now you take that floating **freak** there with you and clear out of here..
..before I smash your pretty little **face** in!

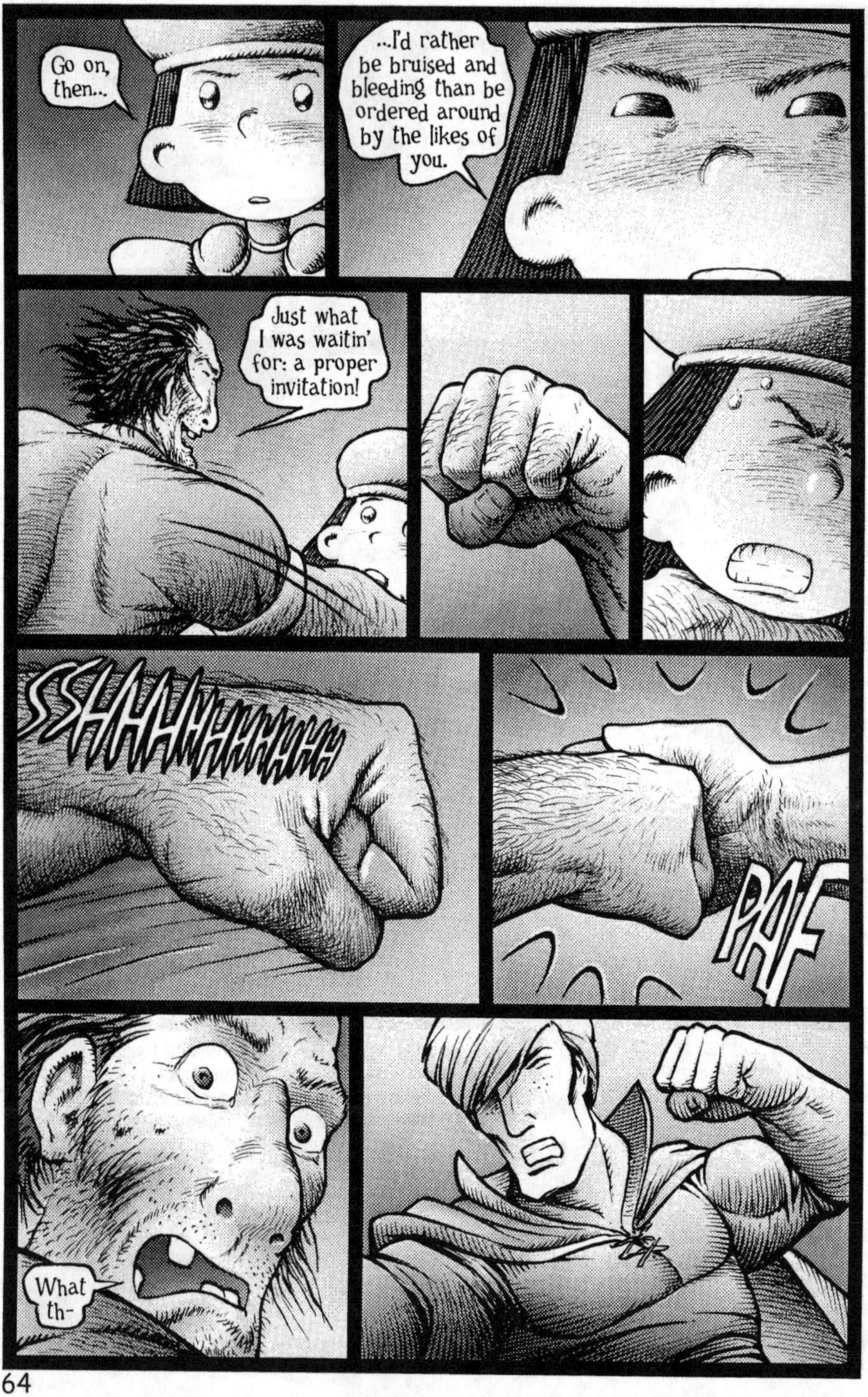
Go on, then...
...I'd rather be bruised and bleeding than be ordered around by the likes of you.
Just what I was waitin' for: a proper invitation!
SSHHHHHHHHHHH
PAF
What th-

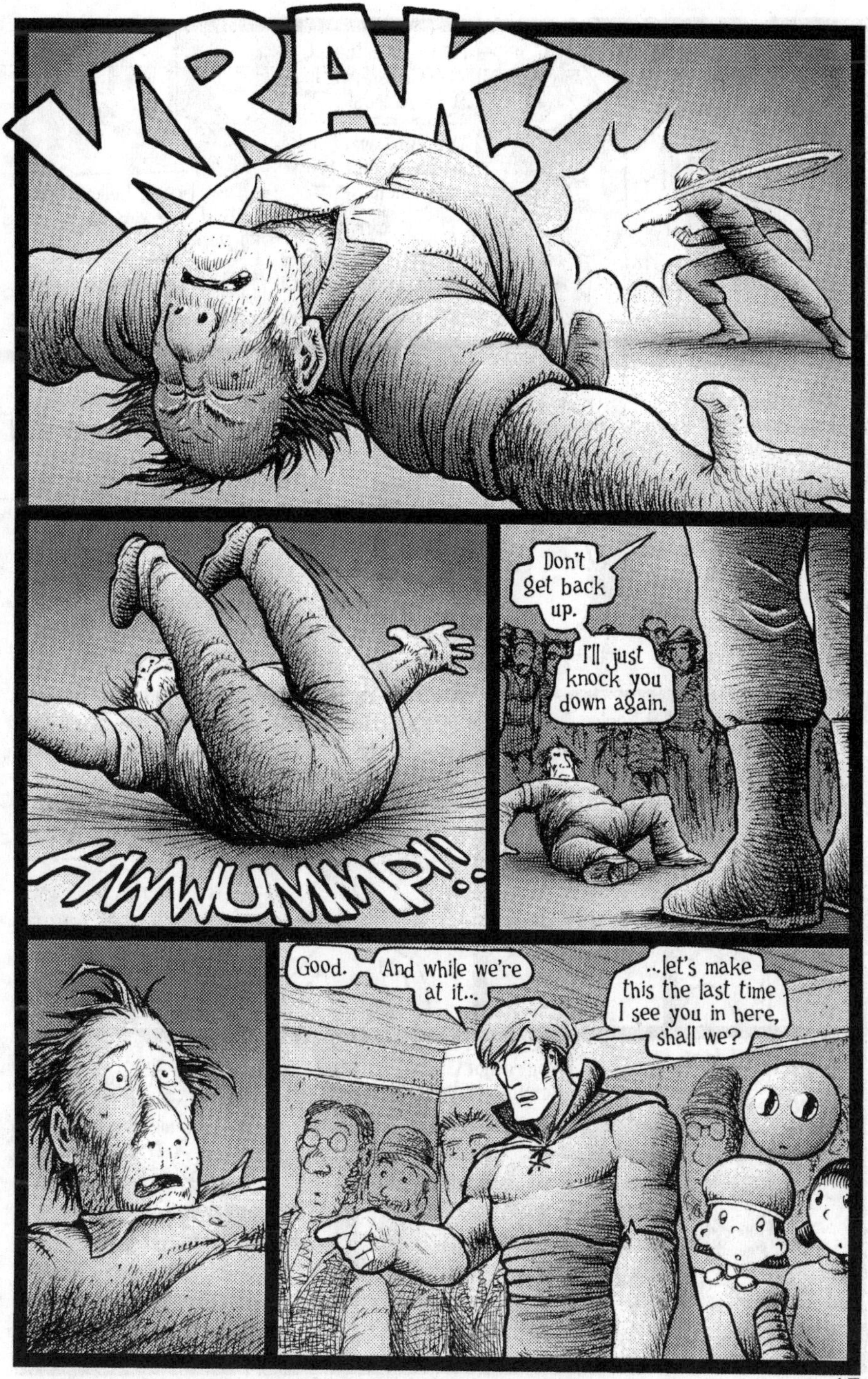
KRAK!
HWUMMP!!
Don't get back up.
I'll just knock you down again.
Good.
And while we're at it...
...let's make this the last time I see you in here, shall we?

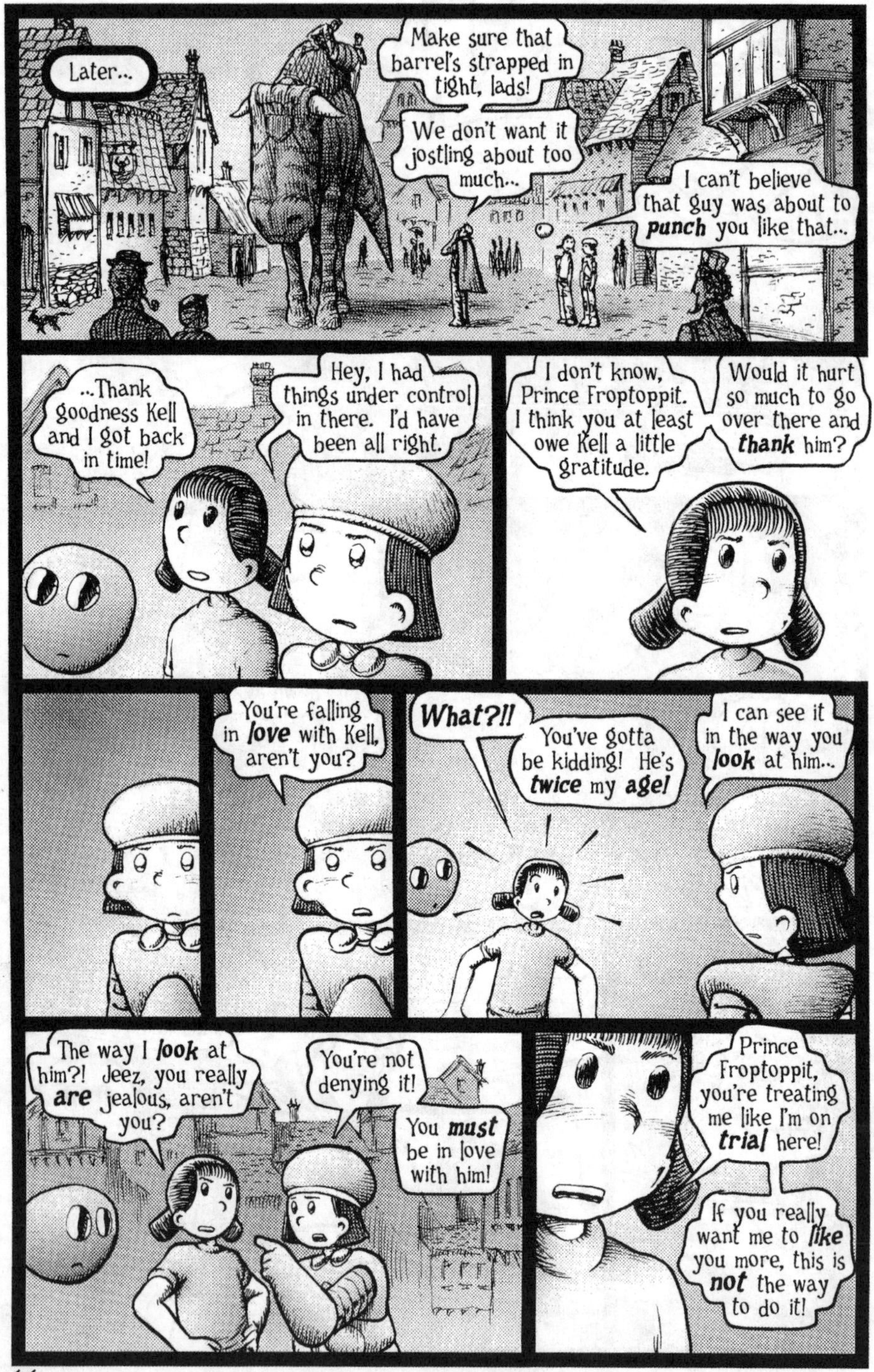
Later...
Make sure that barrel's strapped in tight, lads!
We don't want it jostling about too much...
I can't believe that guy was about to **punch** you like that...
...Thank goodness Kell and I got back in time!
Hey, I had things under control in there. I'd have been all right.
I don't know, Prince Froptoppit. I think you at least owe Kell a little gratitude.
Would it hurt so much to go over there and **thank** him?
You're falling in **love** with Kell, aren't you?
**What?!!**
You've gotta be kidding! He's **twice** my **age**!
I can see it in the way you **look** at him...
The way I **look** at him?! Jeez, you really **are** jealous, aren't you?
You're not denying it!
You **must** be in love with him!
Prince Froptoppit, you're treating me like I'm on **trial** here!
If you really want me to **like** you more, this is **not** the way to do it!

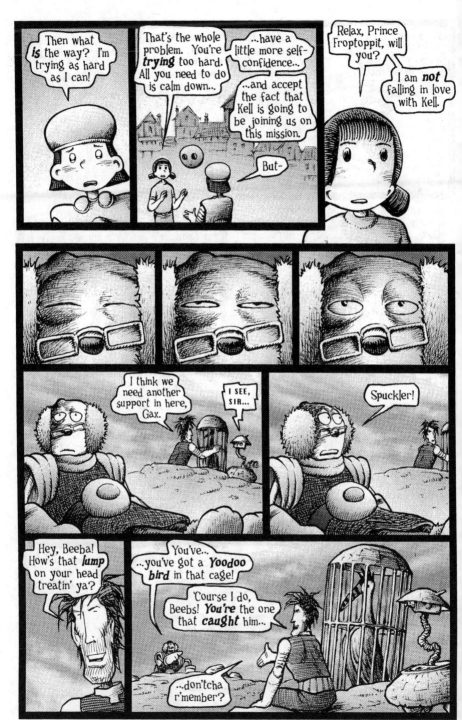

Then what **is** the way? I'm trying as hard as I can!

That's the whole problem. You're **trying** too hard. All you need to do is calm down...

..have a little more self-confidence...

...and accept the fact that Kell is going to be joining us on this mission.

But-

Relax, Prince Froptoppit, will you?

I am **not** falling in love with Kell.

I think we need another support in here, Gax.

I SEE, SIR...

Spuckler!

Hey, Beeba! How's that **lump** on your head treatin' ya?

You've.. ...you've got a **Yoodoo bird** in that cage!

'Course I do, Beebs! **You're** the one that **caught** him...

...don'tcha r'member?

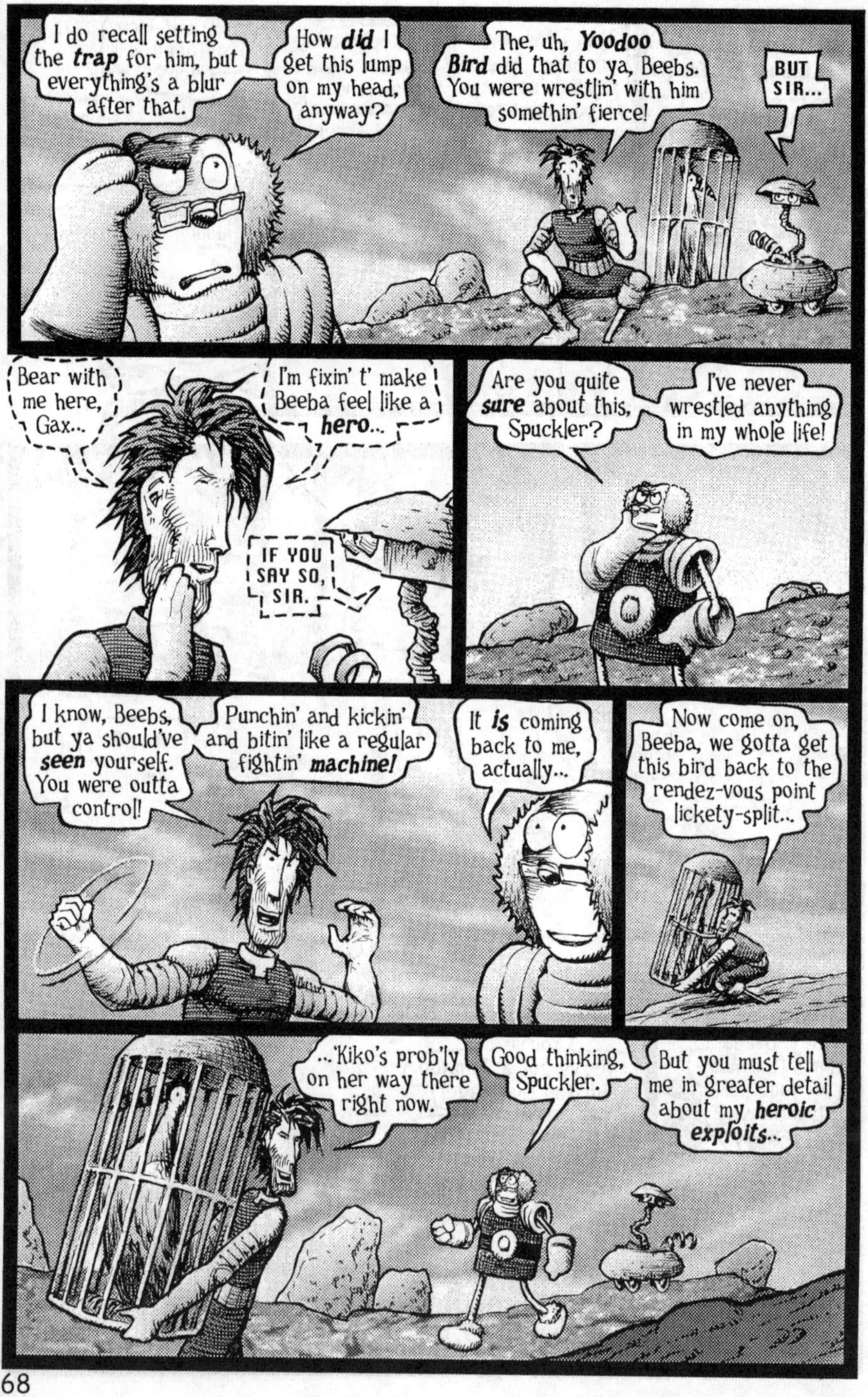

I do recall setting the trap for him, but everything's a blur after that.
How did I get this lump on my head, anyway?
The, uh, Yoodoo Bird did that to ya, Beebs. You were wrestlin' with him somethin' fierce!
BUT SIR...
Bear with me here, Gax...
I'm fixin' t' make Beeba feel like a hero...
IF YOU SAY SO, SIR.
Are you quite sure about this, Spuckler?
I've never wrestled anything in my whole life!
I know, Beebs, but ya should've seen yourself. You were outta control!
Punchin' and kickin' and bitin' like a regular fightin' machine!
It is coming back to me, actually...
Now come on, Beeba, we gotta get this bird back to the rendez-vous point lickety-split...
...'Kiko's prob'ly on her way there right now.
Good thinking, Spuckler.
But you must tell me in greater detail about my heroic exploits...

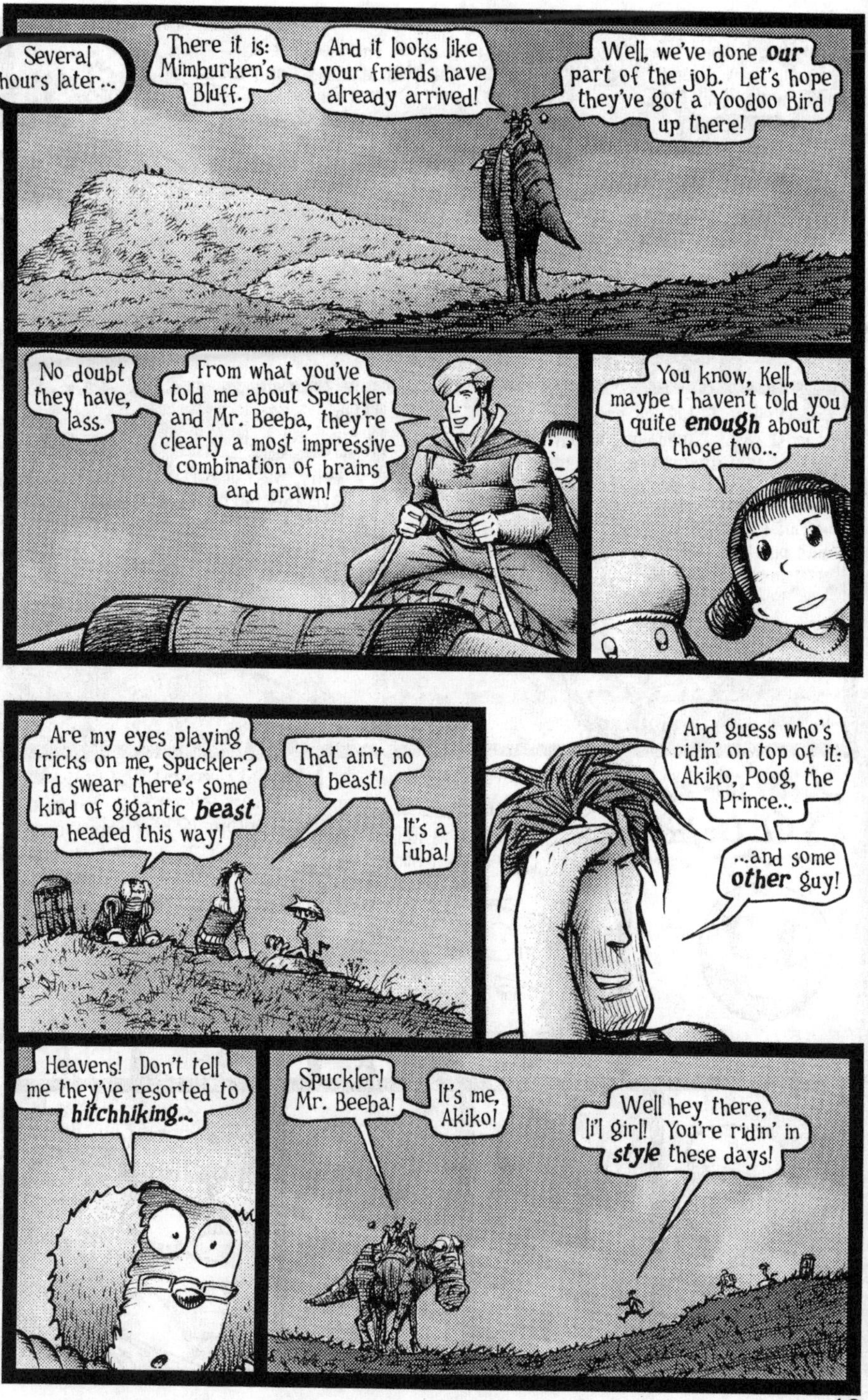
Several hours later...
There it is: Mimburken's Bluff.
And it looks like your friends have already arrived!
Well, we've done **our** part of the job. Let's hope they've got a Yoodoo Bird up there!
No doubt they have, lass.
From what you've told me about Spuckler and Mr. Beeba, they're clearly a most impressive combination of brains and brawn!
You know, Kell, maybe I haven't told you quite **enough** about those two...
Are my eyes playing tricks on me, Spuckler? I'd swear there's some kind of gigantic **beast** headed this way!
That ain't no beast!
It's a Fuba!
And guess who's ridin' on top of it: Akiko, Poog, the Prince...
...and some **other** guy!
Heavens! Don't tell me they've resorted to ***hitchhiking...***
Spuckler! Mr. Beeba!
It's me, Akiko!
Well hey there, li'l girl! You're ridin' in ***style*** these days!

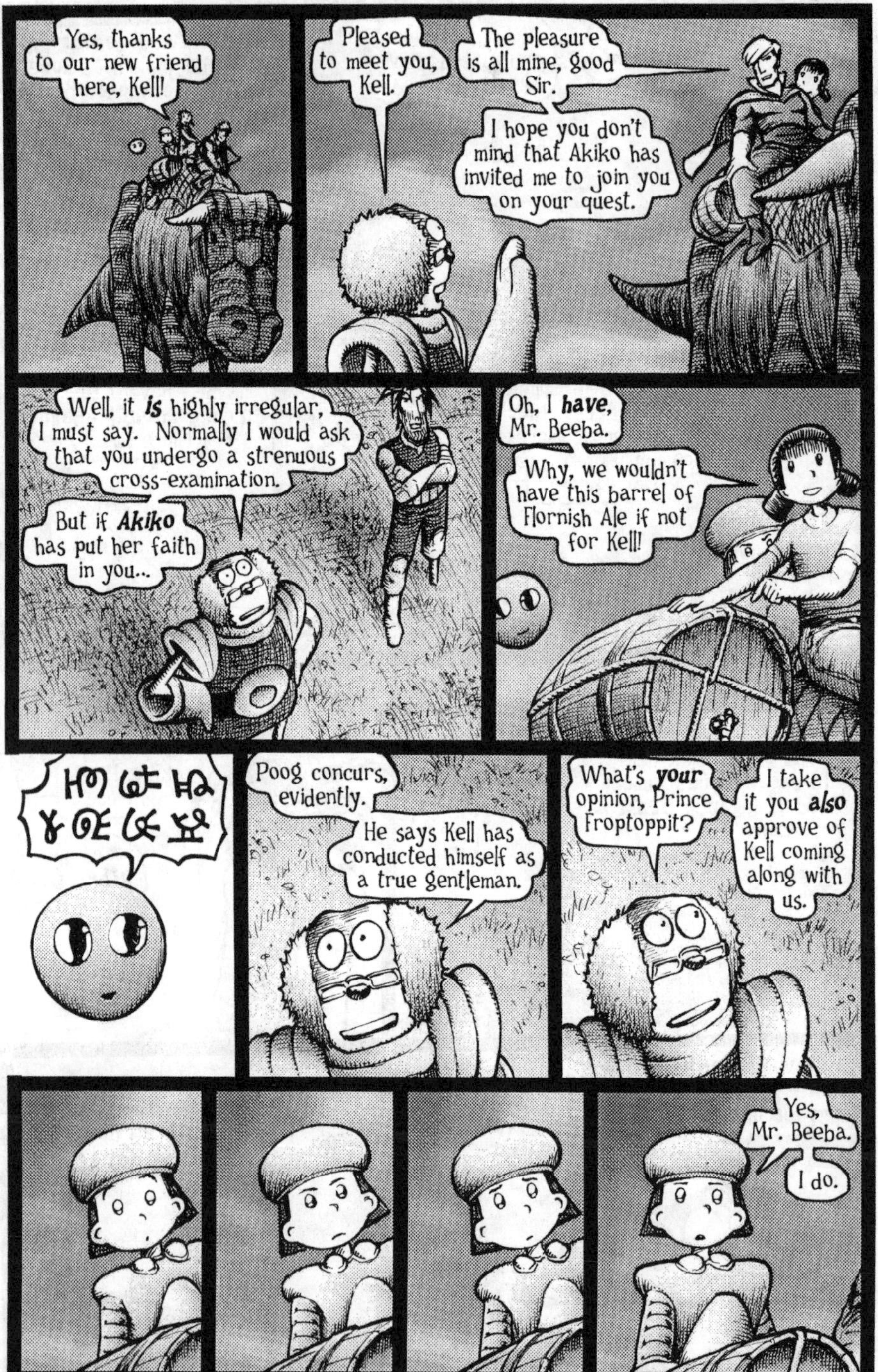
Yes, thanks to our new friend here, Kell!
Pleased to meet you, Kell.
The pleasure is all mine, good Sir.
I hope you don't mind that Akiko has invited me to join you on your quest.
Well, it **is** highly irregular, I must say. Normally I would ask that you undergo a strenuous cross-examination.
But if **Akiko** has put her faith in you...
Oh, I **have**, Mr. Beeba.
Why, we wouldn't have this barrel of Flornish Ale if not for Kell!
Poog concurs, evidently.
He says Kell has conducted himself as a true gentleman.
What's **your** opinion, Prince Froptoppit?
I take it you **also** approve of Kell coming along with us.
Yes, Mr. Beeba.
I do.

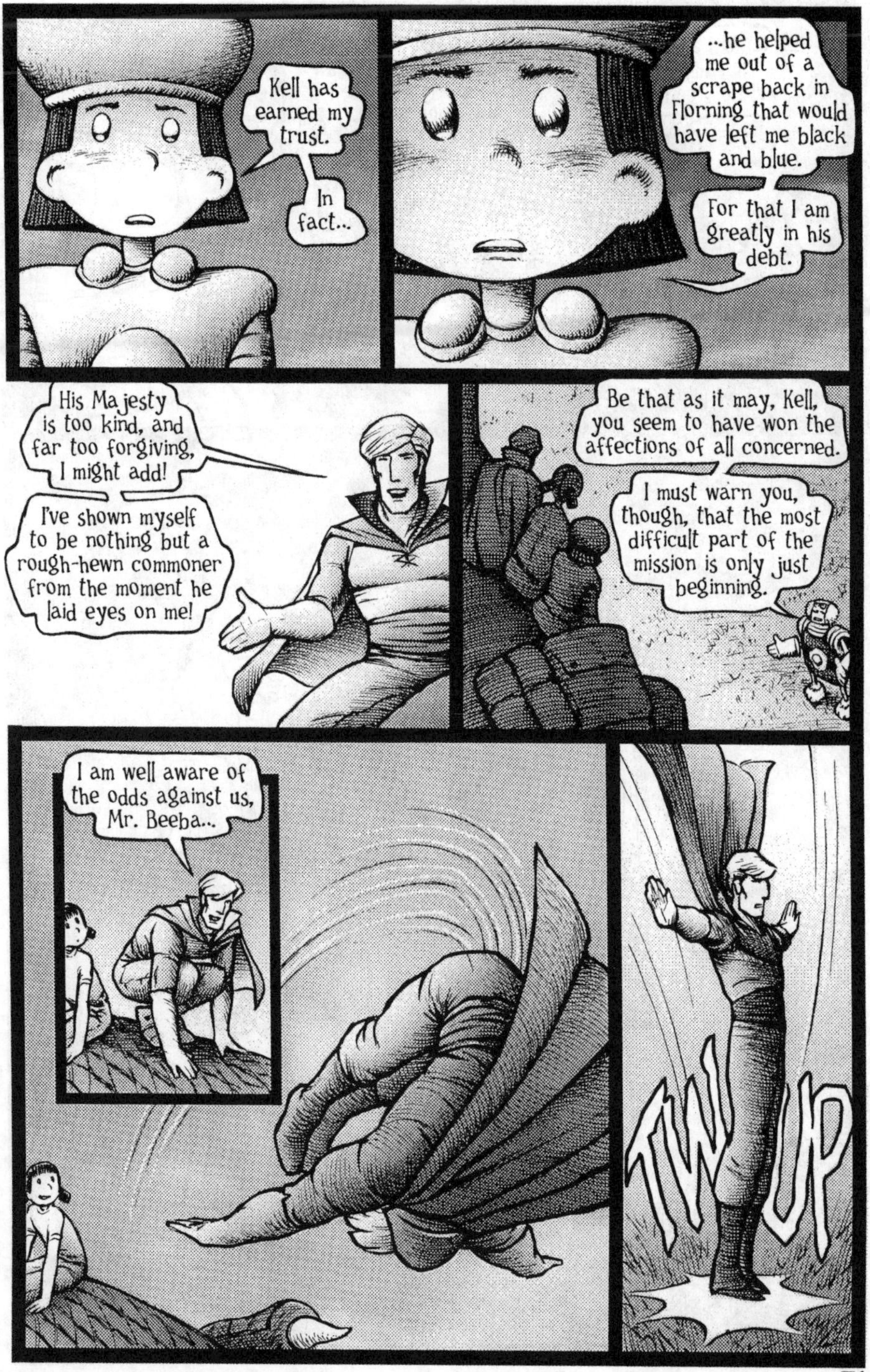

Kell has earned my trust.
In fact...
...he helped me out of a scrape back in Florning that would have left me black and blue.
For that I am greatly in his debt.
His Majesty is too kind, and far too forgiving, I might add!
I've shown myself to be nothing but a rough-hewn commoner from the moment he laid eyes on me!
Be that as it may, Kell, you seem to have won the affections of all concerned.
I must warn you, though, that the most difficult part of the mission is only just beginning.
I am well aware of the odds against us, Mr. Beeba...
TWUP

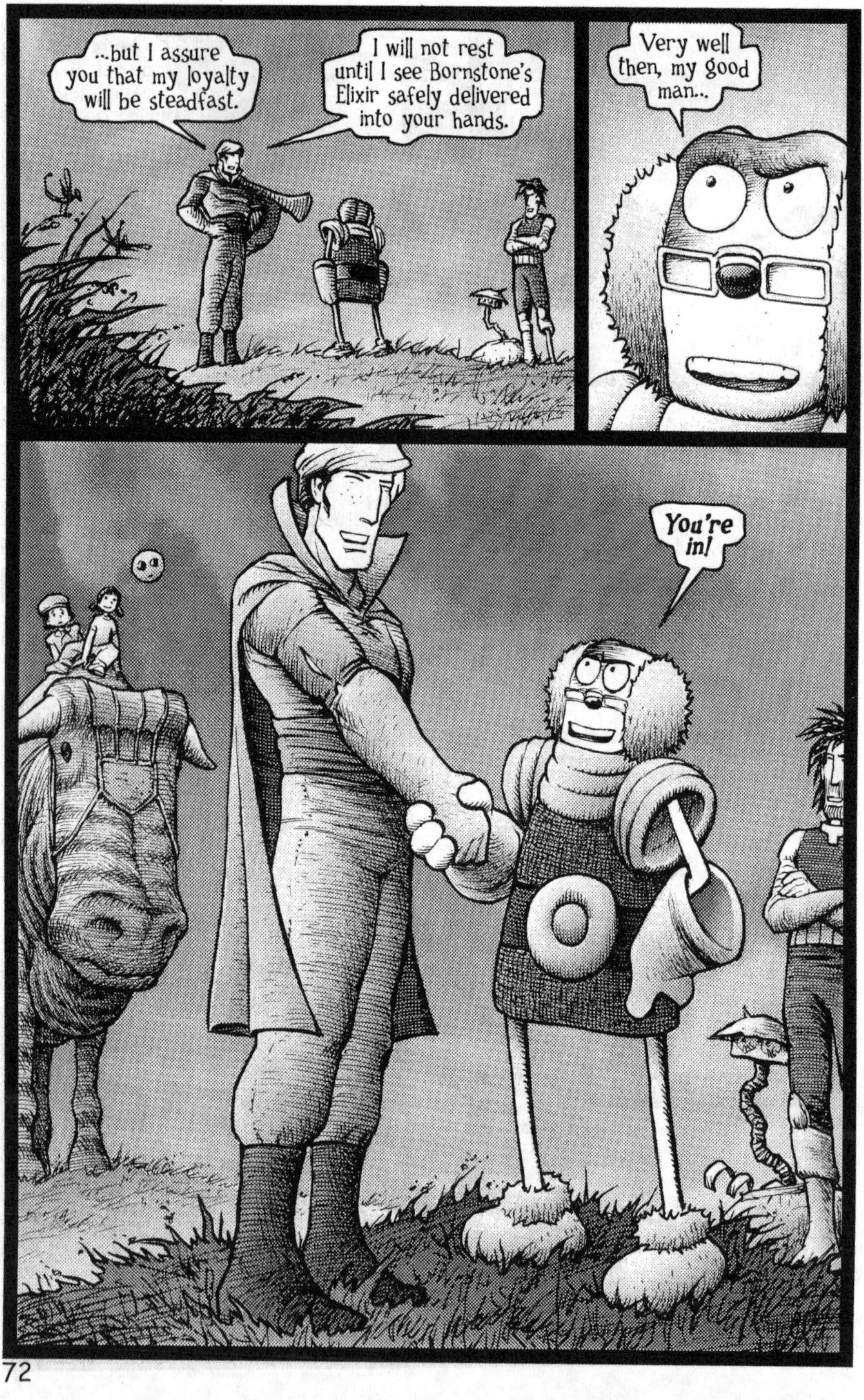
...but I assure you that my loyalty will be steadfast.
I will not rest until I see Bornstone's Elixir safely delivered into your hands.
Very well then, my good man...
You're in!

# BORNSTONE'S ELIXIR

*Chapter 5*

## The Moment of Truth

Pressing onward...

...our heroes make their way across the gently rolling hills...

...until finally they reach the domain of Tholderous Bornstone.

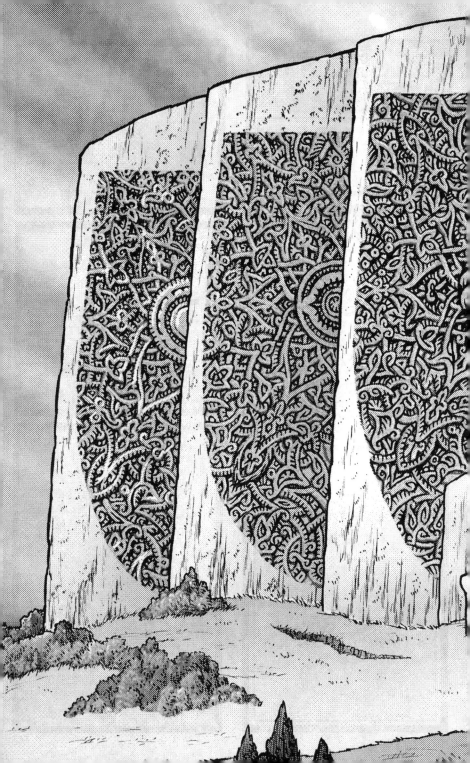

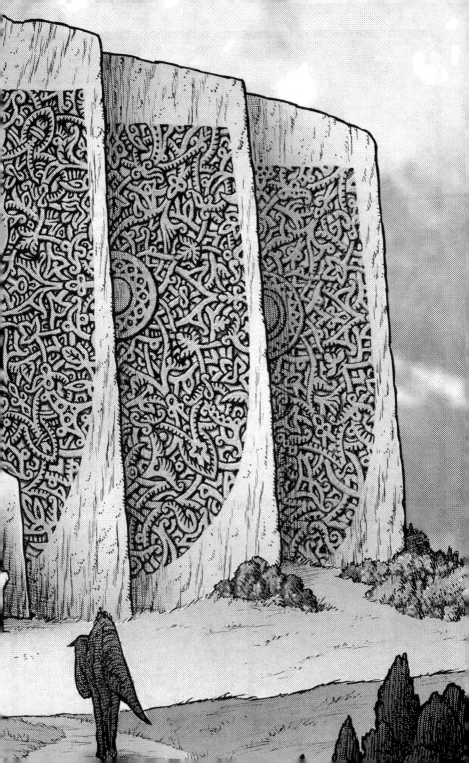

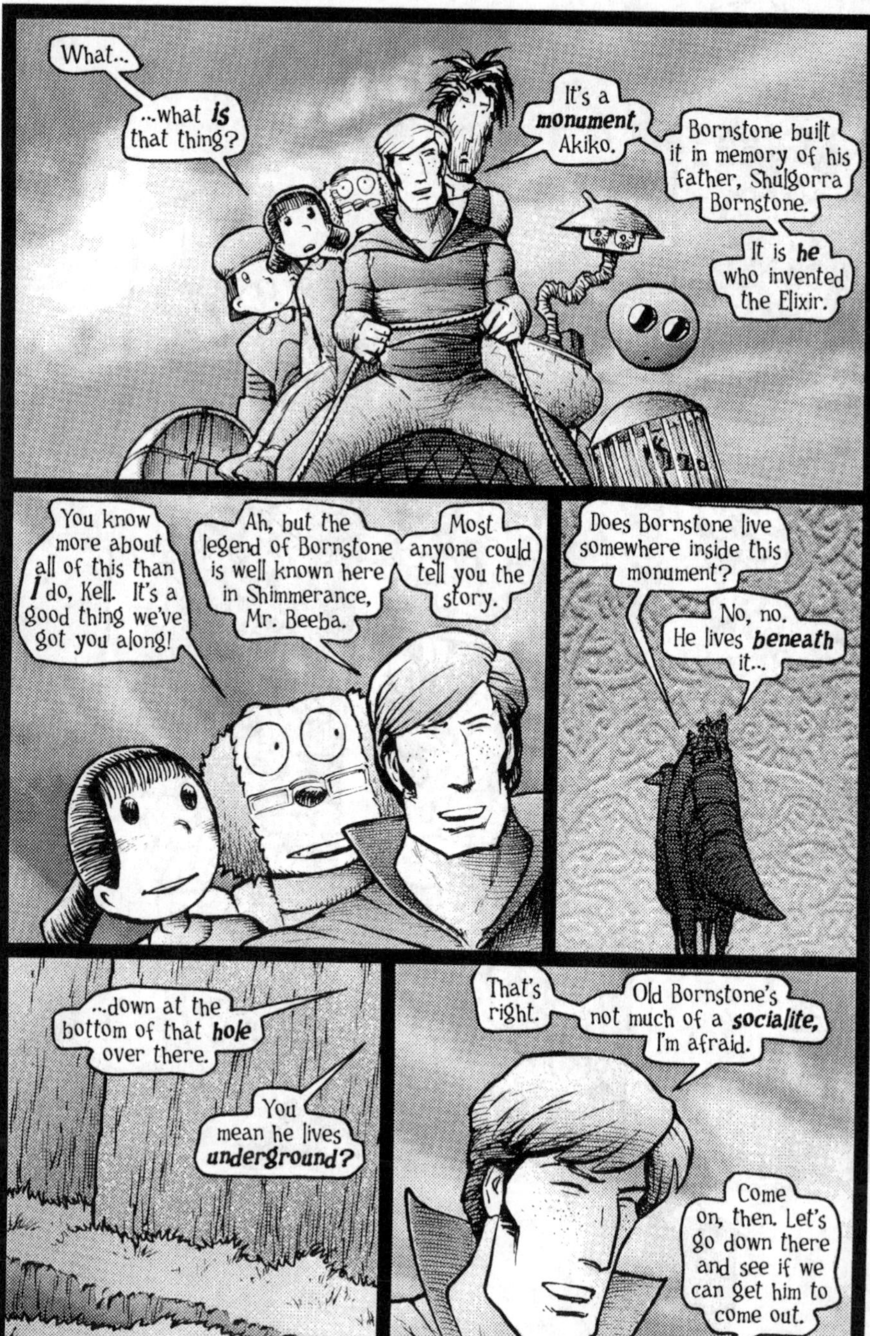
What...
...what is that thing?
It's a monument, Akiko.
Bornstone built it in memory of his father, Shulgorra Bornstone.
It is he who invented the Elixir.
You know more about all of this than I do, Kell. It's a good thing we've got you along!
Ah, but the legend of Bornstone is well known here in Shimmerance, Mr. Beeba.
Most anyone could tell you the story.
Does Bornstone live somewhere inside this monument?
No, no. He lives beneath it...
...down at the bottom of that hole over there.
You mean he lives underground?
That's right.
Old Bornstone's not much of a socialite, I'm afraid.
Come on, then. Let's go down there and see if we can get him to come out.

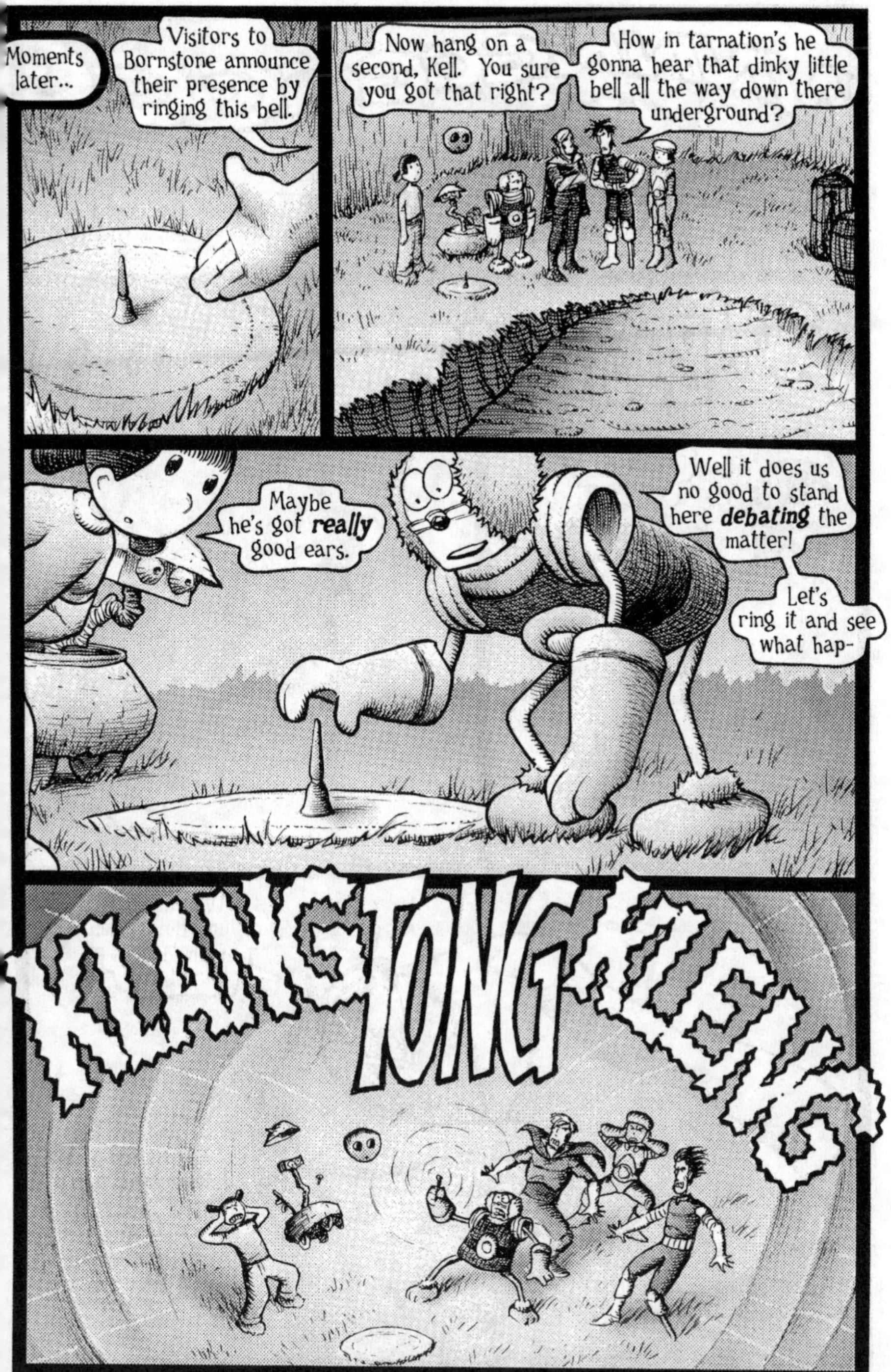
Moments later...
Visitors to Bornstone announce their presence by ringing this bell.
Now hang on a second, Kell. You sure you got that right?
How in tarnation's he gonna hear that dinky little bell all the way down there underground?
Maybe he's got **really** good ears.
Well it does us no good to stand here ***debating*** the matter!
Let's ring it and see what hap-
KLANG TONG KLENG

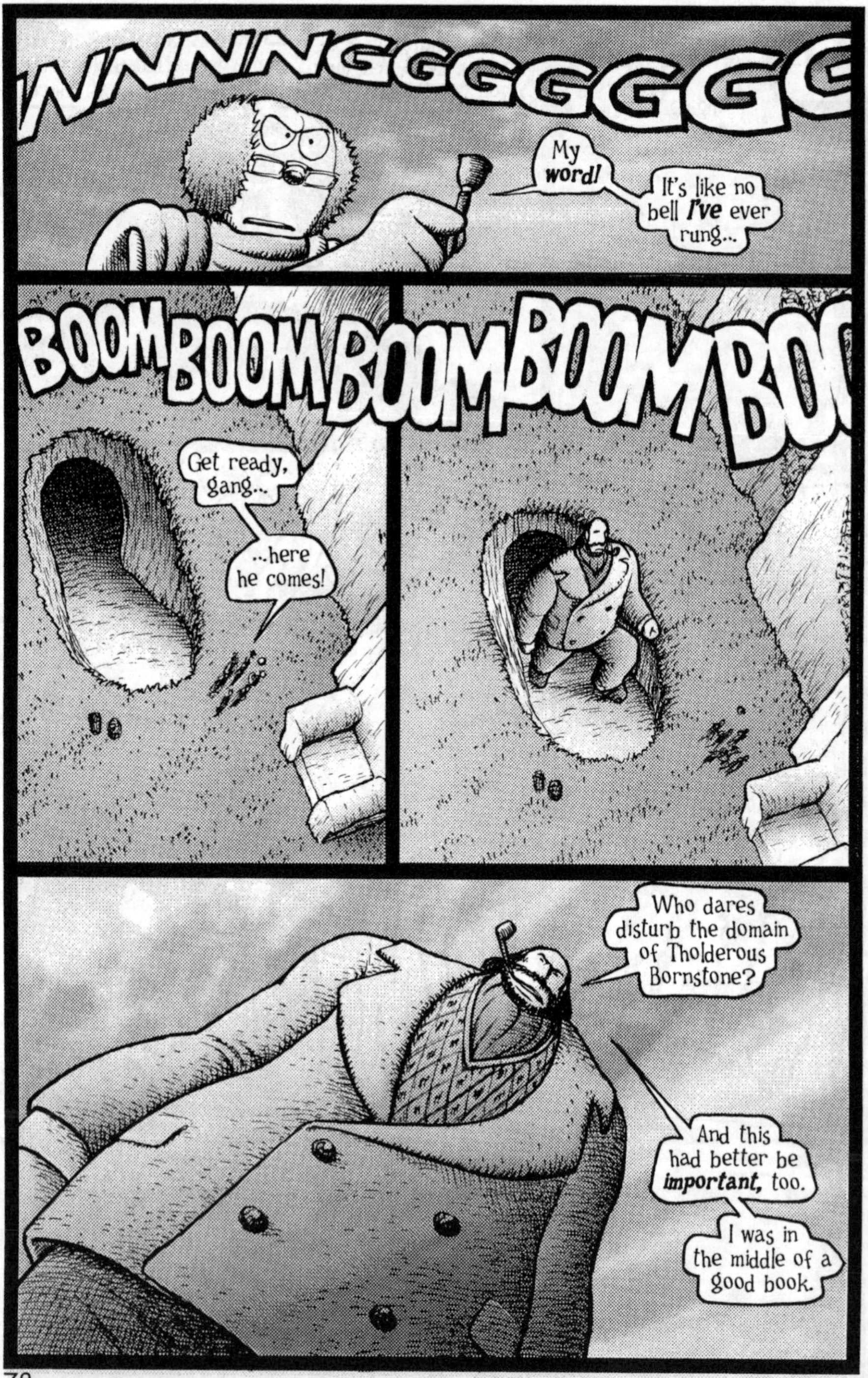
WNNNNGGGGGGG
My word!
It's like no bell I've ever rung...
BOOM BOOM BOOM BOOM BOO
Get ready, gang...
...here he comes!
Who dares disturb the domain of Tholderous Bornstone?
And this had better be important, too.
I was in the middle of a good book.

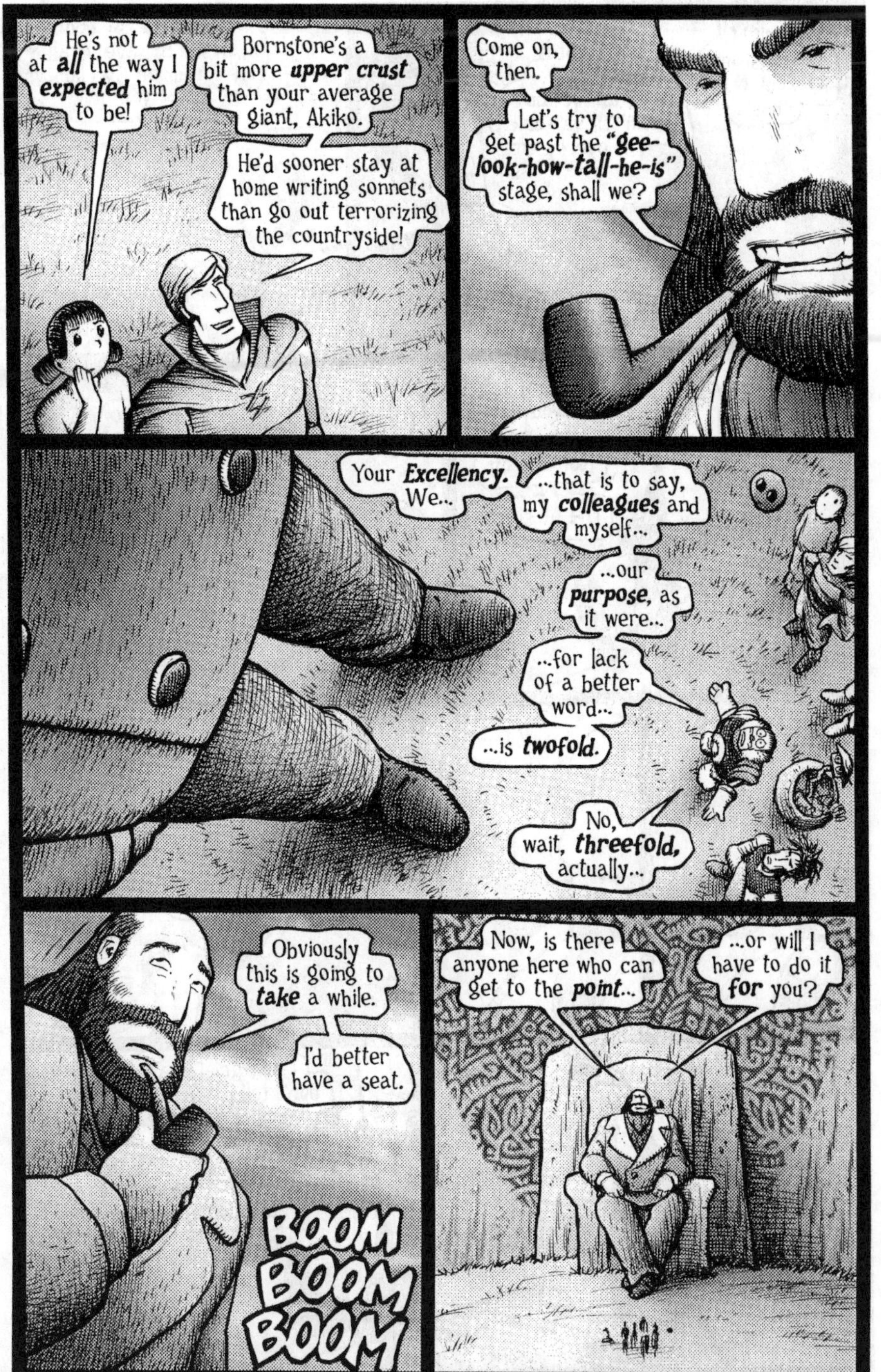
He's not at all the way I expected him to be!
Bornstone's a bit more upper crust than your average giant, Akiko.
He'd sooner stay at home writing sonnets than go out terrorizing the countryside!
Come on, then.
Let's try to get past the "gee-look-how-tall-he-is" stage, shall we?
Your Excellency. We...
...that is to say, my colleagues and myself...
...our purpose, as it were...
...for lack of a better word...
...is twofold.
No, wait, threefold, actually...
Obviously this is going to take a while.
I'd better have a seat.
BOOM BOOM BOOM
Now, is there anyone here who can get to the point...
...or will I have to do it for you?

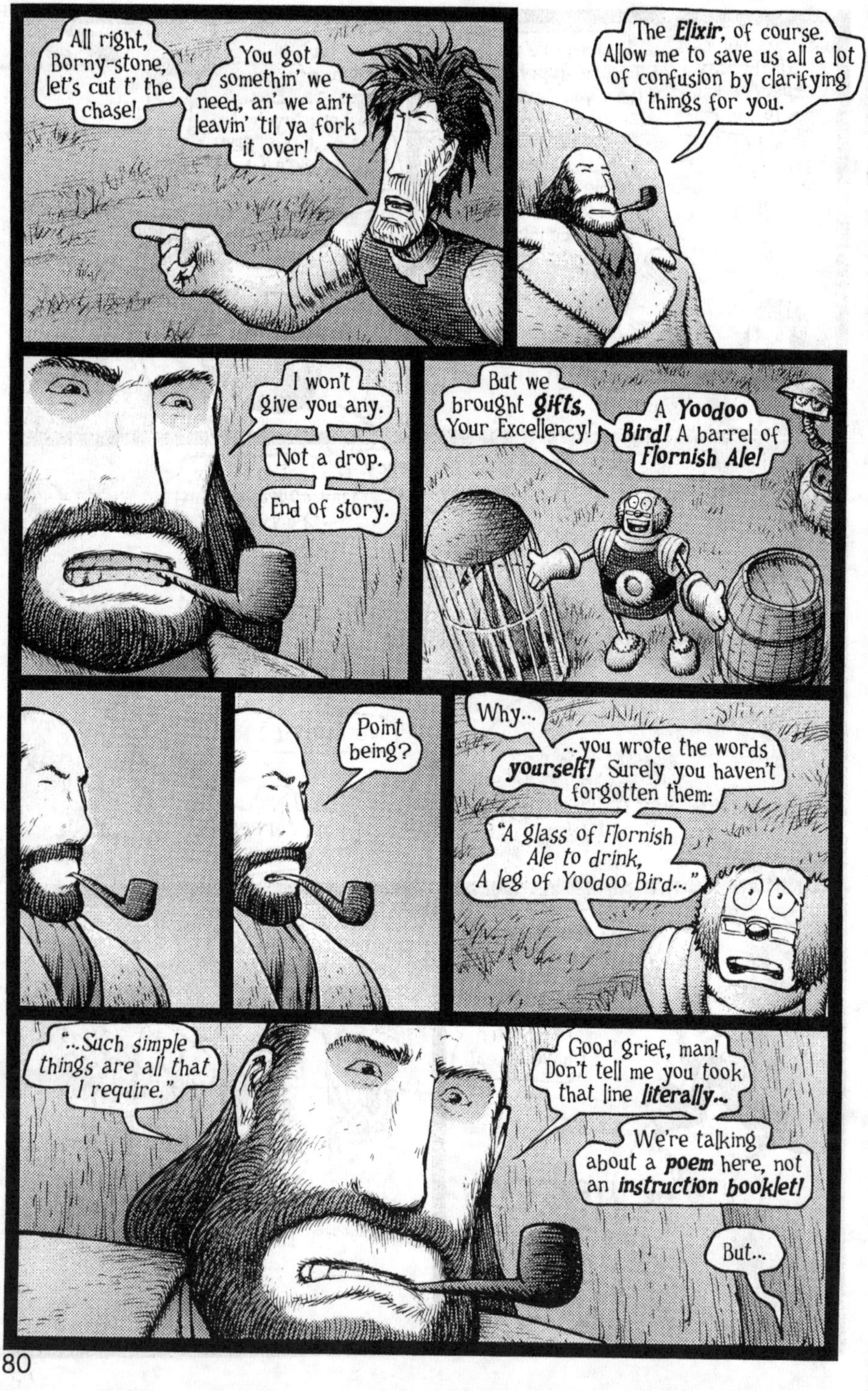
All right, Borny-stone, let's cut t' the chase!
You got somethin' we need, an' we ain't leavin' 'til ya fork it over!
The **Elixir**, of course. Allow me to save us all a lot of confusion by clarifying things for you.
I won't give you any.
Not a drop.
End of story.
But we brought **gifts**, Your Excellency!
A **Yoodoo Bird!** A barrel of **Flornish Ale!**
Point being?
Why...
...you wrote the words **yourself!** Surely you haven't forgotten them:
"A glass of Flornish Ale to drink, A leg of Yoodoo Bird..."
"...Such simple things are all that I require."
Good grief, man! Don't tell me you took that line **literally...**
We're talking about a **poem** here, not an **instruction booklet!**
But...

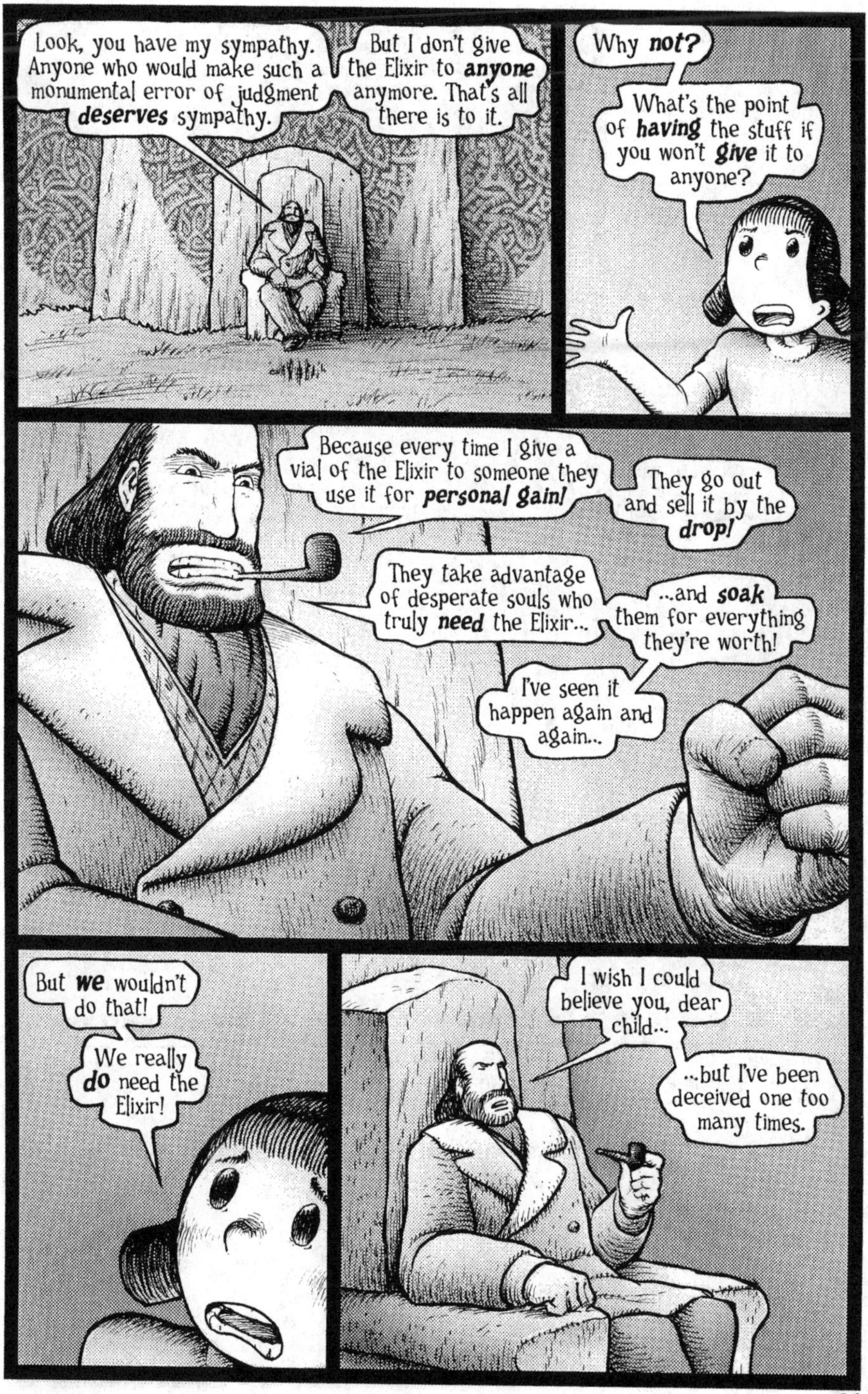
Look, you have my sympathy. Anyone who would make such a monumental error of judgment *deserves* sympathy.
But I don't give the Elixir to **anyone** anymore. That's all there is to it.
Why **not?**
What's the point of **having** the stuff if you won't **give** it to anyone?
Because every time I give a vial of the Elixir to someone they use it for **personal gain!**
They go out and sell it by the **drop!**
They take advantage of desperate souls who truly **need** the Elixir...
...and **soak** them for everything they're worth!
I've seen it happen again and again...
But **we** wouldn't do that!
We really **do** need the Elixir!
I wish I could believe you, dear child...
...but I've been deceived one too many times.

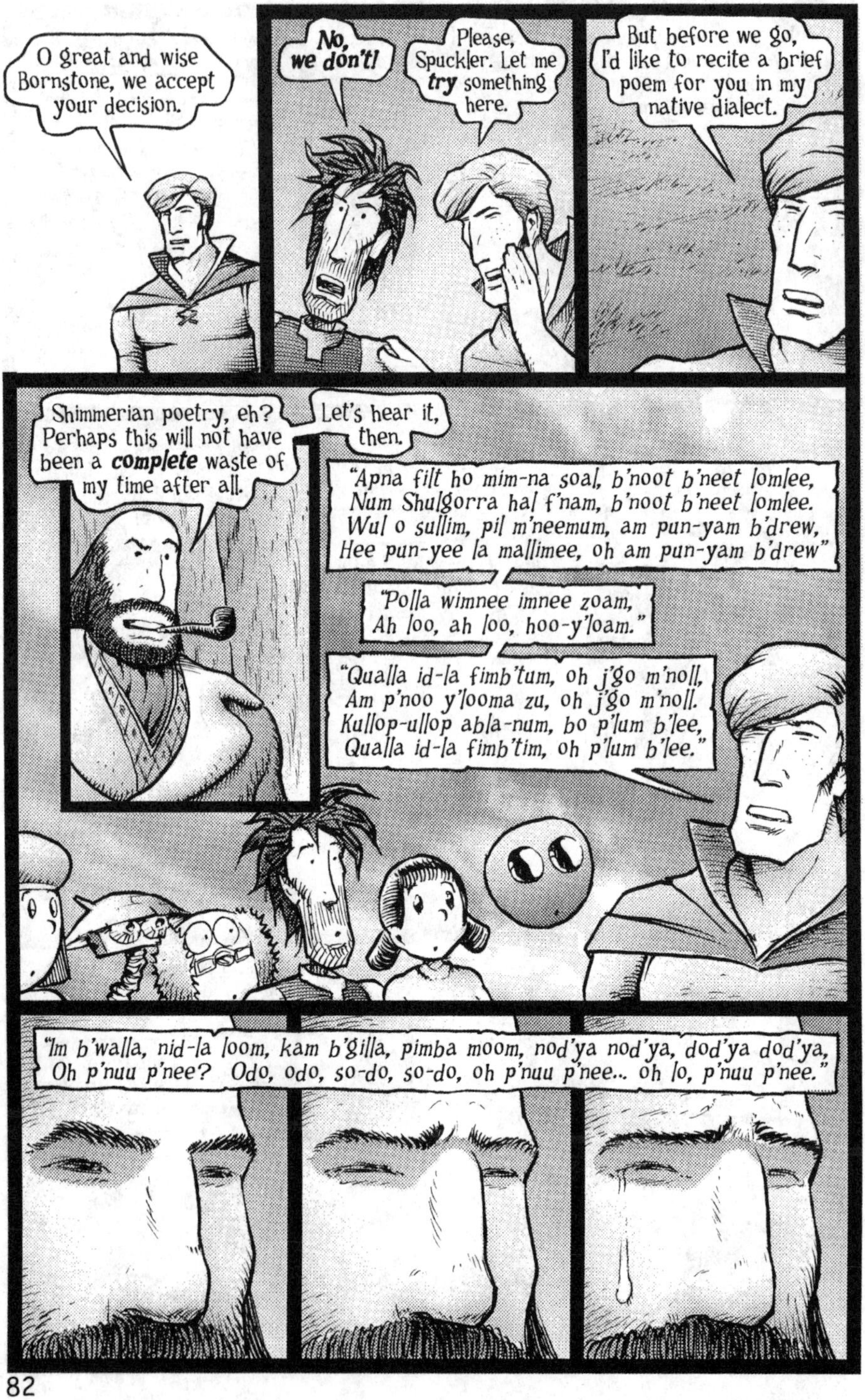

O great and wise Bornstone, we accept your decision.
No, we don't!
Please, Spuckler. Let me try something here.
But before we go, I'd like to recite a brief poem for you in my native dialect.
Shimmerian poetry, eh? Perhaps this will not have been a complete waste of my time after all.
Let's hear it, then.
"Apna filt ho mim-na soal, b'noot b'neet lomlee,
Num Shulgorra hal f'nam, b'noot b'neet lomlee.
Wul o sullim, pil m'neemum, am pun-yam b'drew,
Hee pun-yee la mallimee, oh am pun-yam b'drew"
"Polla wimnee imnee zoam,
Ah loo, ah loo, hoo-y'loam."
"Qualla id-la fimb'tum, oh j'go m'noll,
Am p'noo y'looma zu, oh j'go m'noll.
Kullop-ullop abla-num, bo p'lum b'lee,
Qualla id-la fimb'tim, oh p'lum b'lee."
"Im b'walla, nid-la loom, kam b'gilla, pimba moom, nod'ya nod'ya, dod'ya dod'ya,
Oh p'nuu p'nee? Odo, odo, so-do, so-do, oh p'nuu p'nee... oh lo, p'nuu p'nee."

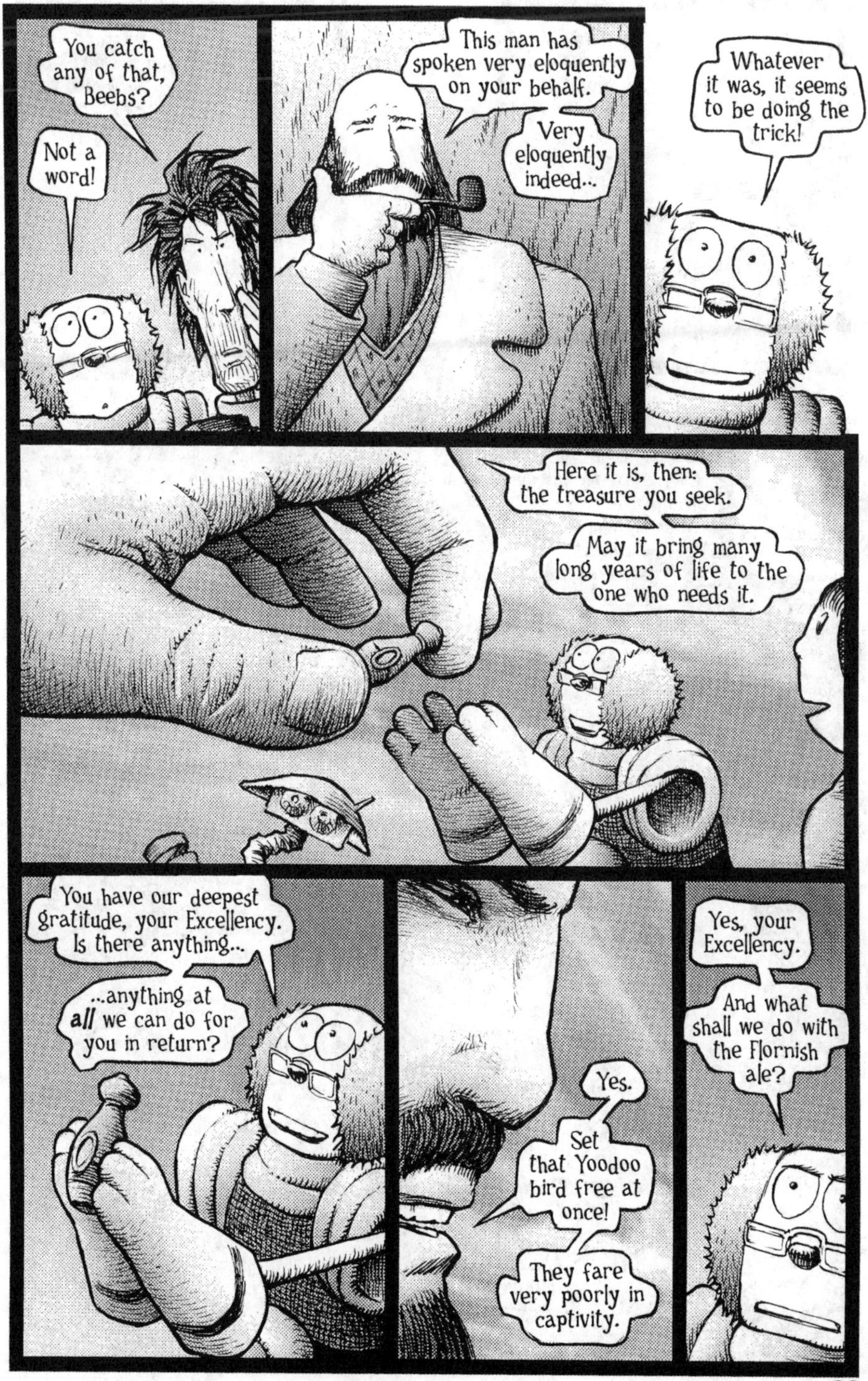
You catch any of that, Beebs?
Not a word!
This man has spoken very eloquently on your behalf.
Very eloquently indeed...
Whatever it was, it seems to be doing the trick!
Here it is, then: the treasure you seek.
May it bring many long years of life to the one who needs it.
You have our deepest gratitude, your Excellency. Is there anything...
...anything at all we can do for you in return?
Yes.
Set that Yoodoo bird free at once!
They fare very poorly in captivity.
Yes, your Excellency.
And what shall we do with the Flornish ale?

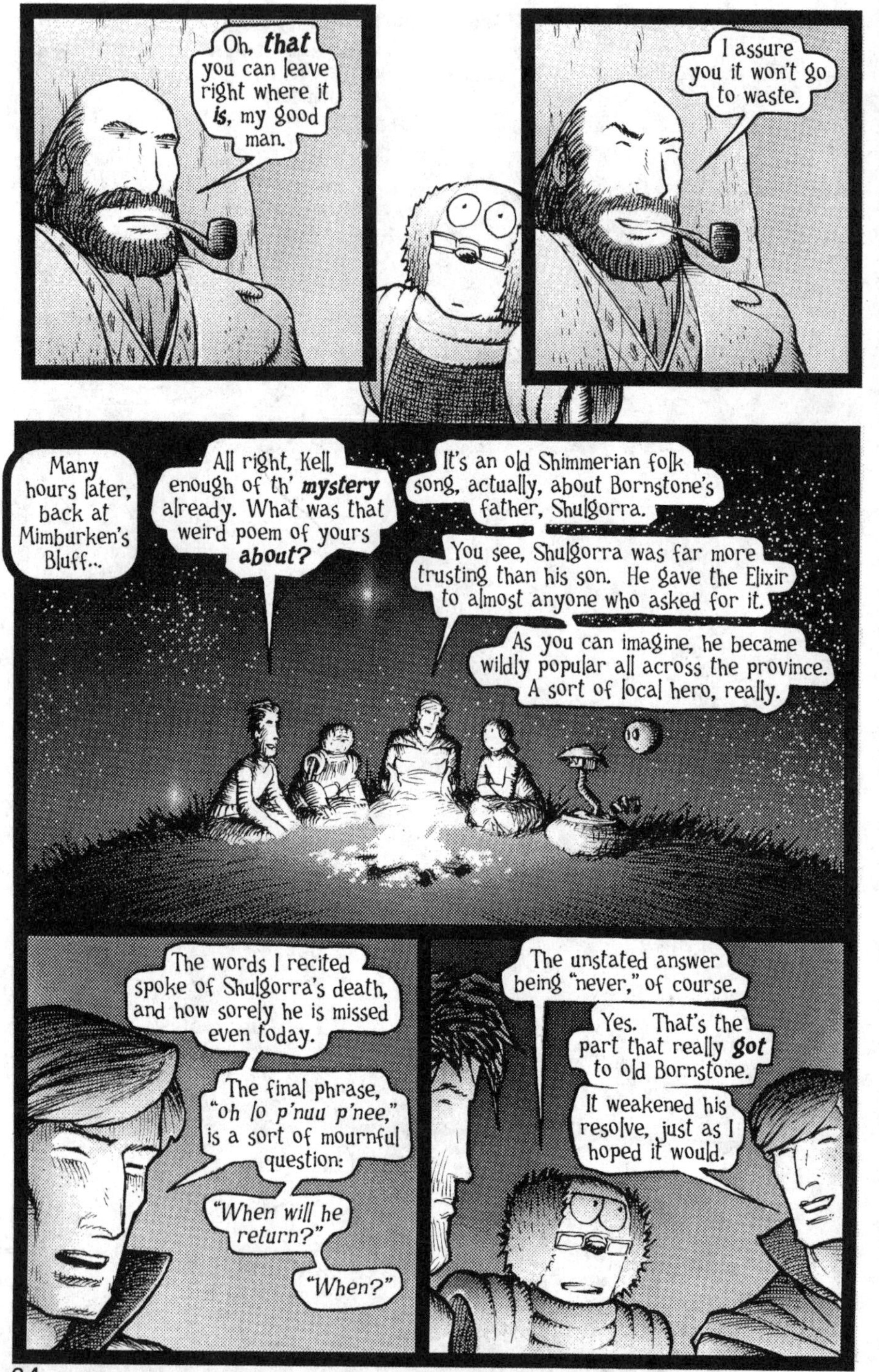
Oh, **that** you can leave right where it **is**, my good man.
I assure you it won't go to waste.
Many hours later, back at Mimburken's Bluff...
All right, Kell, enough of th' **mystery** already. What was that weird poem of yours **about?**
It's an old Shimmerian folk song, actually, about Bornstone's father, Shulgorra.
You see, Shulgorra was far more trusting than his son. He gave the Elixir to almost anyone who asked for it.
As you can imagine, he became wildly popular all across the province. A sort of local hero, really.
The words I recited spoke of Shulgorra's death, and how sorely he is missed even today.
The final phrase, "*oh lo p'nuu p'nee,*" is a sort of mournful question:
*"When will he return?"*
*"When?"*
The unstated answer being "never," of course.
Yes. That's the part that really **got** to old Bornstone.
It weakened his resolve, just as I hoped it would.

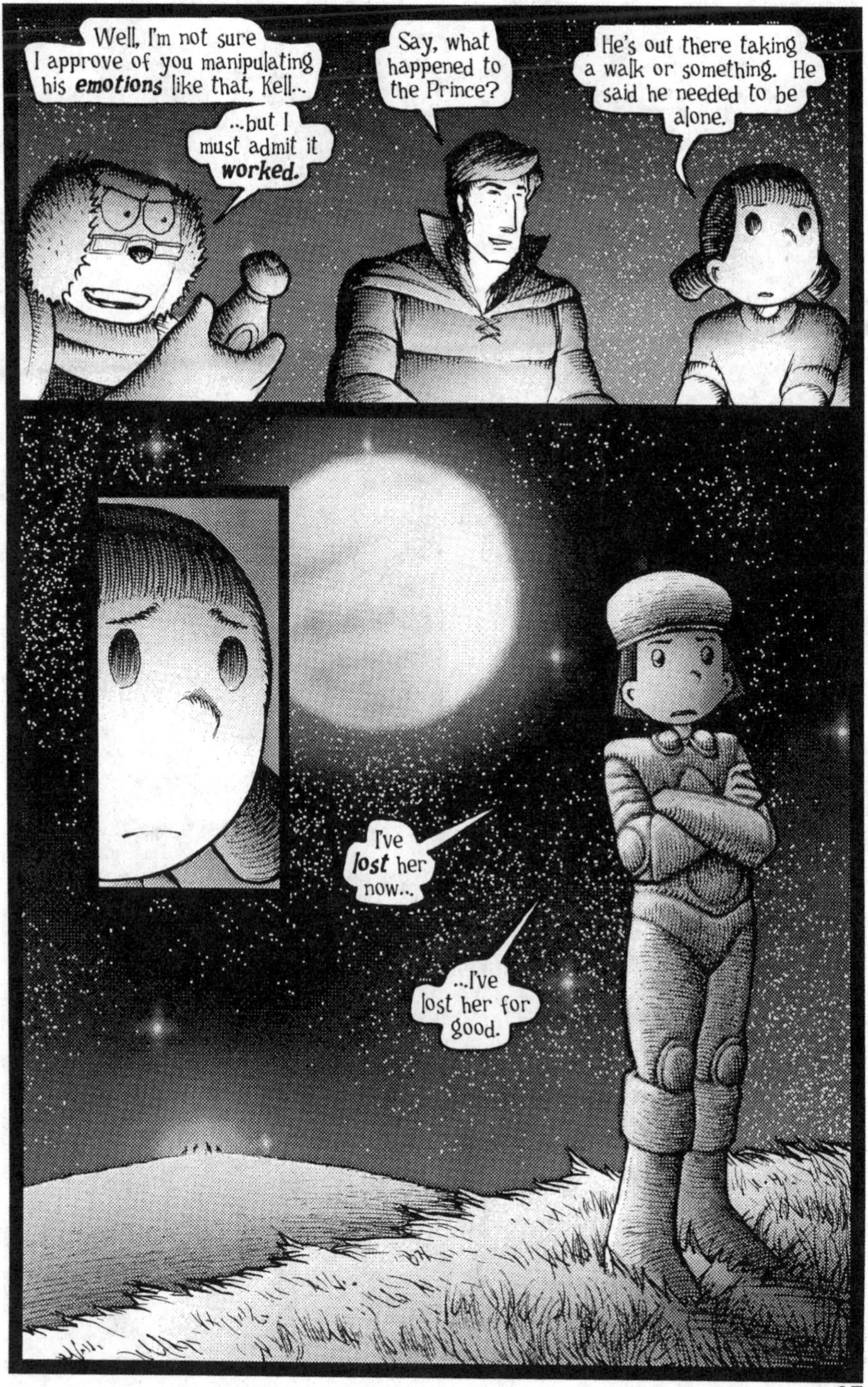
Well, I'm not sure I approve of you manipulating his **emotions** like that, Kell...
...but I must admit it ***worked.***
Say, what happened to the Prince?
He's out there taking a walk or something. He said he needed to be alone.
I've ***lost*** her now...
...I've lost her for good.

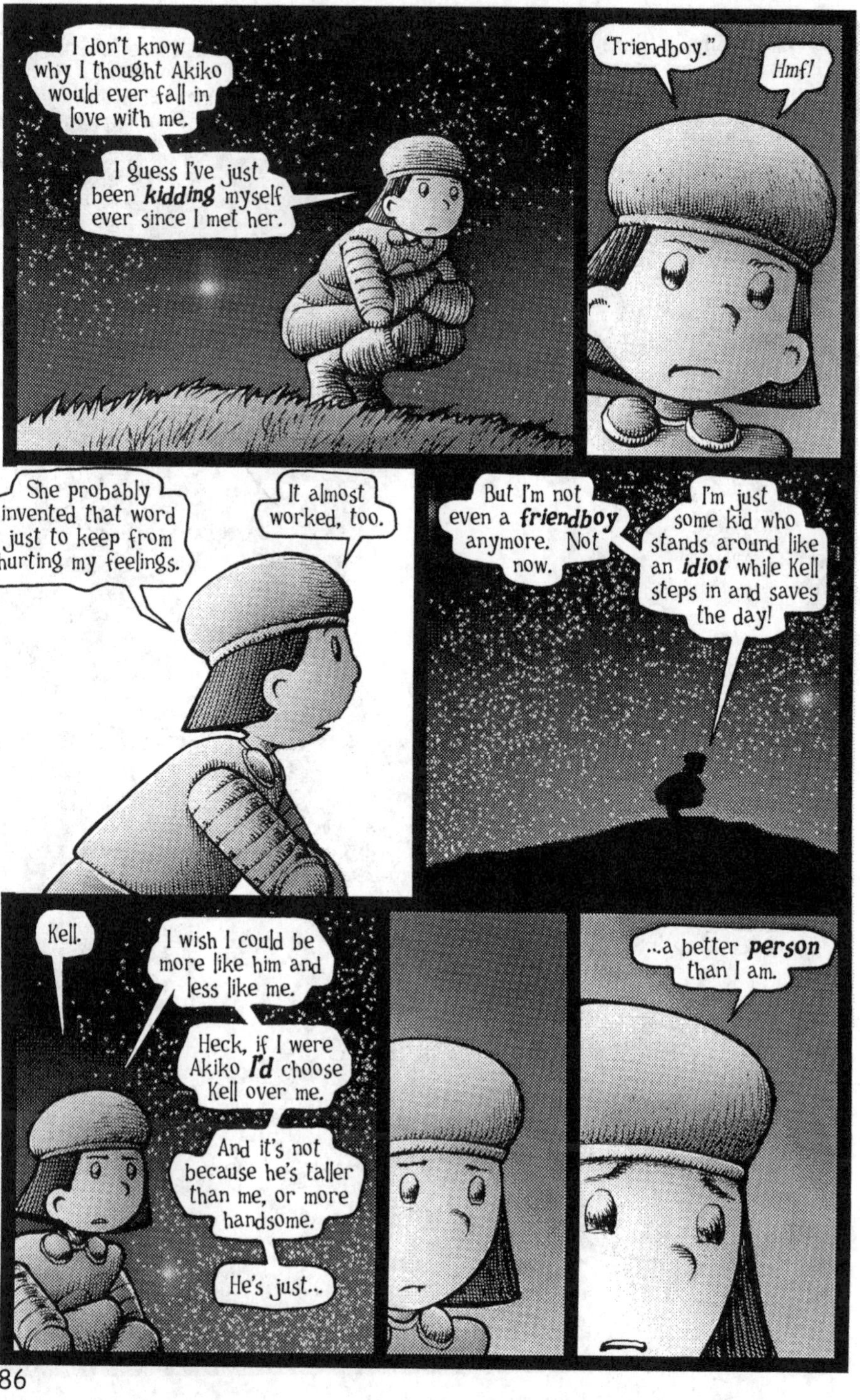
I don't know why I thought Akiko would ever fall in love with me.
I guess I've just been *kidding* myself ever since I met her.
"Friendboy."
Hmf!
She probably invented that word just to keep from hurting my feelings.
It almost worked, too.
But I'm not even a *friendboy* anymore. Not now.
I'm just some kid who stands around like an *idiot* while Kell steps in and saves the day!
Kell.
I wish I could be more like him and less like me.
Heck, if I were Akiko *I'd* choose Kell over me.
And it's not because he's taller than me, or more handsome.
He's just...
...a better *person* than I am.

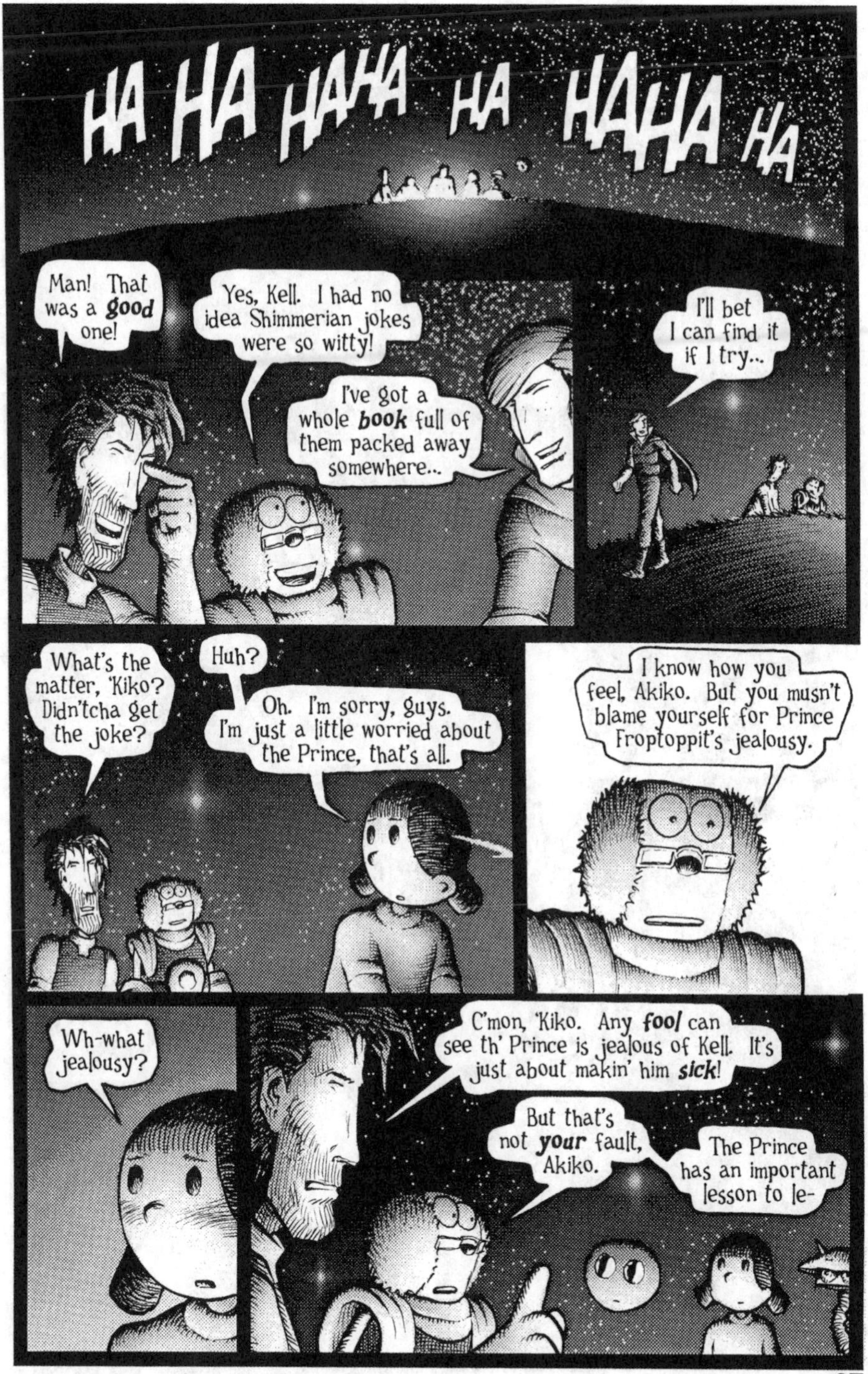
HA HA HAHA HA HAHA HA
Man! That was a good one!
Yes, Kell. I had no idea Shimmerian jokes were so witty!
I've got a whole book full of them packed away somewhere...
I'll bet I can find it if I try...
What's the matter, 'Kiko? Didn'tcha get the joke?
Huh?
Oh. I'm sorry, guys. I'm just a little worried about the Prince, that's all.
I know how you feel, Akiko. But you musn't blame yourself for Prince Froptoppit's jealousy.
Wh-what jealousy?
C'mon, 'Kiko. Any fool can see th' Prince is jealous of Kell. It's just about makin' him sick!
But that's not your fault, Akiko.
The Prince has an important lesson to le-

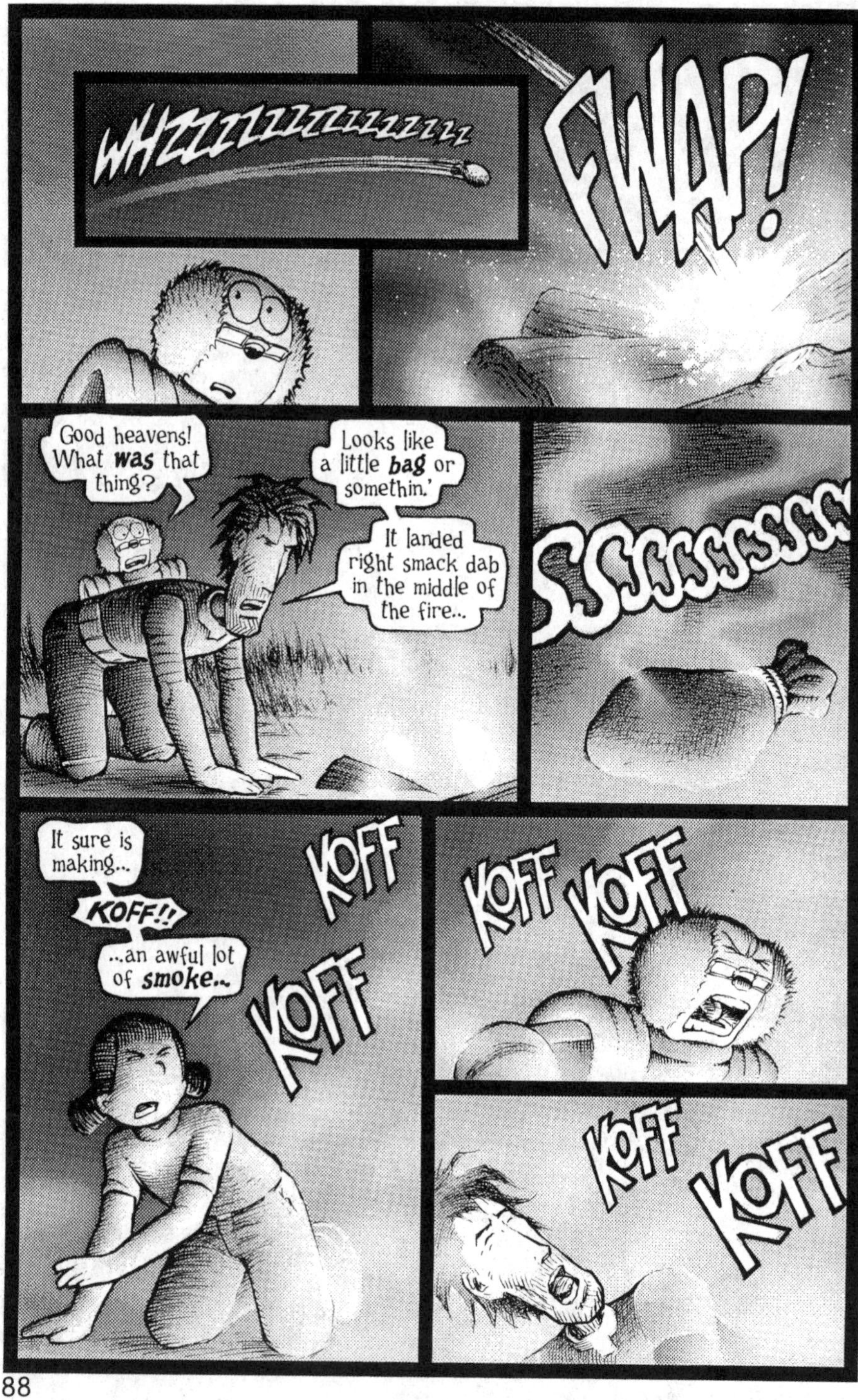
WHZZZZZZZZZZZZZZZZZZZ
FWAP!
Good heavens! What **was** that thing?
Looks like a little **bag** or somethin.'
It landed right smack dab in the middle of the fire...
SSSSSSSSSSSS
It sure is making...
KOFF!!
...an awful lot of **smoke**...
KOFF
KOFF
KOFF
KOFF
KOFF
KOFF

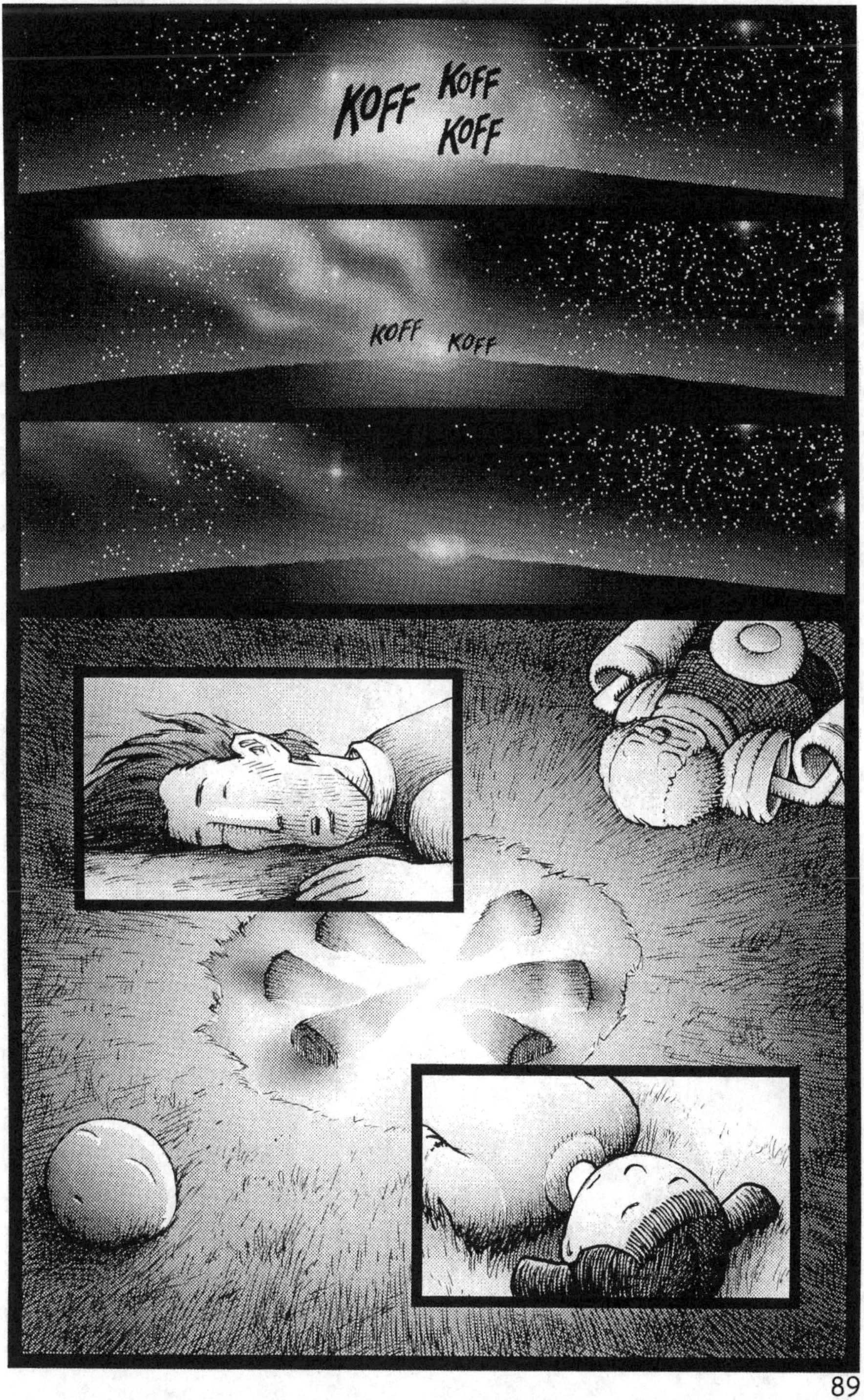
KOFF KOFF
KOFF
KOFF KOFF

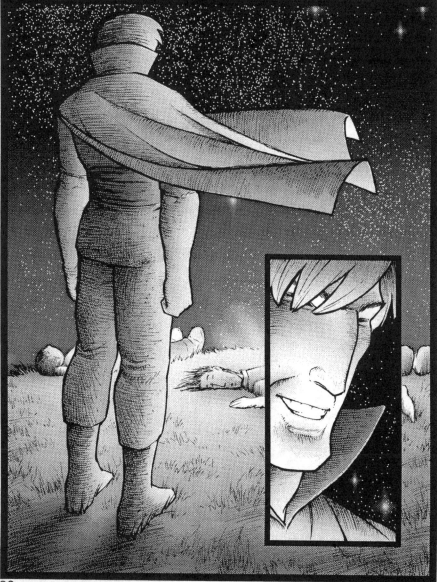

# BORNSTONE'S ELIXIR

*Chapter 6*

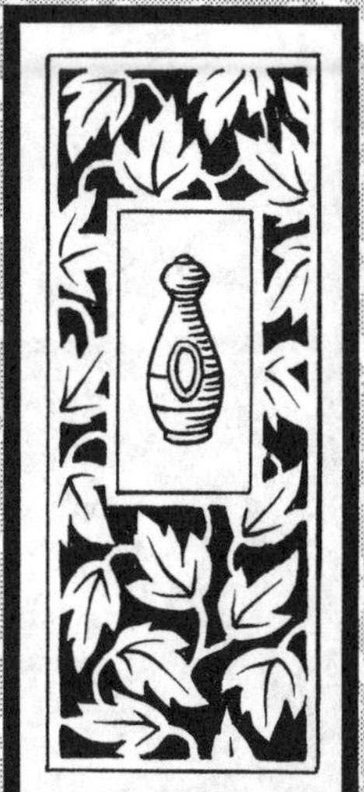

## A Better Understanding

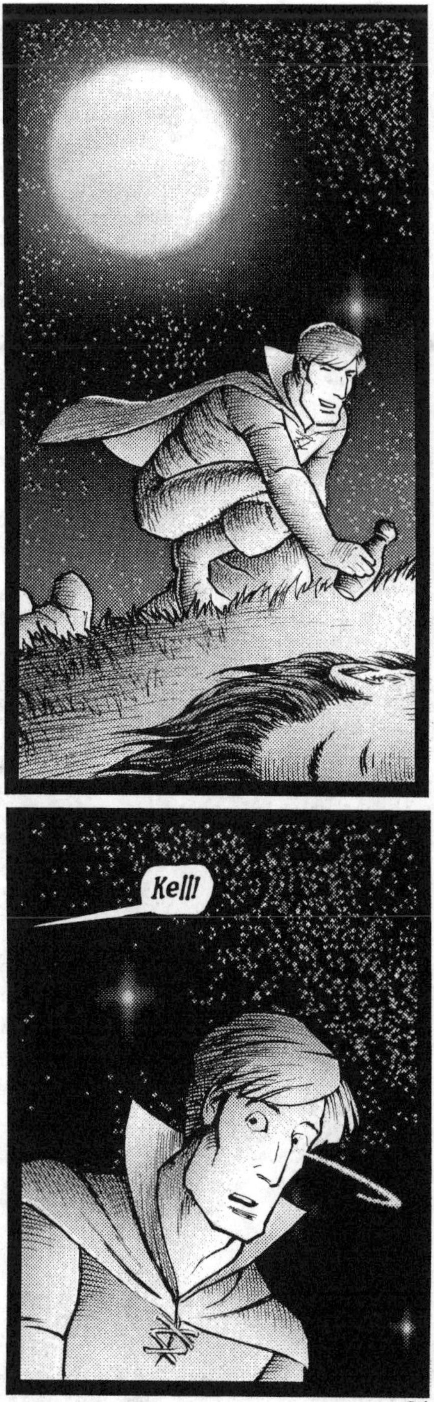
Kell!

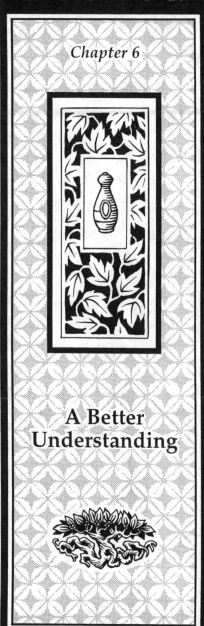

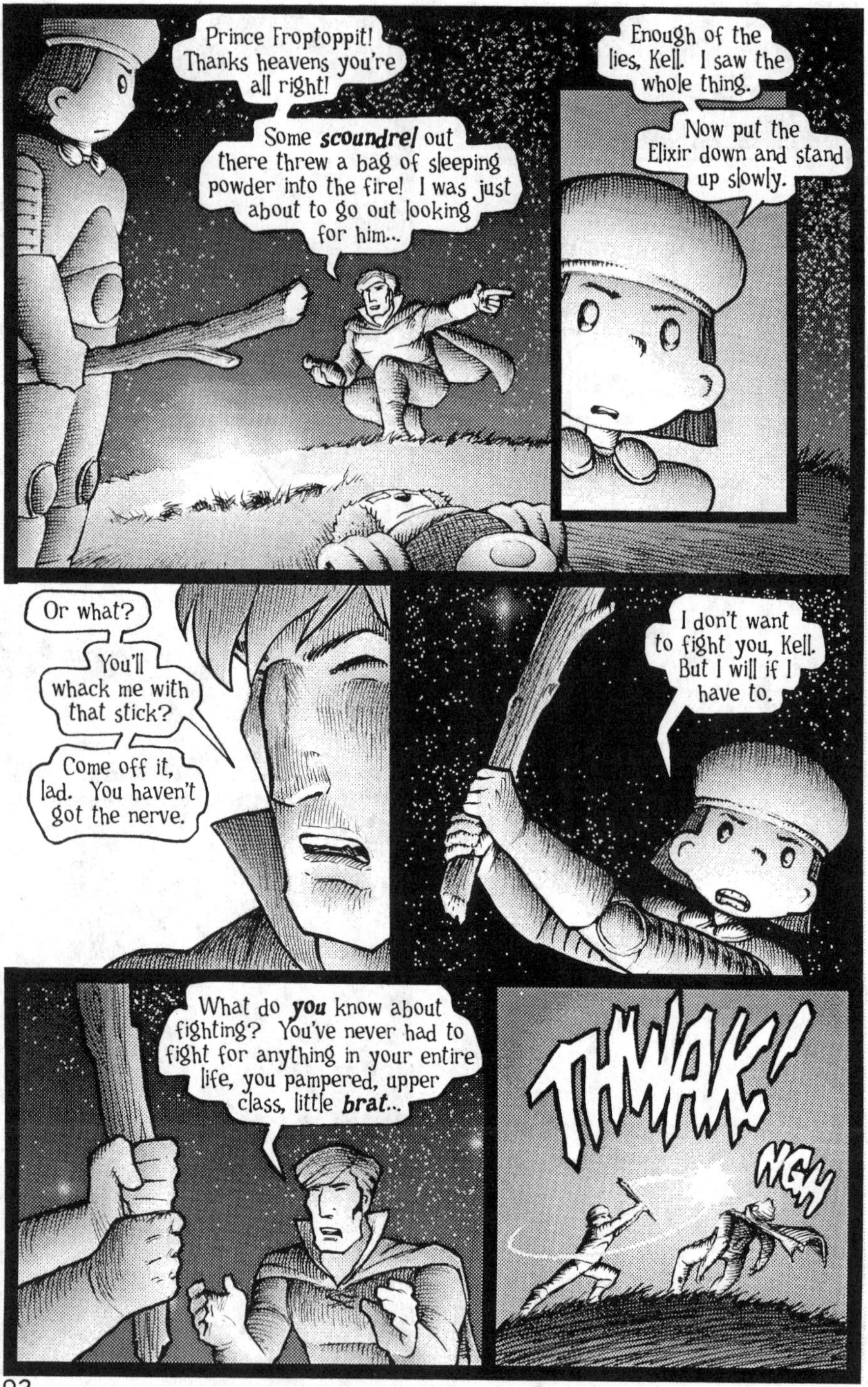

Prince Froptoppit! Thanks heavens you're all right!
Some scoundrel out there threw a bag of sleeping powder into the fire! I was just about to go out looking for him..
Enough of the lies, Kell. I saw the whole thing.
Now put the Elixir down and stand up slowly.
Or what?
You'll whack me with that stick?
Come off it, lad. You haven't got the nerve.
I don't want to fight you, Kell. But I will if I have to.
What do you know about fighting? You've never had to fight for anything in your entire life, you pampered, upper class, little brat..
THWAK!
NGH

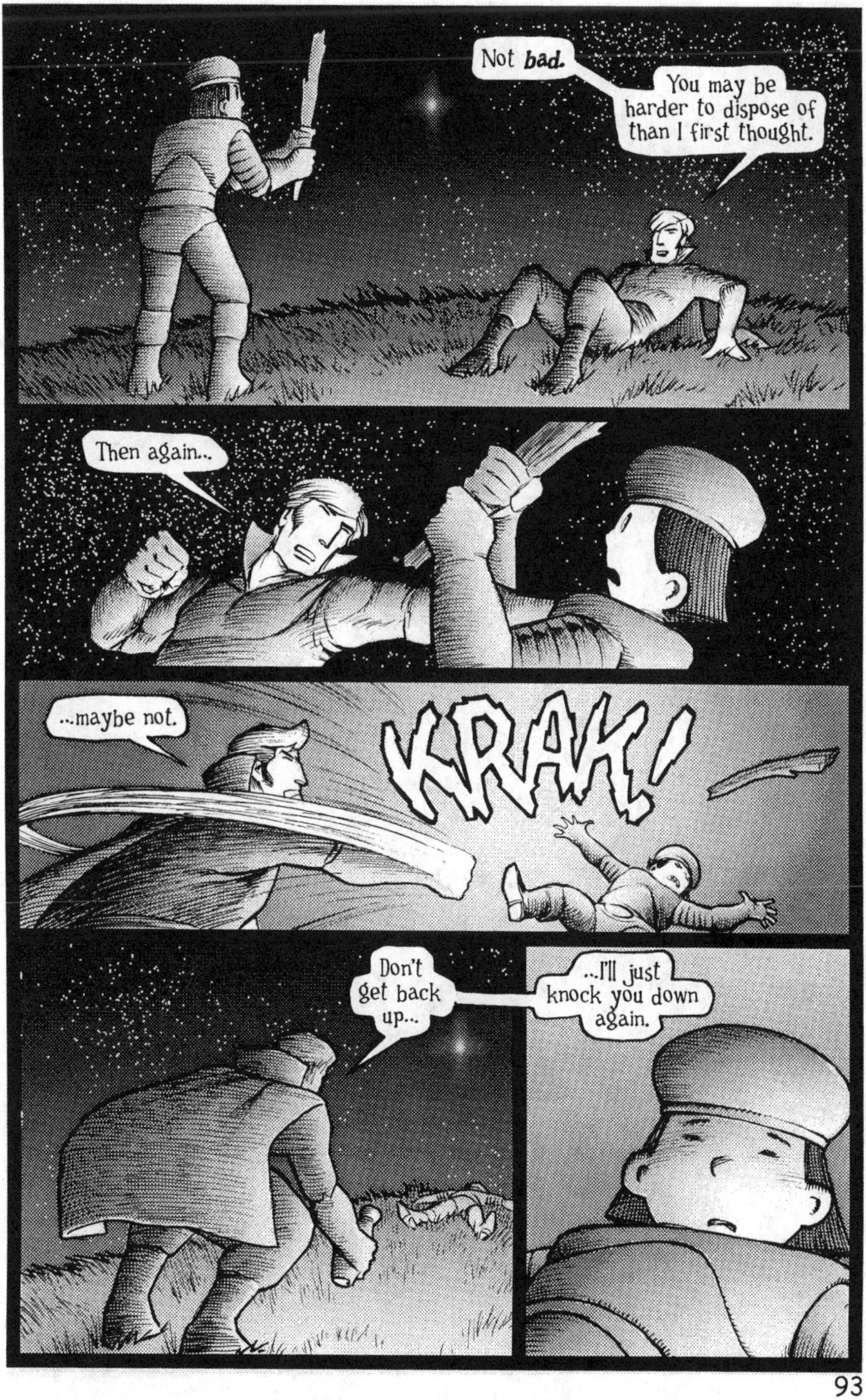
Not bad.
You may be harder to dispose of than I first thought.
Then again...
...maybe not.
KRAK!
Don't get back up...
...I'll just knock you down again.

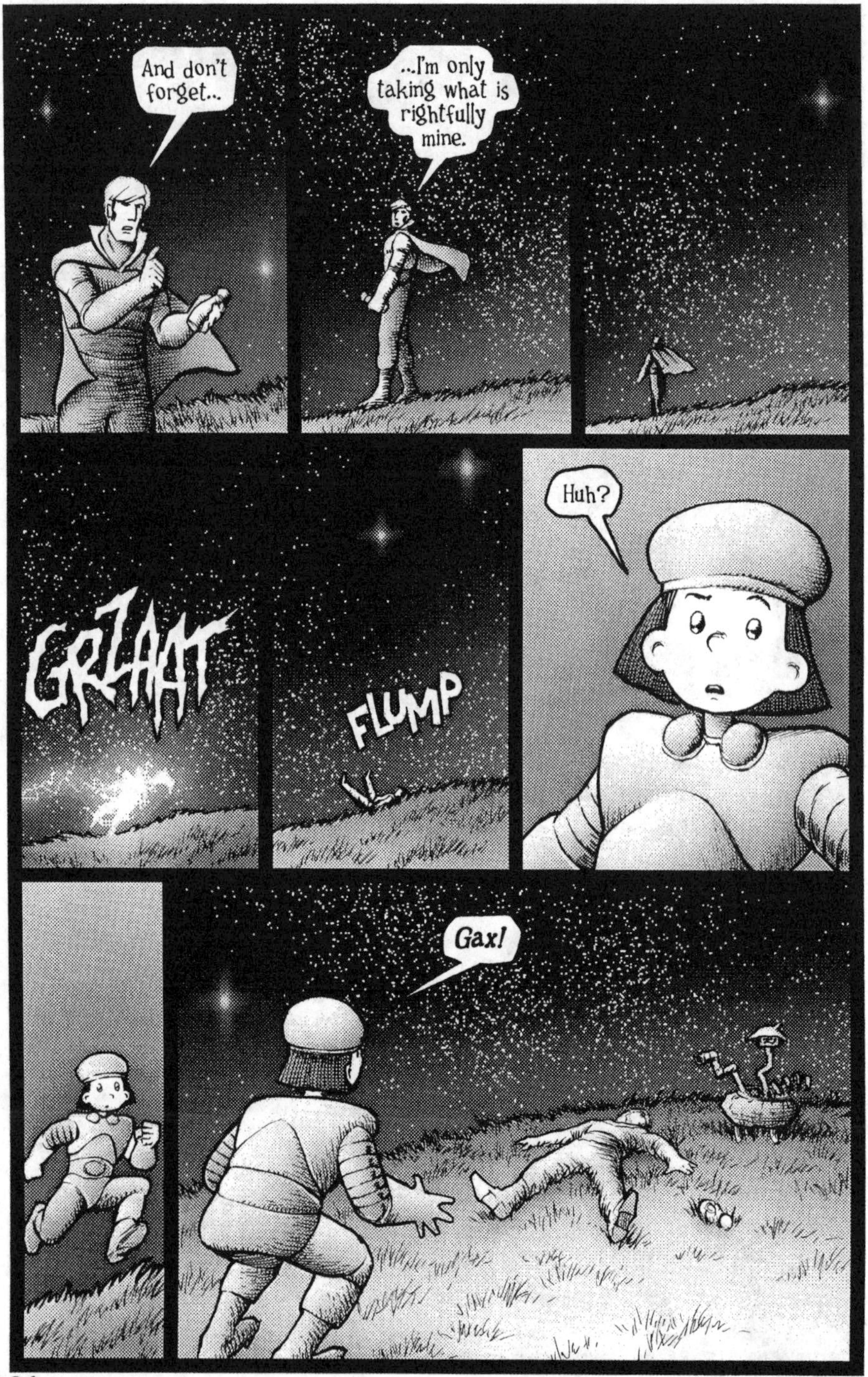
And don't forget...
...I'm only taking what is rightfully mine.
GRZAAT
FLUMP
Huh?
Gax!

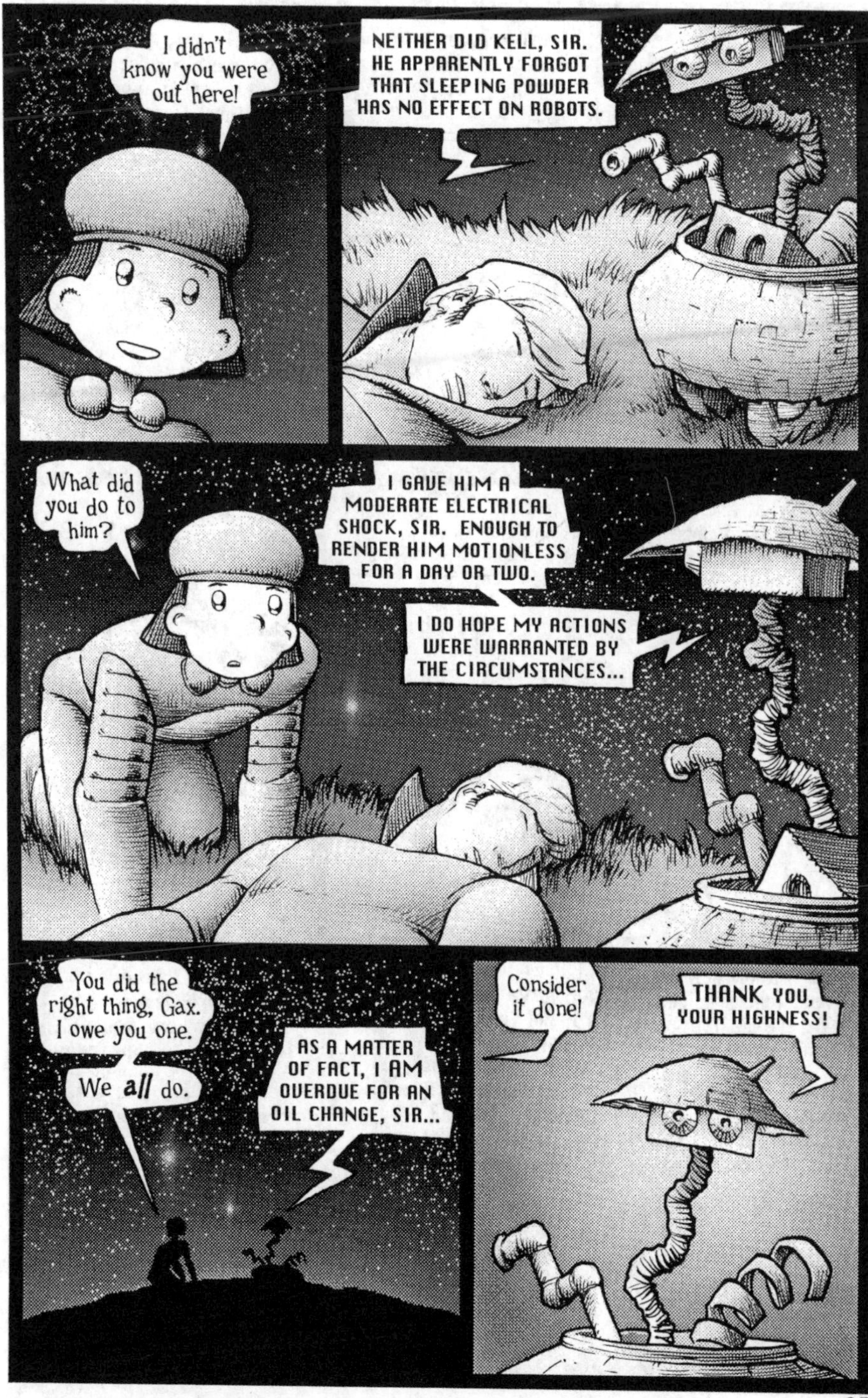
I didn't know you were out here!
NEITHER DID KELL, SIR. HE APPARENTLY FORGOT THAT SLEEPING POWDER HAS NO EFFECT ON ROBOTS.
What did you do to him?
I GAVE HIM A MODERATE ELECTRICAL SHOCK, SIR. ENOUGH TO RENDER HIM MOTIONLESS FOR A DAY OR TWO.
I DO HOPE MY ACTIONS WERE WARRANTED BY THE CIRCUMSTANCES...
You did the right thing, Gax. I owe you one.
We all do.
AS A MATTER OF FACT, I AM OVERDUE FOR AN OIL CHANGE, SIR...
Consider it done!
THANK YOU, YOUR HIGHNESS!

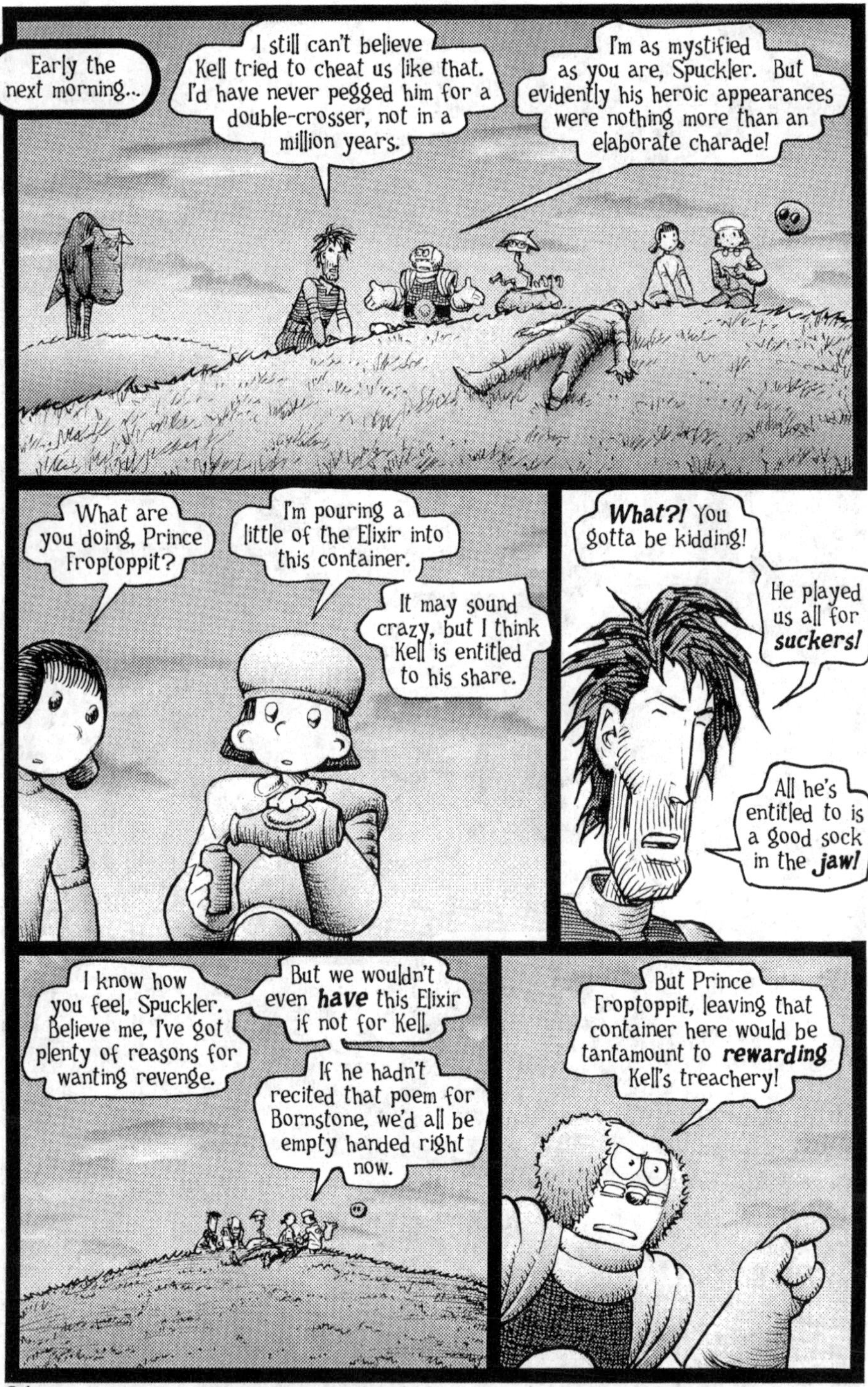

Early the next morning...
I still can't believe Kell tried to cheat us like that. I'd have never pegged him for a double-crosser, not in a million years.
I'm as mystified as you are, Spuckler. But evidently his heroic appearances were nothing more than an elaborate charade!
What are you doing, Prince Froptoppit?
I'm pouring a little of the Elixir into this container.
It may sound crazy, but I think Kell is entitled to his share.
What?! You gotta be kidding!
He played us all for suckers!
All he's entitled to is a good sock in the jaw!
I know how you feel, Spuckler. Believe me, I've got plenty of reasons for wanting revenge.
But we wouldn't even have this Elixir if not for Kell.
If he hadn't recited that poem for Bornstone, we'd all be empty handed right now.
But Prince Froptoppit, leaving that container here would be tantamount to rewarding Kell's treachery!

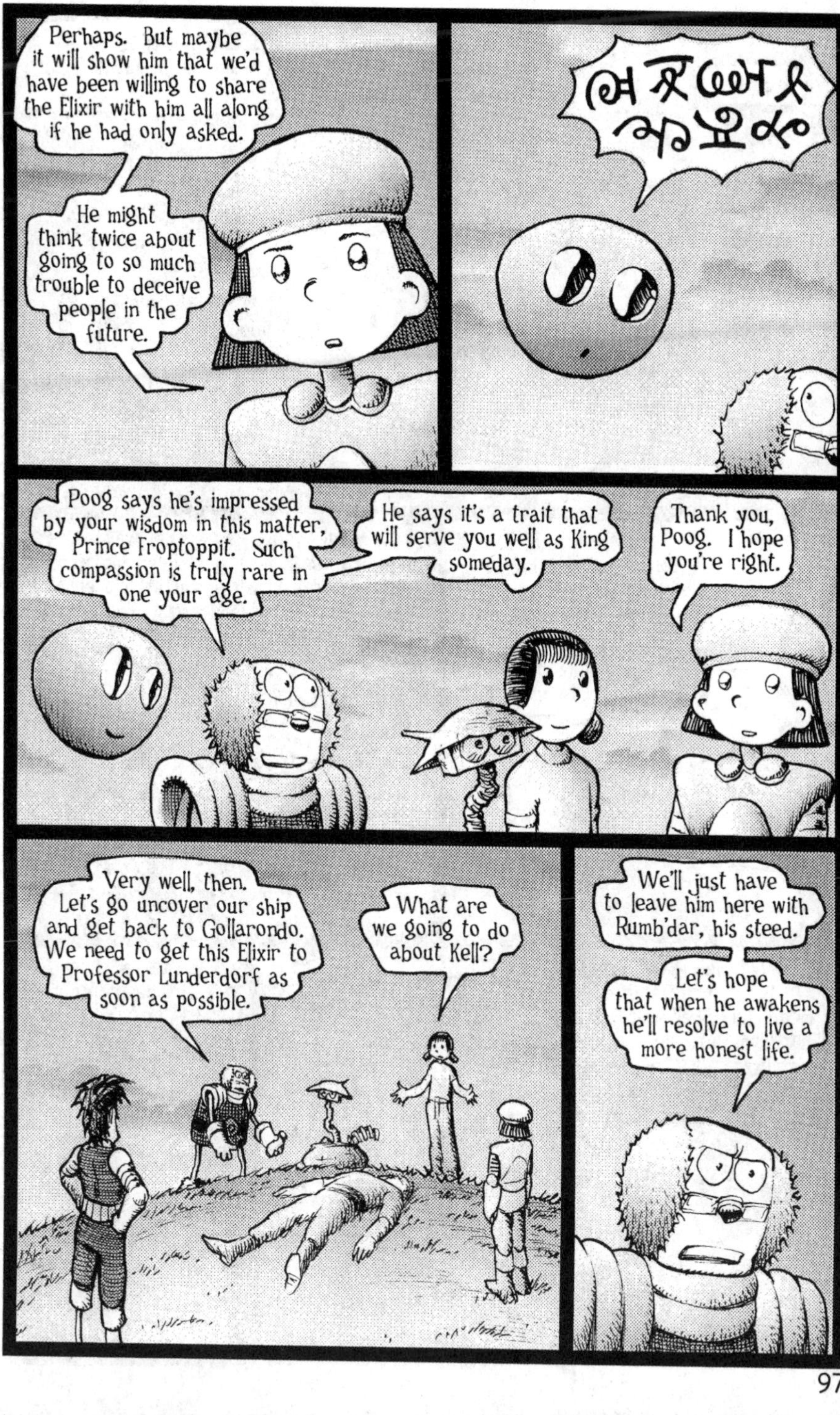
Perhaps. But maybe it will show him that we'd have been willing to share the Elixir with him all along if he had only asked.
He might think twice about going to so much trouble to deceive people in the future.
Poog says he's impressed by your wisdom in this matter, Prince Froptoppit. Such compassion is truly rare in one your age.
He says it's a trait that will serve you well as King someday.
Thank you, Poog. I hope you're right.
Very well, then. Let's go uncover our ship and get back to Gollarondo. We need to get this Elixir to Professor Lunderdorf as soon as possible.
What are we going to do about Kell?
We'll just have to leave him here with Rumb'dar, his steed.
Let's hope that when he awakens he'll resolve to live a more honest life.

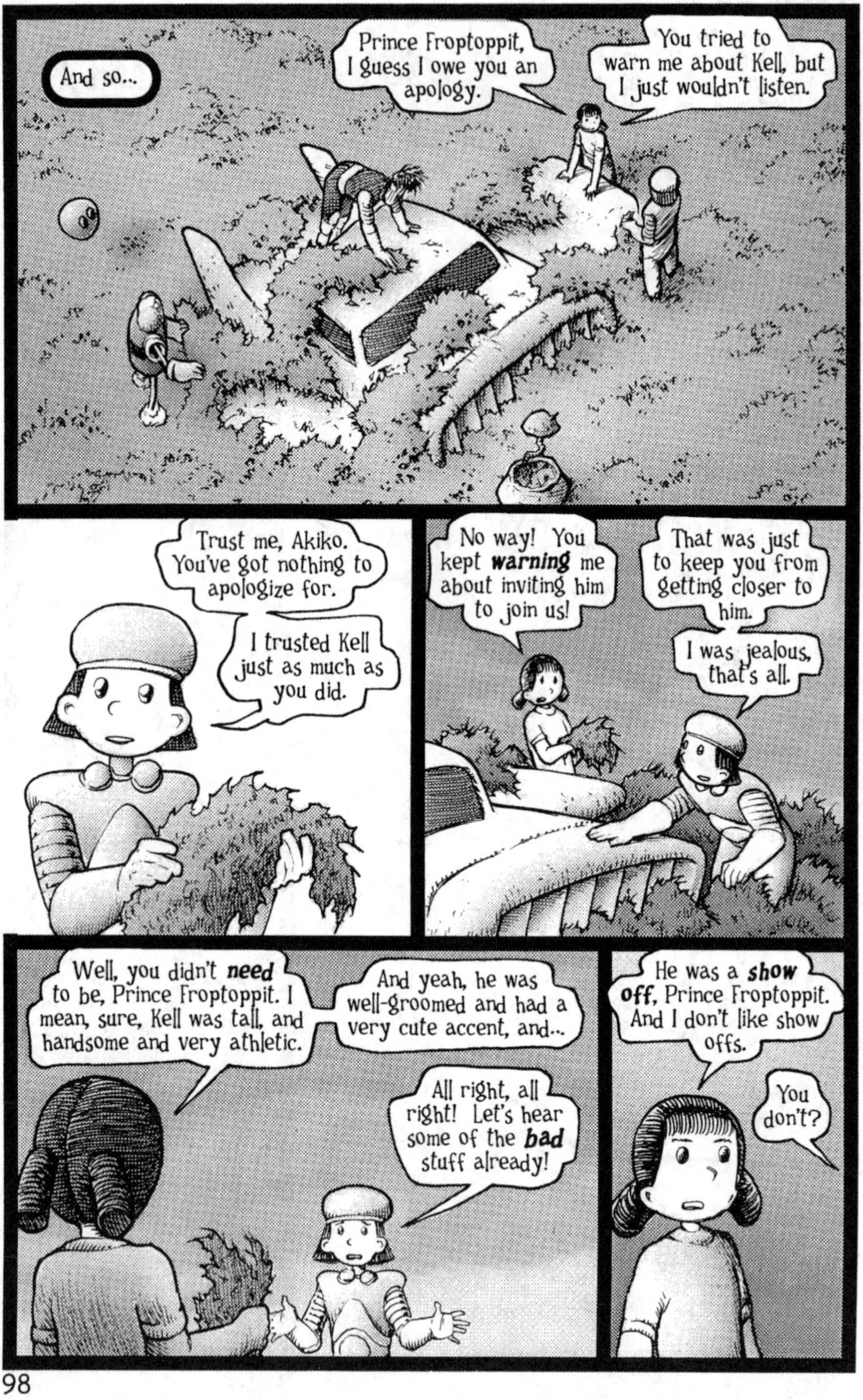
And so...
Prince Froptoppit, I guess I owe you an apology.
You tried to warn me about Kell, but I just wouldn't listen.
Trust me, Akiko. You've got nothing to apologize for.
I trusted Kell just as much as you did.
No way! You kept **warning** me about inviting him to join us!
That was just to keep you from getting closer to him.
I was jealous, that's all.
Well, you didn't **need** to be, Prince Froptoppit. I mean, sure, Kell was tall, and handsome and very athletic.
And yeah, he was well-groomed and had a very cute accent, and...
All right, all right! Let's hear some of the **bad** stuff already!
He was a **show off**, Prince Froptoppit. And I don't like show offs.
You don't?

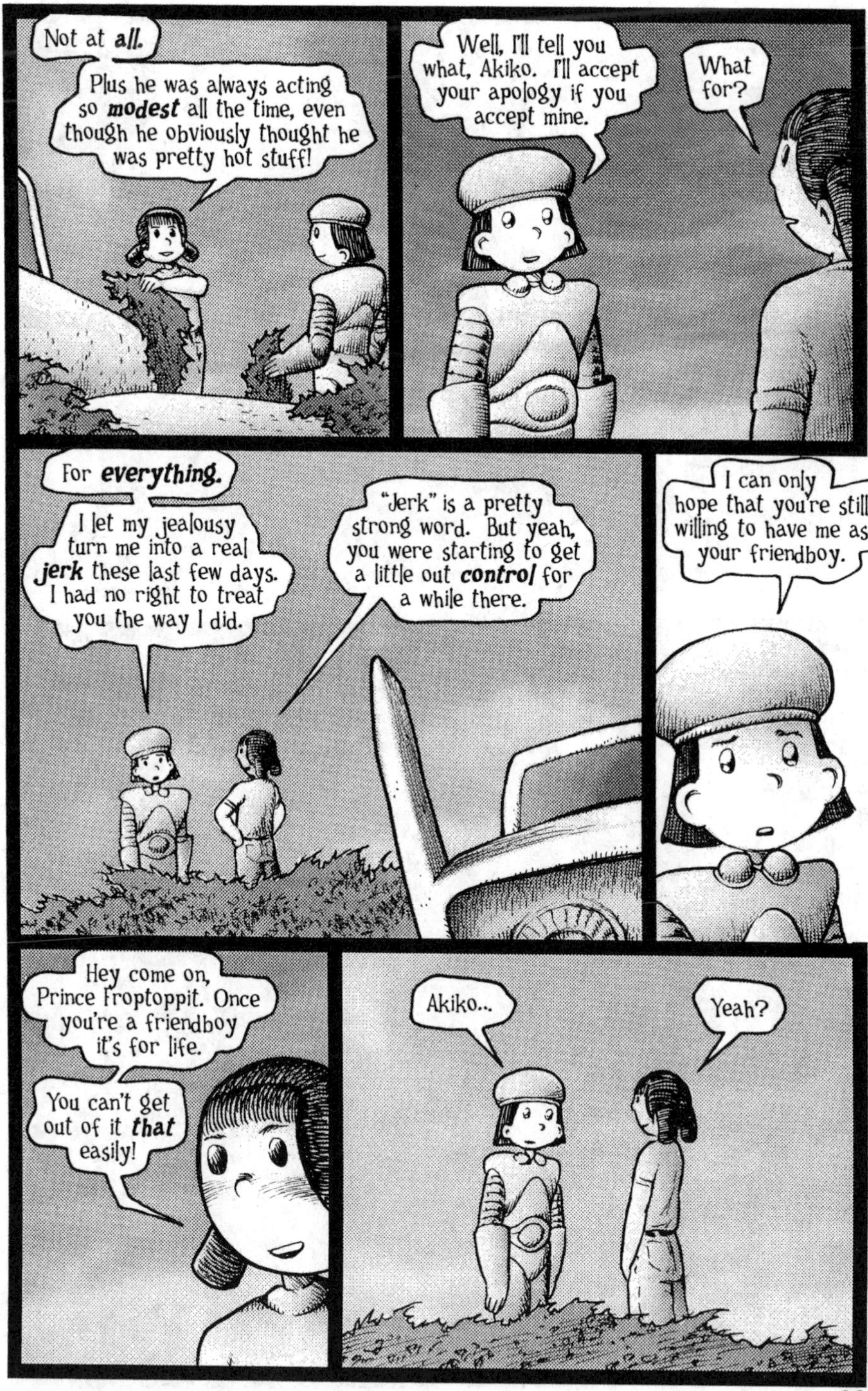
Not at **all.**
Plus he was always acting so **modest** all the time, even though he obviously thought he was pretty hot stuff!
Well, I'll tell you what, Akiko. I'll accept your apology if you accept mine.
What for?
For **everything.**
I let my jealousy turn me into a real **jerk** these last few days. I had no right to treat you the way I did.
"Jerk" is a pretty strong word. But yeah, you were starting to get a little out **control** for a while there.
I can only hope that you're still willing to have me as your friendboy.
Hey come on, Prince Froptoppit. Once you're a friendboy it's for life.
You can't get out of it **that** easily!
Akiko...
Yeah?

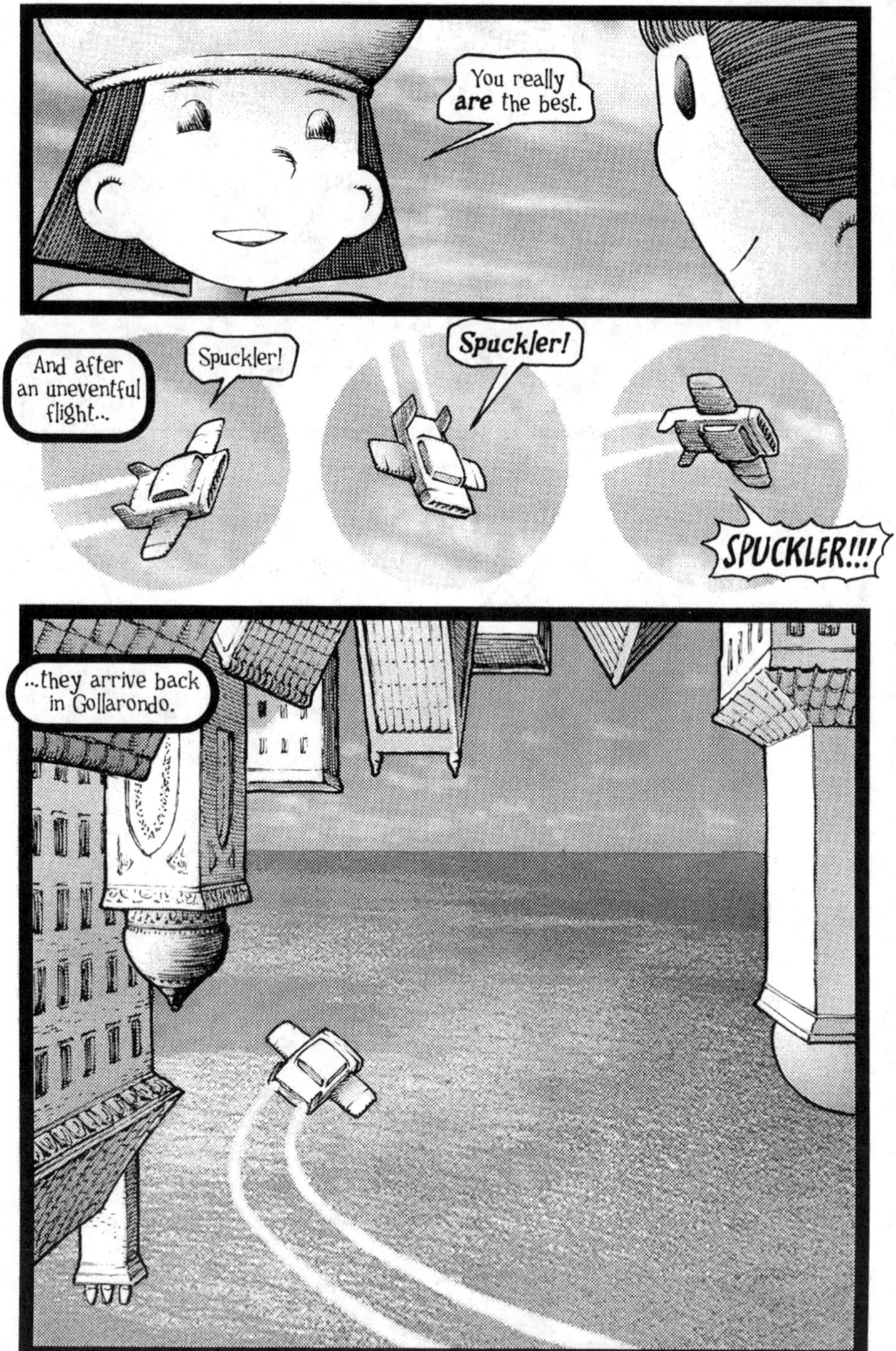
You really **are** the best.
And after an uneventful flight...
Spuckler!
Spuckler!
SPUCKLER!!!
...they arrive back in Gollarondo.

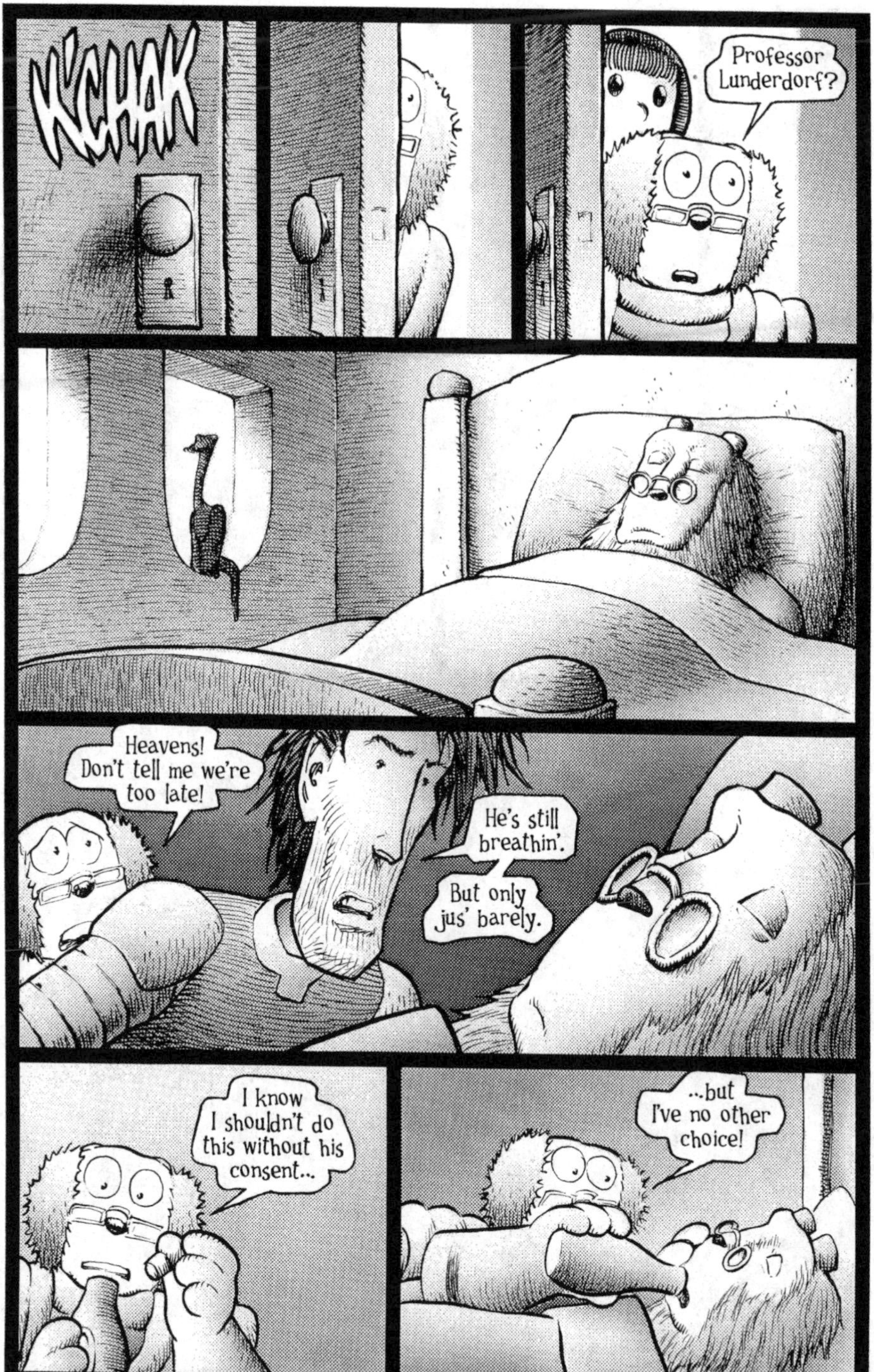
K'CHAK
Professor Lunderdorf?
Heavens! Don't tell me we're too late!
He's still breathin'.
But only jus' barely.
I know I shouldn't do this without his consent...
...but I've no other choice!

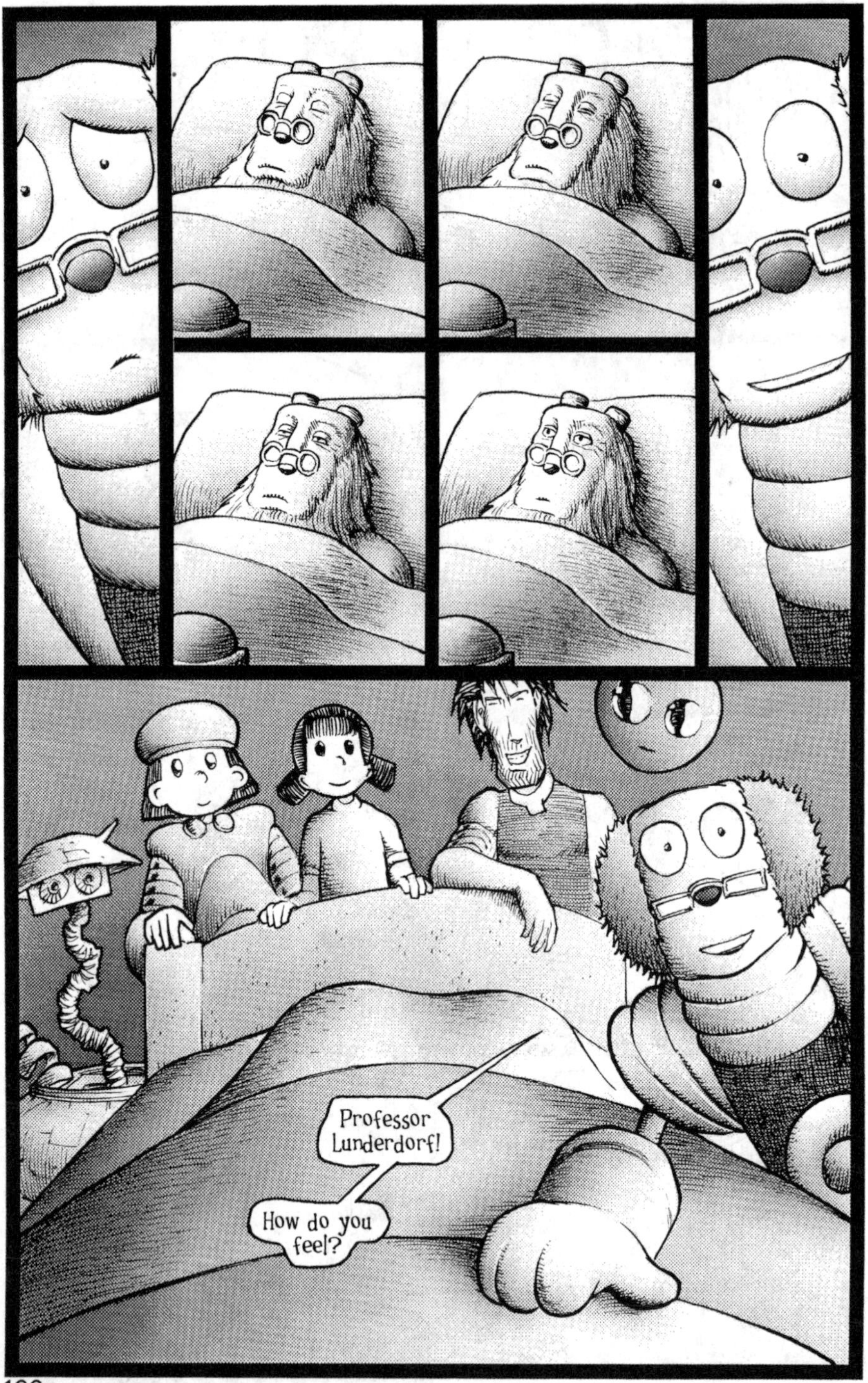
Professor Lunderdorf!
How do you feel?

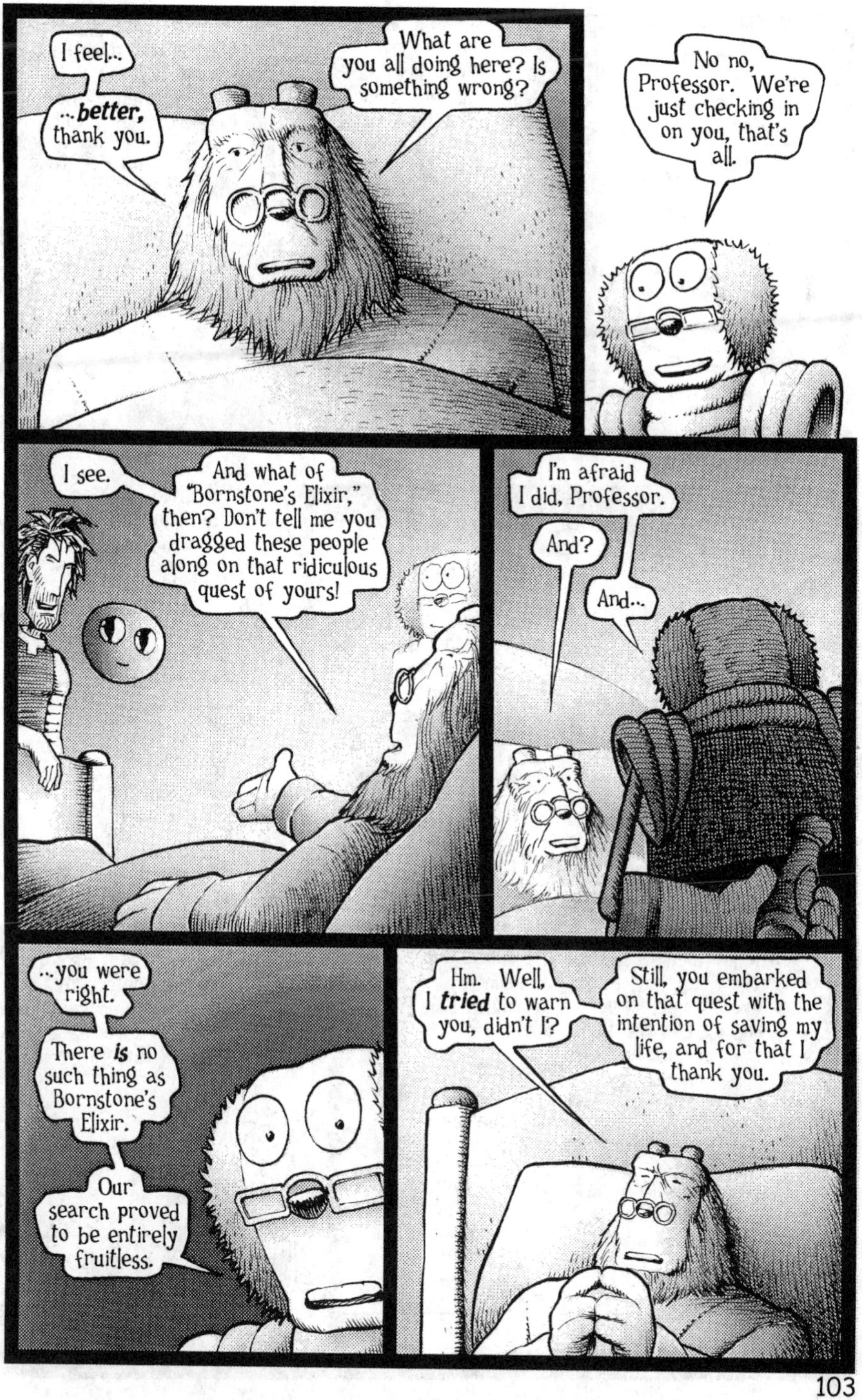

I feel... ...better, thank you.
What are you all doing here? Is something wrong?
No no, Professor. We're just checking in on you, that's all.
I see.
And what of "Bornstone's Elixir," then? Don't tell me you dragged these people along on that ridiculous quest of yours!
I'm afraid I did, Professor.
And?
And...
...you were right.
There is no such thing as Bornstone's Elixir.
Our search proved to be entirely fruitless.
Hm. Well, I tried to warn you, didn't I?
Still, you embarked on that quest with the intention of saving my life, and for that I thank you.

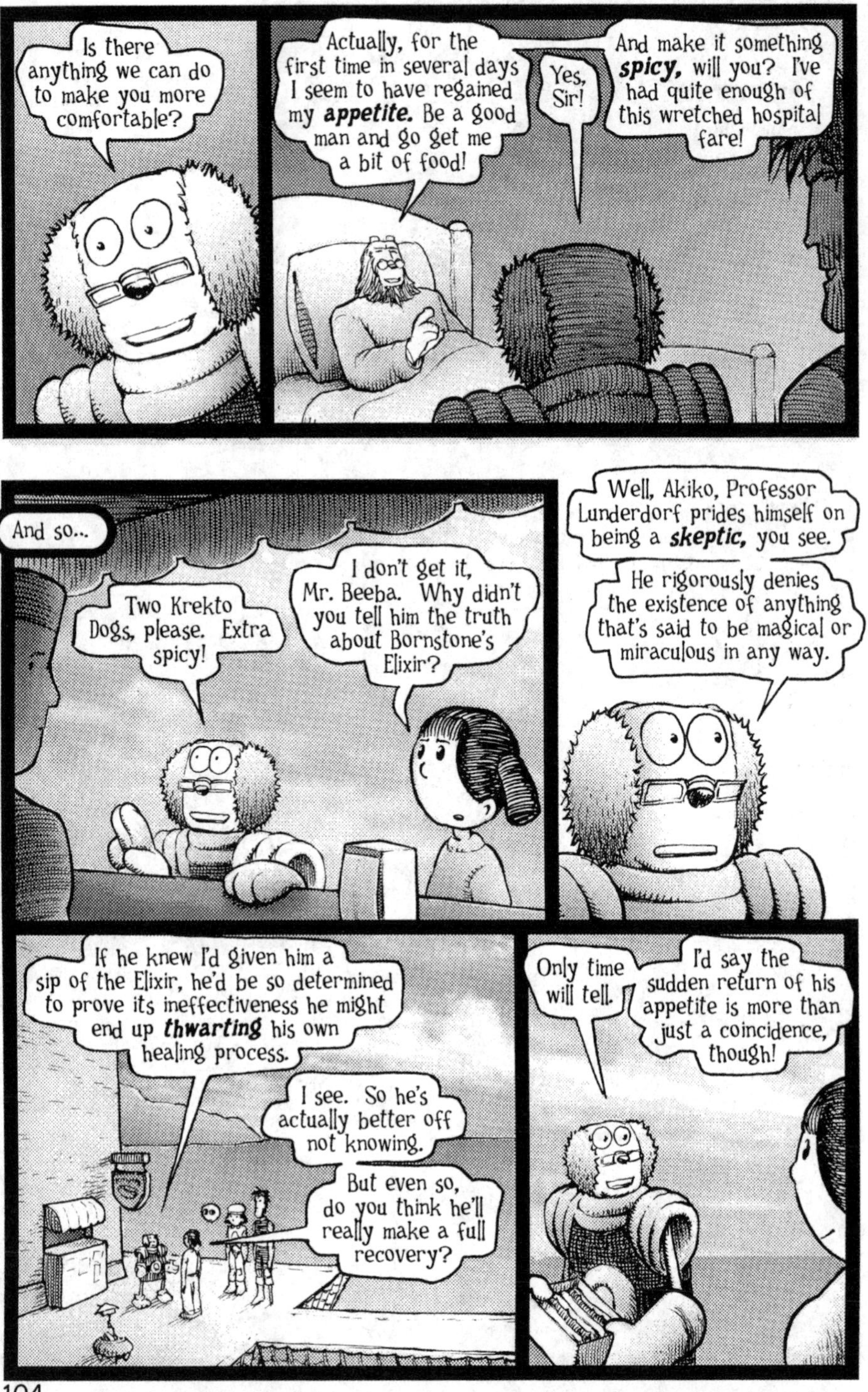

Is there anything we can do to make you more comfortable?
Actually, for the first time in several days I seem to have regained my appetite. Be a good man and go get me a bit of food!
Yes, Sir!
And make it something spicy, will you? I've had quite enough of this wretched hospital fare!
And so...
Two Krekto Dogs, please. Extra spicy!
I don't get it, Mr. Beeba. Why didn't you tell him the truth about Bornstone's Elixir?
Well, Akiko, Professor Lunderdorf prides himself on being a skeptic, you see.
He rigorously denies the existence of anything that's said to be magical or miraculous in any way.
If he knew I'd given him a sip of the Elixir, he'd be so determined to prove its ineffectiveness he might end up thwarting his own healing process.
I see. So he's actually better off not knowing.
But even so, do you think he'll really make a full recovery?
Only time will tell.
I'd say the sudden return of his appetite is more than just a coincidence, though!

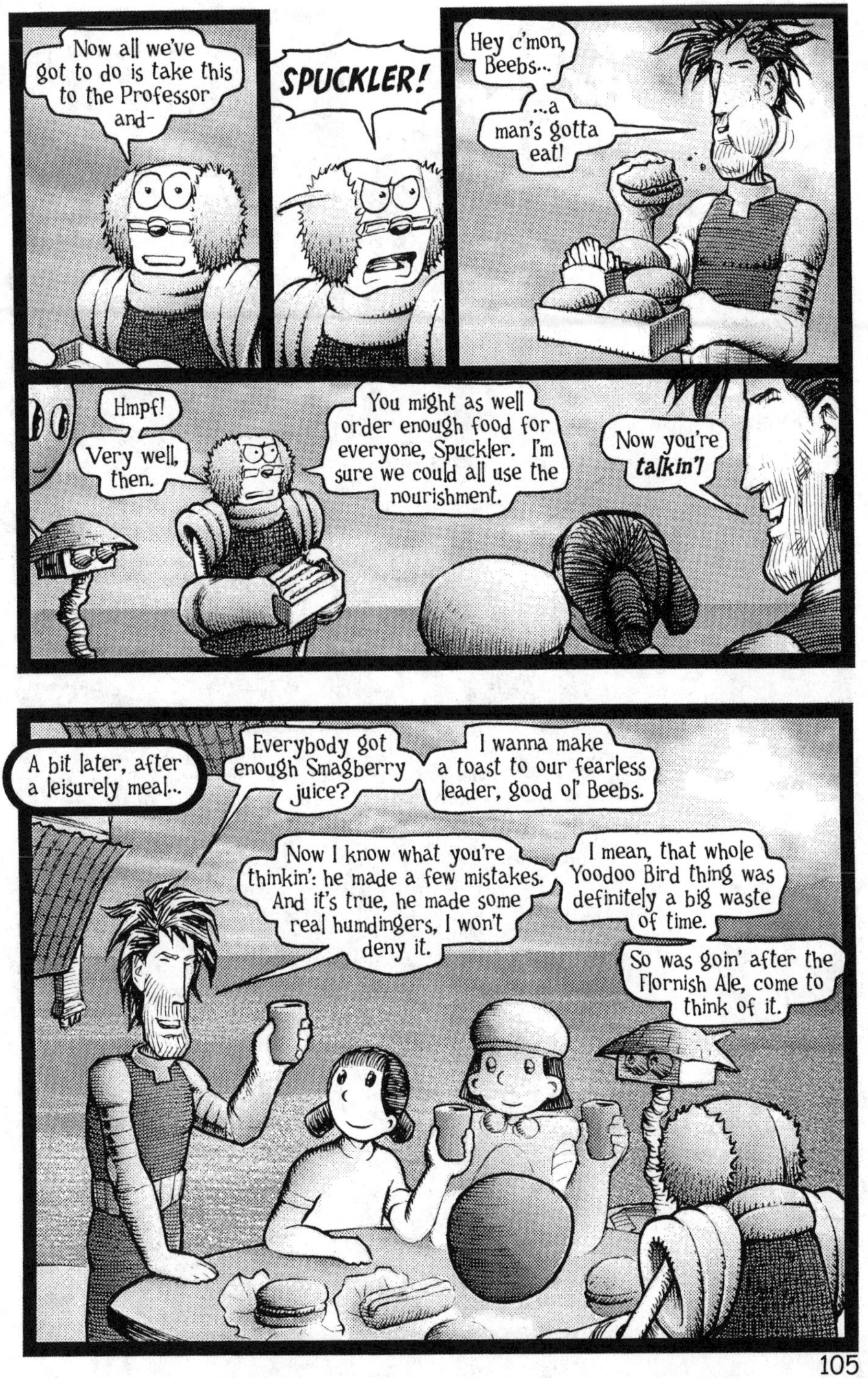
Now all we've got to do is take this to the Professor and-
SPUCKLER!
Hey c'mon, Beebs...
...a man's gotta eat!
Hmpf!
Very well, then.
You might as well order enough food for everyone, Spuckler. I'm sure we could all use the nourishment.
Now you're talkin'!
A bit later, after a leisurely meal...
Everybody got enough Smagberry juice?
I wanna make a toast to our fearless leader, good ol' Beebs.
Now I know what you're thinkin': he made a few mistakes. And it's true, he made some real humdingers, I won't deny it.
I mean, that whole Yoodoo Bird thing was definitely a big waste of time.
So was goin' after the Flornish Ale, come to think of it.

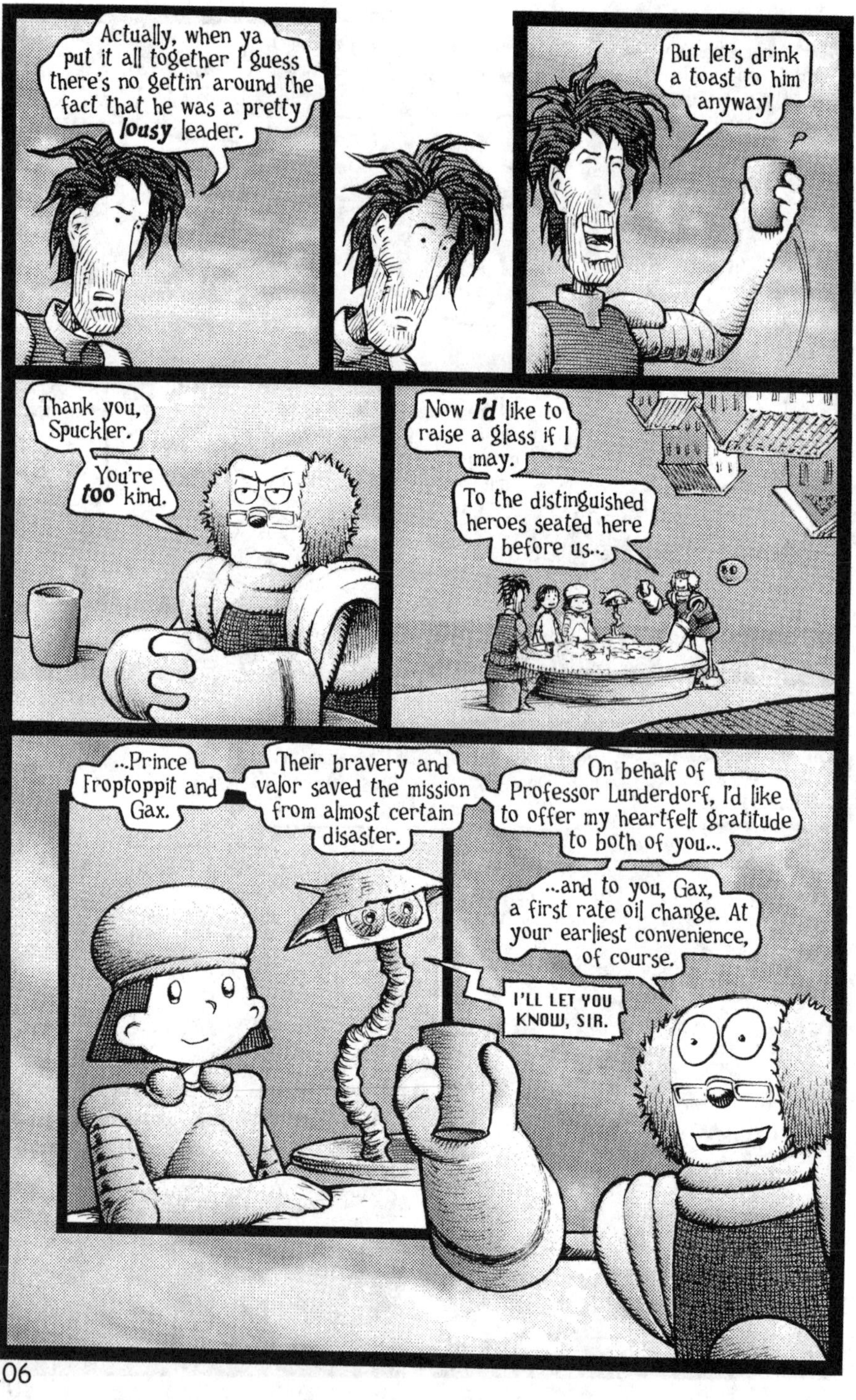
Actually, when ya put it all together I guess there's no gettin' around the fact that he was a pretty **lousy** leader.
But let's drink a toast to him anyway!
Thank you, Spuckler.
You're **too** kind.
Now ***I'd*** like to raise a glass if I may.
To the distinguished heroes seated here before us...
...Prince Froptoppit and Gax.
Their bravery and valor saved the mission from almost certain disaster.
On behalf of Professor Lunderdorf, I'd like to offer my heartfelt gratitude to both of you...
...and to you, Gax, a first rate oil change. At your earliest convenience, of course.
I'LL LET YOU KNOW, SIR.

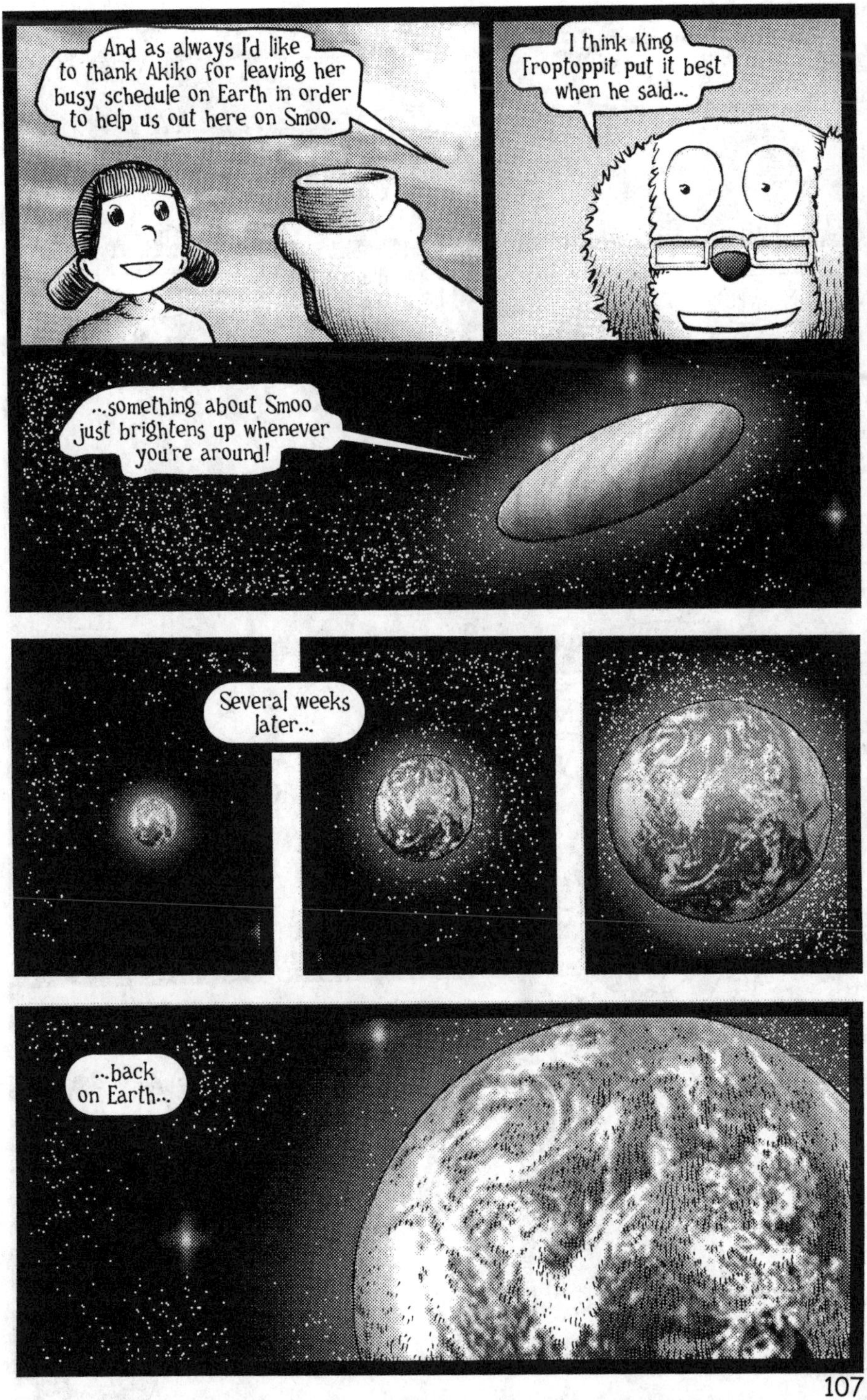

And as always I'd like to thank Akiko for leaving her busy schedule on Earth in order to help us out here on Smoo.
I think King Froptoppit put it best when he said...
...something about Smoo just brightens up whenever you're around!
Several weeks later...
...back on Earth...

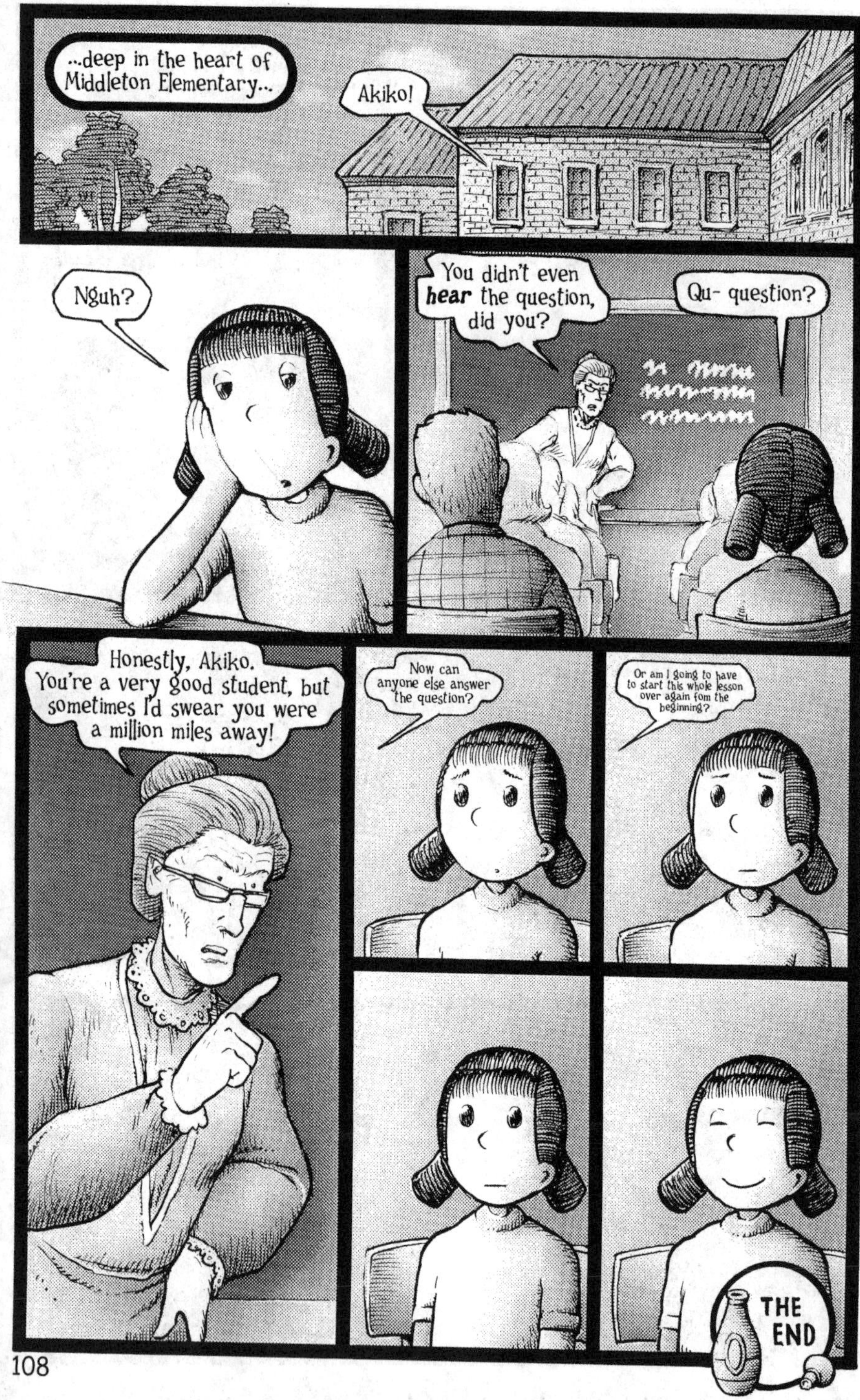
...deep in the heart of Middleton Elementary...
Akiko!
Nguh?
You didn't even **hear** the question, did you?
Qu- question?
Honestly, Akiko. You're a very good student, but sometimes I'd swear you were a million miles away!
Now can anyone else answer the question?
Or am I going to have to start this whole lesson over again fom the beginning?
THE END

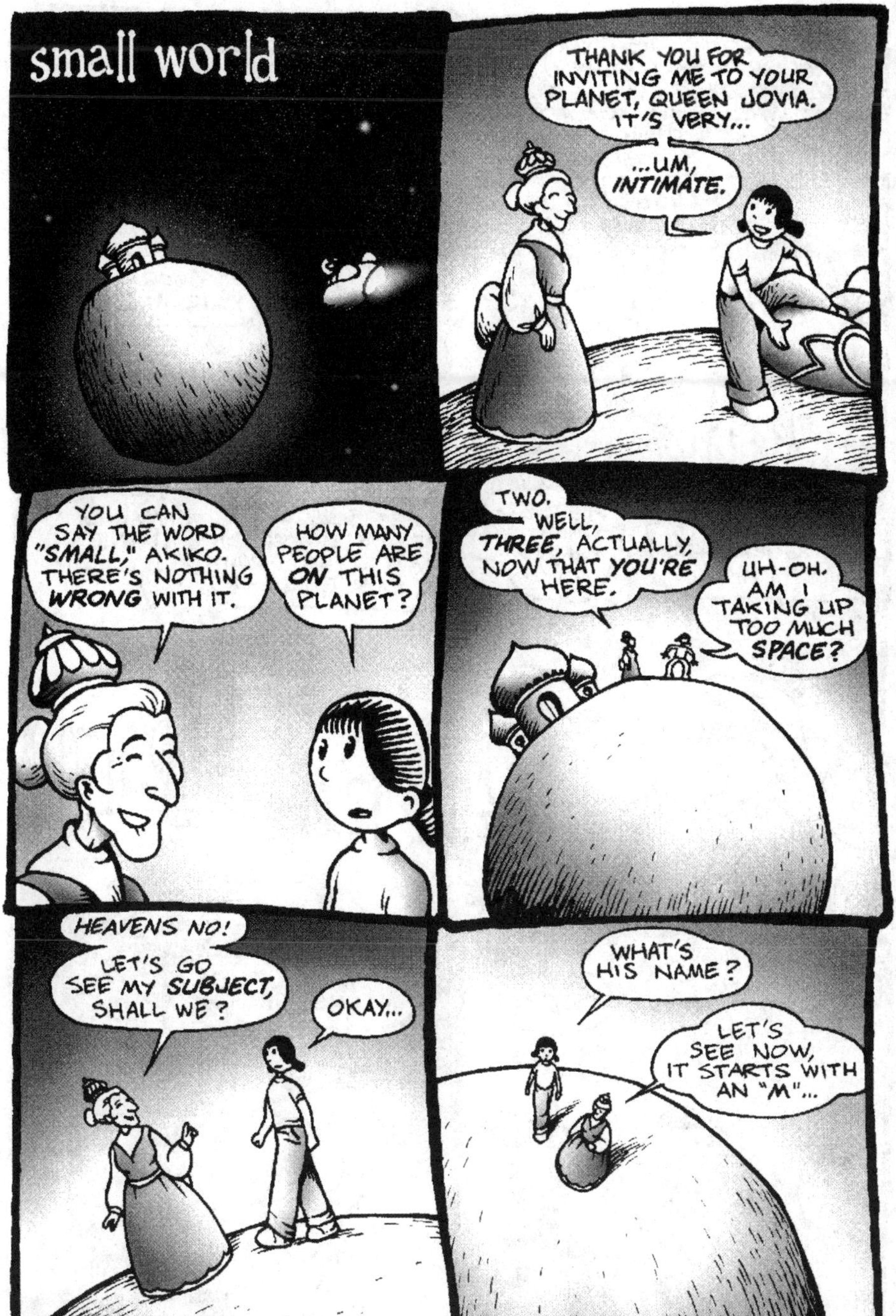
small world
THANK YOU FOR INVITING ME TO YOUR PLANET, QUEEN JOVIA. IT'S VERY...
...UM, INTIMATE.
YOU CAN SAY THE WORD "SMALL," AKIKO. THERE'S NOTHING WRONG WITH IT.
HOW MANY PEOPLE ARE ON THIS PLANET?
TWO.
WELL, THREE, ACTUALLY, NOW THAT YOU'RE HERE.
UH-OH. AM I TAKING UP TOO MUCH SPACE?
HEAVENS NO!
LET'S GO SEE MY SUBJECT, SHALL WE?
OKAY...
WHAT'S HIS NAME?
LET'S SEE NOW, IT STARTS WITH AN "M"...

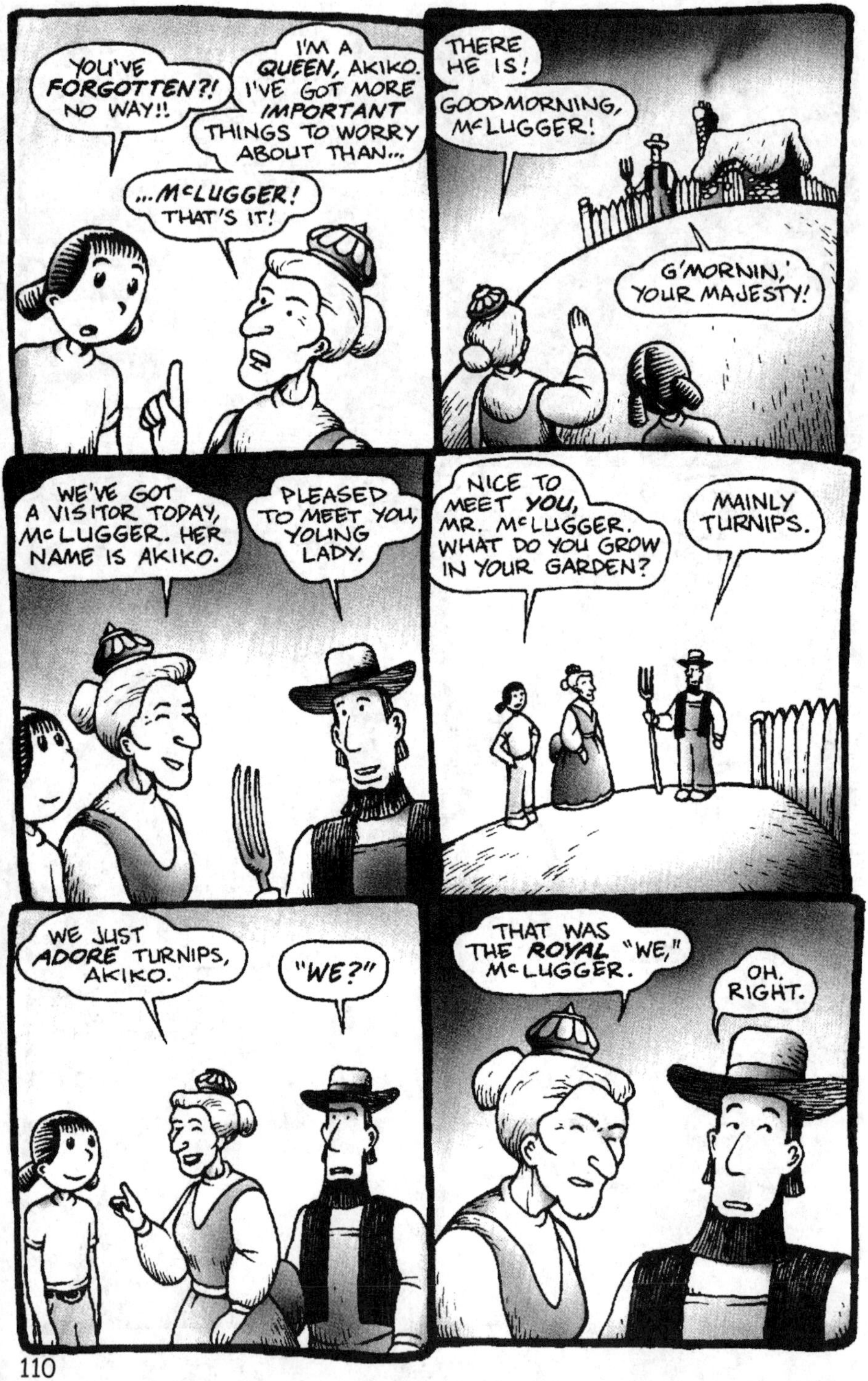
YOU'VE FORGOTTEN?! NO WAY!!
I'M A QUEEN, AKIKO. I'VE GOT MORE IMPORTANT THINGS TO WORRY ABOUT THAN...
...McLUGGER! THAT'S IT!
THERE HE IS!
GOODMORNING, McLUGGER!
G'MORNIN,' YOUR MAJESTY!
WE'VE GOT A VISITOR TODAY, McLUGGER. HER NAME IS AKIKO.
PLEASED TO MEET YOU, YOUNG LADY.
NICE TO MEET YOU, MR. McLUGGER. WHAT DO YOU GROW IN YOUR GARDEN?
MAINLY TURNIPS.
WE JUST ADORE TURNIPS, AKIKO.
"WE?"
THAT WAS THE ROYAL "WE," McLUGGER.
OH. RIGHT.

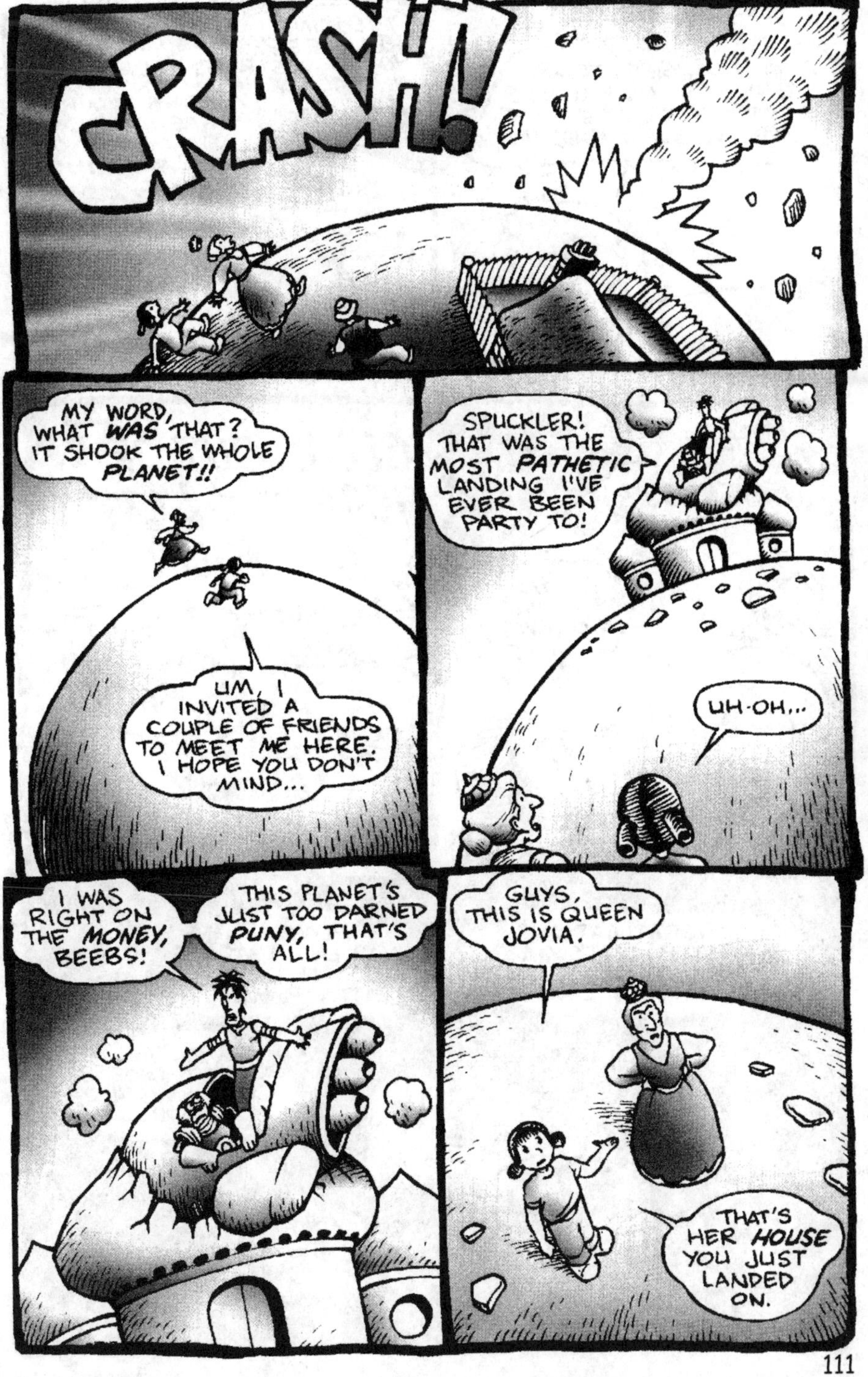
CRASH!
MY WORD, WHAT WAS THAT? IT SHOOK THE WHOLE PLANET!!
UM, I INVITED A COUPLE OF FRIENDS TO MEET ME HERE. I HOPE YOU DON'T MIND...
SPUCKLER! THAT WAS THE MOST PATHETIC LANDING I'VE EVER BEEN PARTY TO!
UH-OH...
I WAS RIGHT ON THE MONEY, BEEBS!
THIS PLANET'S JUST TOO DARNED PUNY, THAT'S ALL!
GUYS, THIS IS QUEEN JOVIA.
THAT'S HER HOUSE YOU JUST LANDED ON.

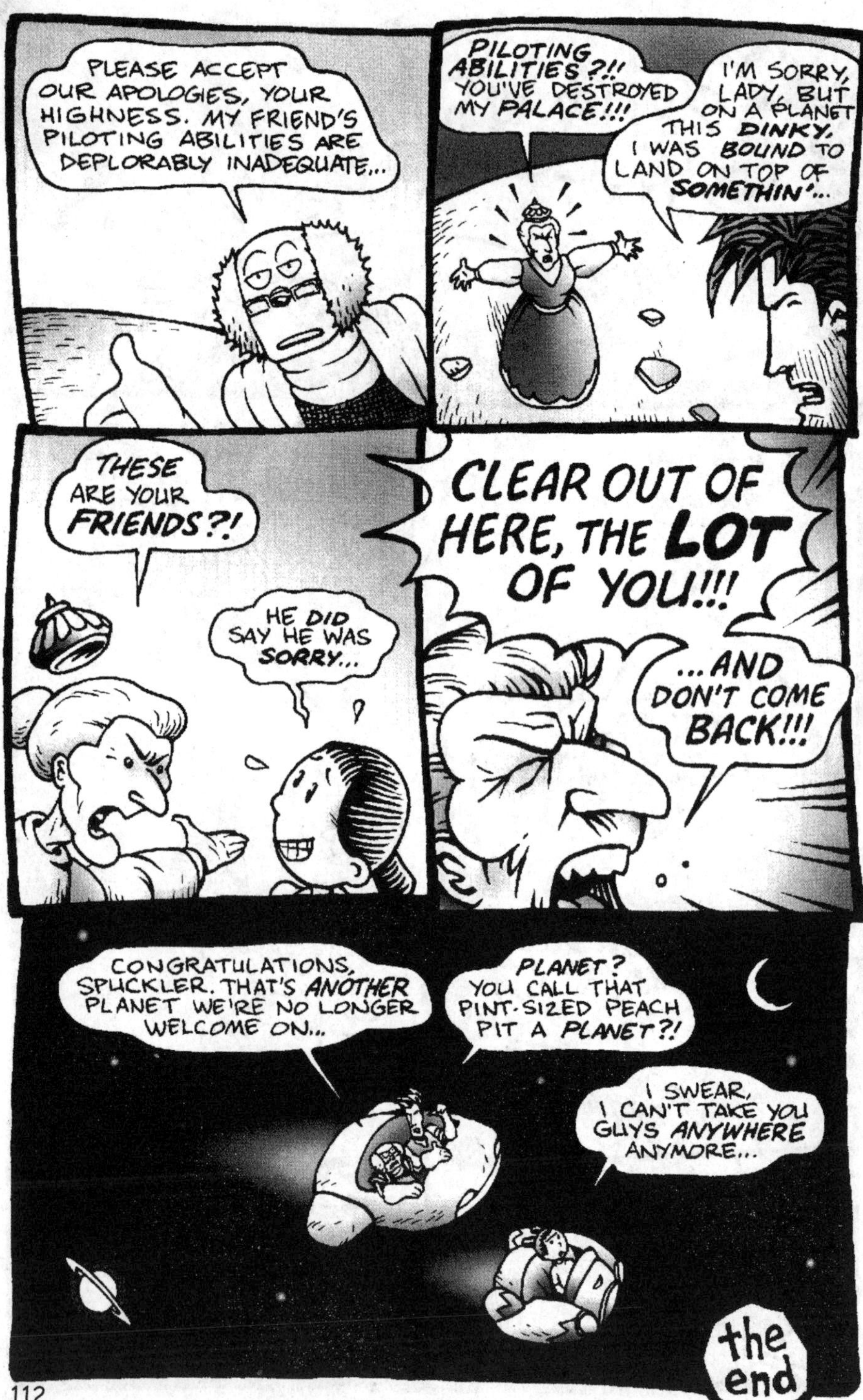
PLEASE ACCEPT OUR APOLOGIES, YOUR HIGHNESS. MY FRIEND'S PILOTING ABILITIES ARE DEPLORABLY INADEQUATE...
PILOTING ABILITIES?!! YOU'VE DESTROYED MY PALACE!!!
I'M SORRY, LADY, BUT ON A PLANET THIS DINKY, I WAS BOUND TO LAND ON TOP OF SOMETHIN'...
THESE ARE YOUR FRIENDS?!
HE DID SAY HE WAS SORRY...
CLEAR OUT OF HERE, THE LOT OF YOU!!!
...AND DON'T COME BACK!!!
CONGRATULATIONS, SPUCKLER. THAT'S ANOTHER PLANET WE'RE NO LONGER WELCOME ON...
PLANET? YOU CALL THAT PINT-SIZED PEACH PIT A PLANET?!
I SWEAR, I CAN'T TAKE YOU GUYS ANYWHERE ANYMORE...
the end